KITTYHAWK
DOWN

Also by Jonathan Nicholas:

Hospital Beat
Kibbutz Virgin
The Tragic Romance of Africa
Oz – A Hitchhiker's Australian Anthology
Who'd Be a Copper?
Cherry Picking – Life Between the Sticks

KITTYHAWK DOWN

DENNIS COPPING & ET574

Jonathan Nicholas

The Book Guild Ltd

First published in Great Britain in 2020 by
The Book Guild Ltd
9 Priory Business Park
Wistow Road, Kibworth
Leicestershire, LE8 0RX
Freephone: 0800 999 2982
www.bookguild.co.uk
Email: info@bookguild.co.uk
Twitter: @bookguild

Typeset in 12pt Adobe Jenson Pro

Printed and bound in the UK by TJ International, Padstow, Cornwall

ISBN 978 1913208 561

British Library Cataloguing in Publication Data.

A catalogue record for this book is available from the British Library.

Dedicated to all the young men of the Allied nations who fought in the deserts of North Africa during World War Two; we will always remember.

All the places described in this book are real,
as are the majority of the people and events,
although some facts have been altered to suit the story.

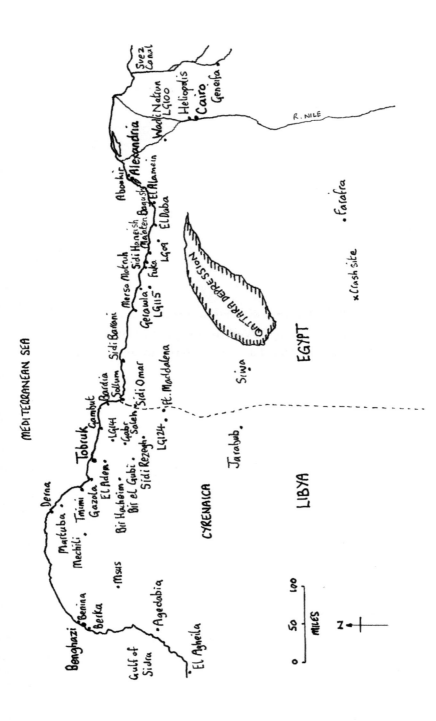

Prologue

ON THE AFTERNOON OF SUNDAY 28TH JUNE 1942, Flight Sergeant Dennis Copping took off in a single seat Kittyhawk fighter serial number ET574 from Bi'r Kurayyim in Egypt, a hundred miles west of Alexandria. He was twenty-four years old and an experienced RAF fighter pilot with 260 Squadron, Desert Air Force. His flight that day should have been a simple ferry trip from Landing Ground LG09 to Repair & Servicing Unit No. 53 at LG100 near Wadi El Natrun on the Alexandria–Cairo Road. It should have taken him no more than thirty minutes. He never arrived.

On Monday 5th March 2012, oil exploration worker Jakub Perka found the aeroplane virtually intact a hundred miles west of Farafra Oasis in central Egypt, and three hundred miles south-west of Alexandria. It is believed to have been the first time it had been seen since it crash-landed there seventy years before.

There is overwhelming evidence Dennis Copping survived the crash and stayed with the aeroplane for some time afterwards, but he has never been found.

Why was the aeroplane there and what happened to Dennis Copping?

1

4ᵗʰ March, 2012
Eastern Sahara, Egypt

"YALLA!" AHMED SHOUTED, PUSHING HIS CIGARETTE deep into the hot sand under his desert boot. He climbed back into his vehicle with the other three following. No-one in Jakub's team smoked, but all of Ahmed's did, and they insisted on stopping every time, which was annoying not just because of the delays. Jakub suspected it was more about control than smoking, but he let it go because he had no choice. At least everyone could walk around for a few minutes if they wanted to, so it was probably not a bad thing.

The climate control in Jakub's Toyota Land Cruiser was set at twenty degrees, giving them an unreal sense of separation from outside, and once on the move again the vehicle actually became a little chilly inside. It wasn't Jakub's idea to be this far from the road, but they had their instructions. He'd never been out this way before, but they had enough water, a satnav, and two satellite phones, so they should be okay. They also had

Ahmed and his team, of course, their official escort vehicle, so they weren't alone. Ahead of them deep, rippling pools lured them closer, only to disappear when approached, to be replaced by yet more in endless repeat. Unlike some of his colleagues, Jakub Perka had been in Egypt quite a while, with much of it spent in the desert, and so he'd learned to respect it. He wasn't worried, but he knew that despite all the best technology, even brand-new Toyotas can sometimes get a flat or break down.

They'd left the al-Wahat al-Bahriya main north–south road almost three hours before, passing the last signs of civilisation an hour after that, still heading west. They were no longer following anyone else's tracks; they were now creating their own. If they continued in this direction, they wouldn't encounter anything else until they intersected the Al-Jawf road in Libya, more than three hundred miles into the Sahara. They had prepared themselves for this; they'd spent the previous night relaxing at their hotel in the oasis town of Farafra, now a bustling conurbation of grid-pattern streets. The Badawiya is a modern air-conditioned hotel with a fabulous pool shaded by luxuriant palm trees, where guests can enjoy a well-stocked bar and free Wi-Fi. Only thirty years before this, Farafra was little more than a collection of date palms and a few ancient mud buildings.

The drive from Cairo had taken three days via a first-night stop at another oasis, Bahariya, on the Siwa Road, the modern tarmac lifeline around the Qattara Depression up to the coast at Mersa Matruh.

He knew these places; he'd visited them all now, but he'd already heard of them even before his first visit, not just from work briefings, but classic old British war films such as *Ice Cold in Alex*. Jakub had travelled along all these roads, but never so far away as he was now.

"Give me the map," he said, throwing his left arm awkwardly behind him, his flat palm open with the fingers grasping.

"You don't need a map, Jakub, we have the satnav," Devon said, with undisguised sarcasm from the back seat. Jakub ignored her, his arm still hanging in the air. He now dropped his right boot off the dashboard so he could twist his body even further.

"Just give him the map, Devon, for god's sake," Kasper said, hunched half-asleep with his hat covering his face, directly behind Simon, the driver. Perhaps because they were all now getting very tired, Devon opened her black leather flight bag and handed the map to Jakub.

"Stop the car, Simon," Jakub said, alternately scanning the map and the horizon. Their escort vehicle, always close, pulled up alongside and Ahmed opened his driver's window. Jakub opened his. "Just checking the map a minute, we'll probably stop soon, okay?" he said.

Ahmed nodded. "Okay, okay." Even though they were supposedly just their escort, Ahmed and his men would always have the last word.

Jakub understood this, and so made sure they believed they did. "What do you think, Dev?" he said, turning towards her.

"Yes, I think it's probably the right time and place," she said, sitting upright in her seat, looking around.

The terrain was changing, rising, hardening, and losing the soft sand. These sharp rocks would quickly rip their tyres to pieces, so they needed to find a way around to stay on the sand. It was a good time to stop because it was late afternoon, the light was fading, and they were getting pretty close to where they wanted to be anyway. Perhaps because he was the most experienced, Jakub enjoyed organising the team, and Devon was so easy-going she was more than happy to let him, even though she was in charge. All four of them were geologists and geophysicists under contract to Cannon Oil

Explorations. COE is part of a huge global company, but their job was to find the oil, not to sell it, so you probably won't have heard of them. Using exploration geophysics, they look for it everywhere now; in every ocean, every continent, every desert and in increasingly remote places. If it's there, they'll find it. There are signs which the trained eye and the right equipment can spot. It can't hide forever.

"We'll have to stay here for the night," Jakub said as he opened the door and jumped down. "Is everyone okay with that?" Their silence implied consent, along with some actual nodding approval, mainly from Devon. She could override the decision, but he knew she wouldn't. "I'll just check with the guys," he said, stepping over and leaning into the other vehicle. With no outright dissention, they all opened their doors, relieved to be out of their vehicles for the day. He thought by now the afternoon would be cooler, as the sun was setting fast, but he was wrong.

They began erecting their heavy canvas tents, each one held firm inside by sturdy wooden poles, a huge number of thick guy ropes and an assortment of fearsome steel pegs.

A smaller latrine tent with a chemical toilet was positioned round the back a few yards away. The latter was often disregarded by their escort and even some of their own team, preferring the traditional do-it-yourself desert method. The thick canvas ensured the tents were surprisingly cool inside; modern pop-up nylon would be hell on earth out here. They didn't bring one this time, but on a previous trip they were lucky enough to have a portable air-conditioning unit powered by a diesel generator, but it was noisy, drank fuel and was a cumbersome luxury.

Tents pitched, fire lit, the meals were prepared: chopped vegetables, chunks of lamb, rice, bread and lots of tea, but with no milk. More by accident than design, Devon did most of the cooking. One huge pan over the fire sizzled fiercely with the promise of a tasty meal. She was wearing white linen trousers, a cream cotton blouse buttoned up to the neck, and a black-and-white *kfir* over her head, all appropriate efforts to be modest, or so she thought, but their escort, all four of them, still followed her every movement as she leaned forward in the twilight, her shape increasingly silhouetted by the fire. She was tall and slim, with pretty blue eyes, so why wouldn't they?

They all sat cross-legged or lay on their sides eating, each person occasionally reaching in with their bread to take more from the pan until almost all was consumed. Anything left would then be stored in the cool boxes for breakfast. Jakub wiped his hands, rose to his feet, retrieved a map and a battery lamp from their car, and sat down with Ahmed and Mahmoud. Karim and Amir sat cross-legged opposite them chatting together in Arabic while half-heartedly cleaning their AK-47s, despite the fact they looked brand new. Kasper and Simon rather grudgingly helped Devon collect the plates.

Ahmed had made the fire and so it was his to maintain, which he did with obvious pride. In addition to the smoke breaks, they would occasionally stop while driving to pick up firewood, but this was rare; most of what they used was brought with them. He loaded it with more, prodding it with a stick and sending clouds of embers spinning wildly away like tiny fireworks. He now sat cross-legged facing the fire, gazing into it like he was watching television. He was tall, well-built and good-looking in a classic Omar Sharif movie star kind of way, this image reinforced by his wearing of traditional black robes. "I was an officer in the army, you know. Now I work for the government. They pay me well," he told Jakub the previous day when they first met. He was the oldest of the group, in his early forties, and was very definitely in command. Jakub's team collected them just before they left Farafra, despite Jakub's usual protestations that they really weren't needed, thank you very much, but the authorities insisted.

Mahmood was smaller and a few years younger, with short curly hair, a fresh beard and the only other member of the team to wear traditional robes, this time a mixed shade of cream that should probably be white. He was quietly spoken but was incredibly polite and helpful, and never left Ahmed's side. At night he wore a tartan wool scarf wrapped once around his neck, just like the ones worn in the seventies by the Bay City Rollers, an incongruous addition to his daytime attire. But he was right to do so; coats were needed to keep out the evening cool, with each darkening hour in the cloudless sky the heat of the day evaporated quickly.

2

DEVON JOINED THEM, LEAVING KASPER AND SIMON to finish washing the dishes. She sat on the sand next to Jakub, despite very enthusiastic offers of a place close to Karim and Amir, which she politely but firmly declined in passable Arabic. They had a large-scale map of Egypt, and a smaller one of their immediate locality, spread out in front of them on the cooling sand. The Egypt map was rather pointless, if only to show how vast the place was. They confirmed grid references on the Garmin with the map and agreed on a plan for the next day. They were just over a hundred miles from the southern tip of the Qattara Depression, the north-east tip of which curled around to a point thirty miles south of El-Alamein. It was no coincidence the Allies made a final stand there against Rommel in October 1942; it was a narrow strip of land, with the sea on one side and a soft, unpassable depression on the other.

As evening turned swiftly into night, the stars touched the earth all around far better than any planetarium, and this made them feel even more insignificant than the vastness of the daytime desert. There was nothing in any direction, no artificial light of any sort, no distant city glow and no proof of human existence, just the navigation lights from jet aircraft blinking high overhead, and an occasional satellite cutting across the sky like a wayward star breaking away from its friends. And there was total, absolute silence, with no insect noise of any kind, too remote even for the flies. It was a truly vacuous emptiness that could easily be the surface of Mars. Even in remote parts of Poland Jakub had explored as a kid with his father, there was nothing quite like it. This total isolation never ceased to amaze him, and it was one of the reasons he loved his job.

He checked in with their line manager three hundred miles away; his voice was so reassuringly clear on the satellite phone it was as though he was sitting right next to them. After a few cursory greetings, he passed it to Devon, who was then silent for a while, concentrating, listening intently to the man at the other end. The phone was pressed firmly to her left ear as she idly ran the fingers of her right hand through the full length of her hair down beyond her shoulders and onto the curves of her chest, tilting her head a little, the *kfir* now discarded on her lap. The men were watching her, of course, their faces brightly lit against the black of night as she nodded a few times even though the recipient could not see her, with a very serious expression that completely changed her features, until suddenly she laughed uproariously, followed by, "Sure, sure, no problem," in her usual reassuring tone. Finishing with her hair and the conversation, she tossed her head back and stood up swiftly before handing the phone to Jakub. "He's funny," she said to him, and then, "I'll speak to you later," before moving off to the tent.

It was all sorted with their line manager. In the morning they'd take a look around, beginning early with their seismic equipment and after a few hours' work they'd be heading back to Farafra in the air-conditioned luxury of the Land Cruiser before the worst of the heat. Wandering around the desert at midday with heavy equipment was not recommended. They may find evidence of hydrocarbons, as oil and gas are known in the trade, or they may not. It would be nice if they did, but their lives didn't depend on it. Either way, they all thought nothing unusual would happen this far out because there was absolutely nothing here.

They slept well, and immediately after waking up Devon clambered onto their vehicle to retrieve the equipment, launching herself up onto the roof with ease, her long legs taking her up there in three quick strides. It was before anyone else was around, so for the moment she was merely wearing the shorts and T-shirt she'd slept in. Jakub and the others emerged, and Kasper smiled when he caught him watching her. Jakub could see the unfinished tattoos on the back of both her legs, just below the knee, and he knew yet again that he'd forget to ask her about them. She unlocked the roof box and began passing down the equipment, her heavy blonde plait occasionally falling forwards before she threw it behind her with well-practised flicks of the head. She jumped back down in one leap, and seconds later the battery packs were applied, code words inserted, switches on the instruments were clicked and they all buzzed into life. She was the only one in the team who knew how to operate every piece of equipment and was by far the most qualified. She then disappeared back into the tent to finish dressing, with a characteristic bounce in her step and typical cheery smile.

Simon leaned into the cab and turned the ignition key in the Land Cruiser, catching Jakub with a momentary look of deep seriousness, which was very definitely reciprocated. There was the slightest, almost imperceptible nod of relief between them when it started first time. They would no doubt both deny it, but it was there nonetheless. The desert silence was gone as the first Land Cruiser was left to idle for several minutes, the engine noise and the diesel smoke providing familiar reassurance.

Ahmed and Mahmood then emerged, but much to Jakub's surprise, Amir and Karim appeared from a hundred yards away, their guns casually slung to their front, walking back to camp in step as though on parade. Ahmed checked their vehicle and indicated all was okay. There was little preparation for breakfast, just a buffet of bread, rice and dried sausage for the Westerners, with bread and leftovers for Ahmed's crew. Then there was lots of coffee. The tents were emptied neatly, ready for dismantling, the contents loaded into the vehicles. Over to the right, perhaps five hundred metres away, the rocks were darker, rising in a gentle slope. *This would be a good place to conduct the first of the day's surveys,* Jakub thought.

While the others were busy preparing the instruments and maps, and their escorts were pulling down the tents, Jakub set off on foot alone to take a closer look.

He was seen, and Devon waved, but no-one followed. It was probably assumed he was going for a toilet break, despite the latrine tent still being available. He remembered the line from the film *Ice Cold in Alex*, about a man walking into the desert alone with a spade. He didn't have a spade, but the point was the same. After a few minutes it became clear they certainly wouldn't be able to bring the vehicles up here, Jakub thought, the rocks would be far too risky on the tyres. This would probably be the same thought everyone had who ever passed this way, if at all, thereby ensuring whatever lay ahead would forever remain in permanent isolation. This was good.

It meant from an oil exploration point of view if there was anything there, it would almost certainly still be untouched.

Before disappearing from view, he took a look back at the camp. They were all busy. Good. He only intended to reach the edge of the dark brown rocks before stopping and turning back, but something kept drawing him on. The irresistible lure of the desert, perhaps, or merely something as prosaic as actually wanting to find what they were looking for. He'd be okay, he had the Garmin, his phone and a water bottle on his belt, but even then he didn't wish to be out of visual contact for very long.

Over a small rise there was an object on the near horizon, a long slab of dark rock sitting entirely alone like a toppled monolith, indistinct and blurred; its edges shimmering in the morning heat, the shape and size making it utterly incongruous. Such distinct changes in rock formations could be good news and may be an indication of something promising. He had to get closer, just to be sure. Walking across an area of smaller rocks protruding from the sand like broken teeth, he realised he'd found a way to get up closer in safety with the Land Cruiser should they wish to later. He felt a trickle of sweat run down the centre of his back as he stopped to get his breath. Looking back, the camp was no longer visible down the slope behind him. He was now on top of an isolated low plateau, the entire area of which had most likely never been seen or walked upon by anyone before. As he drew closer to the object, he realised this assumption may be incorrect.

Even from a hundred metres away he could tell it was not a slab of rock, and that what he saw was something astonishing. He stood, wiping the salt sweat from his eyes in disbelief. It couldn't be real, yet here it was, right in front of him.

3

It had obviously crashed, and quite a while ago, perhaps several years at least. Much of it appeared as bare metal, reflecting the sunlight as though never painted, yet the fuselage was a very faint yellowy-green colour, with the right wing almost completely covered with sand. The pilot was clearly dead inside because the cockpit canopy was closed. He'd been unable to bail out or otherwise climb free of the wreck after the crash, so he'd still be in there, what was left of him, slumped over the controls, preserved forever in his last desperate moments. Jakub stepped up onto the left wing, bracing himself for his first sight of the deceased airman as he rubbed an area of Perspex with his right hand. But here was another shock, as the pilot's seat was empty. How could this be? There were no signs of disturbance around the crash site, so who could have closed the canopy?

He tugged at the metal frame, pulling it back a few inches before peering inside. Apart from a gathering of sand on the seat and floor, the inside was perfectly intact. The instruments, though bearing a patina of dust, were undamaged and appeared in full working order. Perhaps the controls were in the same position now as they had been when it touched down? There had clearly been no fire or severe impact that would have killed the pilot; this had been a controlled crash-landing, so why was it here, and where was the pilot?

Jakub rang the other phone, most likely resting on a seat somewhere in the Land Cruiser. No-one answered. He tried again and suddenly there was a woman's voice. "Yo!" she shouted, and then, "Where did you go?"

"Devon, you know where I started walking, you saw me, didn't you?"

"Yes, why, are you lost?" She laughed, but then, in a more serious tone: "Are you okay?"

"Yes, I'm fine, thank you, and I'm *not* lost, I've found something. Leave what you're doing and come and join me up here, will you? I'm over the top beyond where you saw me walking. Bring the others, and I suppose that will have to include Ahmed. You won't believe what I've found. Sadly it's not hydrocarbons; it's something much more interesting."

Intrigued by Jakub's call, the other three appeared twenty minutes later, flanked by all four of their escort, walking so briskly over the horizon they appeared to be jogging. They all stopped in disbelief twenty metres distant in the same way Jakub had done when he realised what it was.

"It's a Spitfire," Devon said with authority, the first to give an opinion.

"It's not, it's a Hurricane. I'd put a year's salary on it, you can tell by the cockpit canopy," Simon said with absolute assurance. "It's an early P51, a Mustang," Kasper said, "from World War Two."

"It can't be that old. Look at it, there's not a speck of rust on it anywhere," Simon said.

"It never rains here," Devon said, throwing him a quizzical look, "you know that, so it's not going to rust, is it? It could have been here a hundred years and it still wouldn't rust. The only damage would be from the sun and the occasional sandstorm."

"Unless it's aluminium, of course," Simon quickly added, which Devon ignored.

"It is Egyptian Air Force," Ahmed said, as the others in his team began nodding as they moved closer.

They all stepped onto the wings either side of the cockpit and crowded around, peering inside, jostling one another to get a better view, the surprise on their faces soon betraying the same thoughts about the pilot that Jakub had.

"Where is he?" Devon said, looking at Jakub. He was now standing, hands on hips at the front of the aeroplane, smiling. They split up and began looking around the crash site, inspecting the numerous bits of wreckage which seemed to follow the aeroplane in a trail across the desert. For a few moments no-one spoke, each person deep in thought, probably all thinking the same. What happened here?

The wheels were some distance back, maybe a hundred metres or more, no doubt broken off on impact, and the propeller hub was detached and away to the right several metres, all three steel blades of which were bent backwards, as though it was still spinning at the time of impact. Kasper removed a wing hatch with a pen knife to reveal a machine gun still inside, and plenty of ammunition. These were huge bullets, much bigger than an ordinary rifle. Seeing this, Ahmed immediately jumped over and took charge, insisting no-one touch the guns but his team.

"I think you're right, Kasper, it's *very* old," Jakub said, running a hand along the fuselage. "The paint's badly faded, but these are RAF markings. They are definitely *not* Egyptian – sorry, Ahmed – it's an RAF aircraft, but where from and when?"

"The pilot must have survived," Devon said, "because he got out after the crash and then shut the canopy after him."

"Why would he do that?" Simon said, looking puzzled.

"Look at this," Jakub said, kneeling beside the fuselage, clearing an area of sand. "It looks like a radio. It's been removed and tampered with, but who did this?"

"Perhaps it was the pilot; perhaps he was trying to fix it," Kasper said, leaning in closer, nodding.

"Or souvenir hunters," Simon replied.

"No-one's been here before us," Jakub said, shaking his head. "The guns would be the first to go, look…" as Ahmed was tugging forcefully at one of them in the right wing. It wouldn't move, and he was cursing loudly in Arabic. "I do hope he knows what he's doing and it doesn't go off in his face."

"My god, look here…" Kasper said, pointing to a patch of sand newly revealed by his cursory digging.

There were some tiny objects, probably six in all, faded and delicate, but there was little doubt what they were. "Cigarette butts, look. The poor bastard tried to fix the radio while smoking his fags."

"You don't know that," Simon said.

"They are cigarette butts, aren't they?" Kasper rebuked, holding one up in his fingers.

"This could only be a few years ago then, surely?" Devon said, jumping in off the wing and leaning over Kasper's shoulder. This prompted them all to begin a more detailed search, both in and around the aeroplane, looking for further clues.

"Here," Jakub said, pulling up some faded white cloth from the sand near the engine. Numerous tattered strings hung from around the edges of the crumpled material. "*Jasna cholera*," he said. It was the first time most of the others had heard him speak his native Polish. He repeated in English, "Bloody hell, could this be a parachute?"

"It certainly looks like it. This proves he didn't use it to jump out, that's for sure," Simon said. "I noticed a small piece of that next to the radio, stained red – well, pink, actually, but you know what I'm thinking."

"If he didn't use his parachute but landed with the aeroplane, climbed out and then shut the canopy, then he's still here, or nearby," Devon said. They each instinctively looked around them, just for a moment.

"Or he walked away. He must have. He's not here, is he? This wasn't yesterday. It was years ago, at least," Simon said. They all knew he was right. If the pilot was still here then they'd find human remains, not a living, walking man. No-one could survive even a few days out here without water. Jakub wasn't the only one now beginning to realise just how old this aeroplane was and how long it had been there.

"Maybe he was picked up and returned home?" he said, suddenly breaking a momentary silence.

"We need to take some details, serial numbers and so on if we can find any, so the right people can be notified," Devon said, shielding her eyes with the flat palm and straightening the fingers of her right hand like a navy salute. Ahmed and his team were noisily heaving long belts of bullets from the wings, photographing each other in turn with them slung over their shoulders, laughing. Devon scanned the horizon all around and back at the aeroplane before capturing the moment with everyone's thoughts: "Poor man."

"Agreed," Jakub said, staring into the cockpit again. "There must be something with a name or number on it, but I can't see anything in here. Maybe there's something written on the engine."

"Guys, I've found something." Simon's voice echoed from inside the fuselage, his head buried in an open hatch on the left-hand side. He shouted again. *"Curtiss Aeroplane Division, Curtiss-Wright Corporation."* He pulled his head out from inside and stood upright, deliberately looking straight at Devon. "They didn't make Spitfires, did they?"

"No, nor Hurricanes or Mustangs, not as far as I know," Kasper said. "Unless it was under licence, of course."

"Then what is it, a Curtiss, what's that? I've never heard of it," Jakub said.

"It rings a bell, but I'm not sure," Simon said. "We ought to take some photos, though, while we're here, we never know if we'll ever see it again. Jakub, you found it, stand next to it so I can get some shots of you with the plane." Ahmed and his colleagues were still scrambling all over it, pulling at the other guns and anything that moved. By now they'd created a huge pile of live bullets, though what they were going to do with them was a mystery. Simon asked them to stand clear of the wreck while photographs were taken.

Jakub stood on the left side of the aeroplane just in front of the cockpit, his right foot on the left wing root, knee bent, leaning with his right hand on the engine. The parachute remains were at his feet just in front of him in the sand. Then they all took photos with their phones, including detailed shots of the engine and anything with serial numbers that might help identify it. Jakub looked at his Garmin and made a note of their location: 27° 23' 52" north and 27° 37' 41" east. It was indeed the very middle of nowhere.

Simon stomped off for several hundred metres back in the direction of where the aeroplane must have touched down, past the wheels and other wreckage. Others made their own searches for quite some distance around the crash site, prepared to discover something tragic and unsightly, but he never appeared. There was no trace of him.

Ahmed was busy on his satellite phone, shouting loudly in Arabic. The secret was now out. After half an hour they left the aeroplane to its silent isolation. Who knows how long it had been there avoiding detection, quietly poised to tell its story and that of its pilot to anyone who found it?

There was something about the site that prevented them from ripping pieces off the wreck to begin carting it across the desert, almost as though the pilot was sitting nearby watching over them and his aeroplane. Ahmed's team took a few bullets, but they were heavy, and so they contented themselves with just a few samples, for 'official reporting', so they said. But other than this, it just didn't feel dignified to steal from that place, even though they all dearly wanted to reveal it to the world, and maybe to preserve it somewhere safe forever. No-one knew at the time that it had been sitting there untouched and unseen for the last seventy years.

As they reached the Land Cruiser to resume work, Simon stood rock still as though hit by a lightning bolt. He was wondering where he'd seen that name before. He knew all along, but it had been hiding in a part of his brain that had been temporarily smothered by the excitement of the find. Then he remembered. "I know what it is," he said, shaking his head and smiling. "It's a Curtiss P40, a Kittyhawk."

4

9th September, 1940
Southend-on-Sea, England

I SAW IT COMING IN FROM OVER THE SEA LONG BEFORE I realised what it really was, and by then it was too late. I was sure it was an RAF Blenheim, perhaps on a training flight, skimming the surface of the water fast and low as they so often do. It had to be one of ours because there was no air raid warning, and no-one was shooting at it. As it turned inland, sweeping along the Esplanade towards me, I began to see people diving for cover behind walls, into buildings, behind cars, anything they could find. This wasn't right, what on earth were they doing, frightening people like this? It was only a hundred feet above the road when just in front of me a young woman in a desperate panic launched the pram she was pushing towards the side of the road, hitting the opposite kerb and almost toppling over. The moment I realised it wasn't a Blenheim was the exact same moment I saw the woman fall forwards onto her face with her arms by her sides, dropping like a felled tree. There was a dull thud and a quiver from her body, and then silence.

My face was pressed into the road and I was cursing my bad timing, suddenly realising I had been lucky after all, filling one of the gaps between bullets. I turned my head briefly skywards to see the pale blue of the aeroplane's underside flash overhead with the unmistakeable black crosses on the wings. The man in the glass front never stopped firing his machine gun as they covered the full length of the Esplanade. We clearly weren't soldiers, but even if we were, shooting someone in the back as they ran away just isn't right.

I stood up and, instinctively crouching as I ran over to her, I nudged the woman firmly on the shoulder. "Come on, get up…" but there was no response. I shoved my hands under her arms and tried to pick her up, but she was surprisingly heavy for someone so slim. I tried again and this time she was much lighter as three men grabbed us both and, collecting the pram on the way, they dragged us into a shop doorway. The baby was crying but the woman remained silent.

Sitting on the floor with my back to the wall, I noticed bright red marks on my shoes and across the floor all around her; there was a thick trail of blood that had followed us into the shop, and someone, perhaps all of us, had stepped in it because there were smudged shoe prints all around. "Come on, love, you'll be alright," one of the men said tenderly as he laid her on the floor, face up. They lifted her up a little, leaning her against the wall opposite me, hoping she'd greet us with a smile because her blue eyes were wide open and staring. It was then that we saw the enormous hole in the front of her blouse from which her stomach began pouring out all over the floor. One of the men took a step back with just one word: "Shit…" Another shook his head. "She's a goner," he said, as they gently eased her back down onto the floor. We all stared in a moment of stunned silence.

"Are you alright?" one of them asked. Was he talking to me? I didn't reply. I couldn't. I wasn't there anymore; it all seemed so unreal. "Is she yours?" he said to me.

Finally I shook my head. "No," I said. One of them ran outside with his hands dripping blood. I saw him standing in the street hurling abuse and waving his fist at a distant speck, the low hum of the Ju88's engines barely audible as it disappeared back out to sea. He was crying, as I was, as we all were. We didn't know her; we didn't need to. It was just one of those moments the war presented to us. Dreadful events were happening more often now, but still they were always unexpected. The Hun had been given a damned good pasting in the skies above southern England, and so in revenge he was doing things like this. They couldn't beat us in a fair fight, so in typical Hun fashion, they decided to kill civilians instead. What cowardly bastards they were.

These were the times we were living in, times where you could be machine-gunned in the back without warning while pushing your pram along the seafront. Think about that for a moment. Of course I volunteered, and I was bloody glad I did, even though I had absolutely no idea what to expect. The RAF desperately wanted pilots in the Volunteer Reserve and so I enlisted. I love aeroplanes and I always have, so what else was I going to do? God knows I didn't want to become cannon fodder in the army.

I'd never heard of RAF Padgate, and so I didn't realise when I set off from my home in South Benfleet the next morning that the journey would take the best part of a day. I had hoped it would be somewhere in southern England, but I suspected this was unlikely due to the night bombings, which had become pretty bad at that time, as well as the occasional daytime raids. Sergeant Grey, a cheery middle-aged chap in the recruiting office, had hinted at Padgate's location. "It's up north, Mr Copping, quite a way up north," he said, and of course my return Rail Warrant named it, but I had no idea it was near Warrington, so close to Liverpool and Manchester, just about bang in the middle actually. You didn't discuss specifics in public anymore, particularly those of military bases; you didn't know who might be listening. 'Loose lips sink ships', as they say.

The Hun was just about to invade our islands and so I'd no doubt they had hundreds or even thousands of spies in the country, with quislings and Fifth Columnists ready to strike. But we were not going to make it easy for the invaders. There were long rolls of barbed wire on the beaches stretching as far as you could see, with land mines and huge concrete tank traps all over the place and sandbags piled up everywhere. Soldiers with fixed bayonets were on watch twenty-four hours a day, and the blackout was strictly enforced.

The war was everywhere, there was no escaping it; from everything we ate being strictly rationed to air raid shelters in all public places and in everyone's back garden. Even when you looked out the window the world was only visible between diagonal strips of scrim tape all over the glass.

The man at Southend Station was very helpful; he told me exactly which trains to catch and where to change. How did he know in such great detail? The station was really busy, and every single train was delayed and jam-packed, mainly with hopeful people like me still in civilian clothes, but many with all the accoutrements of uniform: kitbags, suitcases, gas masks and guns. It seemed like the whole country was on the move. Not that I had a gun; I didn't. I was still a civilian, not a soldier. I'd never even seen a gun, let alone fired one, and probably never would, not if I became a pilot. It hadn't occurred to me yet that if I flew an RAF aeroplane I might soon be shooting at people. How would I feel about that? I'd be aiming for the machine, though, not the person, unlike that Hun bastard over Southend Esplanade. It would be nice to have a crack at him.

When I finally arrived at Padgate Station I bought two packs of Black Cat cigarettes for sixpence each and stuffed them in my pockets. It was a good job I did. RAF Padgate wasn't officially open yet, it was only half-finished and there was nowhere to buy anything. As I walked into the camp off Cinnamon Lane, everything looked brand new and thrown together in a blinding hurry, with more workmen milling around than RAF personnel. I was shouted at by an angry flight sergeant at the main gate because when he saw my ID card he told me I was an hour late. I'm sure he was probably a nice chap underneath all that barking. I was too tired to argue with him and knew I probably shouldn't anyway. I was directed to a brand-new Nissen hut and passed another with the words 'Aircrew Board' handwritten on the door in chalk.

I took the third bed in, on the left. I opened my suitcase and the first thing I did was hang up my shirts in the wardrobe, thinking of my Aunt Margaret, who had kindly ironed them so well only the day before, despite my protestations that I was happy to do it myself. The chap sitting on the next bed jumped up and suddenly threw his right hand at me, shaking mine so firmly I thought he'd break the bones. He was taller than me, blond, athletic and tanned, with sea-green eyes and freckles, looking every bit like one of those Hun soldiers we see in the newsreels. He had an accent I'd heard a few times before, when he stated he was from 'Sarth Ifrikka'. In the months to come I would become very familiar with this accent. There were Aussies too, and Canadians, and a Yank, even though they weren't in the war yet. On my other side there was an Englishman like me, and about the same age, but he was much posher than me. He'd been to university. I'd never met anyone like him before. He looked and sounded like a younger version of my bank manager.

In another hut that was supposedly a dining hall and was called the airmen's mess we were given a meal of fried eggs, sausages and bully beef, and the conversations between us were restrained, almost hesitant, as though no-one was willing to trust anyone else and make the first move.

I passed my cigarettes around as we sipped our tea, and all ears centred on one chap who stated he'd already done a lot of flying in his uncle's Tiger Moth and there really was nothing to it. I wondered how true this was because if so, why was he here and not already in the skies above southern England in a Spitfire?

Back in our accommodation hut, some chaps had gathered around one bed and were playing cards, which soon made the atmosphere a little more relaxed. It seemed we were mostly from similar backgrounds, all united in a desire to fly aeroplanes as a way of getting back at the Hun. I wasn't to know at the time, but half our number would never make it to an operational squadron; such was the length and stress of the process.

5

AT SIX O'CLOCK THE NEXT MORNING A SERGEANT
burst in, stomping around noisily in hobnail boots which were
no doubt ruining the new wooden floor, with the peak of his
cap bent almost vertically down over his nose, shouting and
prodding our beds with a yard stick, telling us to, "Get up, if
you please, gentlemen." The hut was freezing cold, even at that
time of year. There was a stove, but it wasn't lit. I wouldn't like
to spend too much time there in winter. I hate being cold. Back
in the mess hut we ate a fantastic breakfast which was merely
a variation on the previous evening's meal, but wonderful
nonetheless; the eggs for which I later found out were from
a farm just across the road. At nine-thirty I straightened my
tie and had a last cigarette before sitting patiently with some
of the others in the hut marked Aircrew Board. I was wearing
my best shoes with my grey suit and a brown tie. Not too bold,
but not understated either.

The chap before me was the posh bloke with the degree. He was in there for almost half an hour. When he came out, he was beaming, jumping around with a clenched right fist, shouting, "Yes! Yes!" over and over under his breath, with a, "Good luck, old man," to me before disappearing out the door. The next one wasn't so lucky. He emerged with such a glum face I thought he'd start crying at any moment, like a little boy who'd just had his new bicycle stolen. He merely shook his head and was gone without saying a word. I never saw him again, the first of many who would never make it. My thoughts drifted to my own circumstances if the same thing happened to me, until I was snapped out of it when the door opened suddenly and a man's voice shouted from inside: "Copping!"

I'd spent weeks preparing for this moment. I followed the news broadcasts on the Home Service and read the newspapers daily, listening intently to the progress of the war as much as I could. I had no idea what they would ask or indeed what they were looking for. I'd done what I could and so I decided that it was now out of my hands. If they liked me, they'd take me on; if they didn't, then they wouldn't. It was a simple as that. Maybe then I'd try the Royal Navy or the Fleet Air Arm.

I was ushered into the centre of the room and onto a very ordinary wooden chair facing an extremely wide desk. Behind it were four men, only two of whom were in RAF uniform; the others wore dark suits. The oldest uniformed man had quite a few rings around his sleeves, at the very least a squadron leader, or so I thought. He also had pilot's wings above his left breast pocket and a dozen medal ribbons. He was the first to speak.

"Dennis Charles Hughmore Copping," he said, reading out my full name from papers in front of him. "Why the Air Force, Copping?" he said, now staring right into my eyes over the top of his half-moon glasses.

"To fly aeroplanes, Sir, of course," I replied, suddenly realising I might have sounded a little abrupt.

"How old are you, Copping?" he said. He must have known the answer; my file was right in front of him.

"I'm twenty-two, Sir," I replied, leaning forward a little in order to see more of the desk.

"Any connection with the Air Force?" the man on his right said.

"No, Sir," I replied.

"Army?" the older man said.

"Yes, I have a brother, Gordon, in the army," I replied. They must have known this as there followed some mutual nodding of heads as one of them wrote something down, passing it to the others who all nodded in unison with raised eyebrows. Gordon was doing well, working in London with the top brass somewhere, all very hush-hush. That was as much as he would tell me. A wide shaft of light suddenly hit me like a spotlight through the tiny window behind them as cloud cover broke, briefly blinding me and putting them in silhouette. My mind wandered a little. There was a strong smell of newly planed timber and boot polish, just as in the accommodation hut, now with the addition of cigarette smoke as one of my interviewers lit up.

"You don't live with your parents, why is that?" one of the men in plain clothes asked, staring at me, pen poised in his left hand. I wondered if this was relevant. Why were they asking this? What should I say?

"They separated, Sir," I replied, not really knowing whether to call him sir or not, but erring on the positive side, and continued, "five years ago. I now live with my Aunt Margaret." There was some scribbling from two of them, with more staring, and I felt uncomfortable.

"What does your father do, Mr Copping?" the first chap asked, smiling.

"He's a dentist, Sir," I replied. "He has his own practice in Warrior Square, Southend." I could see they were impressed. The scribbling was now accompanied by vague nods of approval.

"What do you do with yourself at the moment?" the other suited one asked. I assumed he meant what was my occupation. Surely they knew all this? I'd written it all down on the application form.

"I work for Cable and Wireless, Sir, electrical stuff, wireless sets, that sort of thing." More nods of approval. I'd heard a rumour they approved of technically minded people. They then asked me questions about my journey to Padgate. I told them it was a long way from Southend, but I didn't mind at all, if it meant I could eventually get my hands on an aeroplane. I told them I'd always loved aeroplanes, ever since I was a boy. I used to ride my bike to watch the activity at our local aerodrome, but up until then I'd never even been near one, let alone flown in one. There was more nodding of heads. Everything was going fine until the last few minutes. The younger chap in uniform put down his pen and looked directly at me. He also had pilot's wings on his tunic.

"Right, Copping, there you are, flying along in your brand-new Spitfire, perhaps having just had a tangle with the Hun and given him a bloody nose, when you look down and realise you're miles away from your home airfield. Your fuel gauge says you have around forty gallons left and you're somewhere over the North Sea. Let's assume your aircraft is using twenty-four gallons an hour at ten thousand feet and at 200 mph. How much flying time do you have left?"

My brain froze for a moment. This certainly caught me by surprise. You cannot possibly prepare for this, obviously, and they knew it. I began to work it out in my head as quickly as I could. Two hours is forty-eight gallons. I don't have that much, I have forty, which is twenty-four plus sixteen. Sixteen is two thirds of twenty-four. Converted to time, two thirds of an hour is forty minutes.

"I think it's about one hour and forty minutes, Sir," I replied, adding, "or thereabouts."

There was silence. Was I right? I thought I was. I went over it again in my head. Yes, I think it was right. The older chap smiled. There was some more scribbling and whispering. They ignored me for what seemed like hours. Then one of the suits said,

"You've got half an hour before you must get yourself to the last hut on the right for a medical. Good luck."

That was it. It seemed I'd passed.

6

THE MEDICAL WAS RELAXED BY COMPARISON. I'D never had any major health problems and my eyesight was fine. A corpulent middle-aged doctor with Harold Lloyd spectacles, bad breath and cold hands held onto my balls for a little longer than necessary, I thought, but everything was fine. It all seemed a bit of a formality, really, and in less than an hour I was back in the accommodation hut, having eaten another wonderful meal. I was shocked to find quite a few of the men had gone, already sent home after not making the grade, for whatever reason. I sat on my bed and wrote a letter home and then after tea some of the other chaps stated they were determined to find The Plough, a pub rumoured to be somewhere nearby, and would I like to come along?

We left the camp via the Blackbrook Avenue gate, over the bridge and into RAF Orford. I wasn't even aware this other camp existed until then. We were challenged by two armed

RAF police and asked to produce our identity cards before continuing. They confirmed the existence of the pub and gave us directions. Out the other side we crossed two fields of freshly cropped wheat before reaching The Plough, a tiny pub that wouldn't have looked out of place in an Essex village. An RAF sergeant was playing a piano with an impromptu choir of mixed uniforms gathered around him, all holding their pint pots and singing in a packed room thick with cigarette smoke.

We smiled as we walked through and eventually settled in one corner with our pints, the conversation soon focussing on the future. Rumours were flying around about where we would be sent for flying training if we passed the initial selection. Canada was the strongest possibility, with South Africa, and even Palestine, a possibility. It had to be done so far away because the Hun enjoyed the easy pickings of fledgling pilots undergoing training, like vultures circling overhead. We all understood this and so were prepared to travel. I had some tentative family connections with South Africa and so this was my preferred choice. Canada would be very cold in winter too.

It was approaching ten o'clock before our group left The Plough and returned to Padgate. There were a couple of chaps who I could become quite fond of but at that stage none of us knew where we would be going and with whom. As it turned out, this initial group would be dispersed across all corners of the empire when finally achieving operational service and I never saw any of them again. One of them was eventually posted to Singapore and the other to Bomber Command in Lincolnshire. We exchanged scribblings regularly, but a few months after becoming operational, the letters from both abruptly stopped arriving. I never found out why, but I could guess. This was always on one's mind when making friends during wartime, as I was to learn all too often.

I was prodded awake at six o'clock in the morning by the angry sergeant with his stick and told to report to the Aircrew Board promptly at nine.

My head was a little fuzzy, but it wasn't quite a hangover. After breakfast I walked in, expecting to be seen by someone official in uniform. Instead I was handed a buff envelope marked 'Confidential' by a smiling young woman in a grey blouse and plain blue pencil skirt. Inside was a letter, telling me in very formal RAF language that I was free to return home, but I must be ready to report back at any time. It was a curious way of welcoming me to the RAF, by not saying that I had failed. I knew I'd been accepted because I was given my service number, 785025, and the basic rank of Aircraft Charge Hand, Aircrew Under Training, RAF Volunteer Reserve, but still no uniform. I was in, so to speak, but sitting precariously on the very bottom rung of a very tall ladder.

I spent the next two weeks at home in a kind of limbo, patiently waiting for my call-up. Home for me at the time was 493 Kents Hill Road, South Benfleet, where I lived with my Aunt Margaret. She was delighted with my news and as soon as I'd slurped a quick cup of tea with her, I took the bus to Warrior Square in Southend to inform my father, Sydney, at his surgery. Now I was back in my hometown I felt quietly big-headed about my situation; I was going to be a fighter pilot and none of the other ordinary people on the bus were aware of just how important I was. They'd be thanking me and saying what a wonderful chap I was if they knew, that's for sure.

I sat in the waiting room for ten minutes reading an old *Picture Post* with other patients until the receptionist summoned me and I knocked on the surgery door before stepping inside. My father was drying his instruments thoroughly, laying each one out on a tin tray very methodically, totally engrossed in his work. He had a very important job and I didn't want to disturb him. He knew where I'd been because I'd told him beforehand, so it wouldn't be a complete surprise.

"I'm in, the RAF has accepted me," I said, feeling oddly nervous standing at the door, my right hand gripping the handle tightly. He didn't reply but paused briefly, laying a shiny dental spike onto the tray beside him. "I'm just waiting for my call-up papers now," I continued, "sometime in the next two weeks," I said, taking a step forward, abandoning the door handle and standing alone in the middle of the highly polished parquet floor.

"That's good," he said finally, picking up another instrument, rubbing it gently with both hands in a cloth before laying it down. "Have you told your mother yet?" he said, glancing round at me for an instant before resuming.

"No, not yet, but I will," I said, as the surgery door was then opened and his receptionist appeared.

"Your next patient is anxious to see you now, Mr Copping, are you ready?"

"Yes, send them in, Miss Clarke," my father said, moving over to his chair. "Well, good luck, old chap," he said, extending his right arm. I shook it just as the door was opened and a middle-aged man entered. My father dropped my hand and turned around to his instruments. I stepped out into the hallway where the receptionist smiled at me and then looked down at the floor. Outside the late summer sunshine warmed my face. I lit a cigarette and after some long, hard pulls on it, the nicotine rush almost caused me to stumble as I walked along the path to the street. This was the last time I saw my father.

My mother Adelaide occasionally lived with us in Kents Hill Road but was now working for a wealthy family in a huge house just outside Southend. She kissed me warmly on my right cheek, and I noticed there were tears in her eyes. She looked very tired in the same way my father did. Wartime must be particularly worrying for parents of five children, wondering where each of them were and what they were doing. My brother Gordon was soon to be posted overseas in the army, my brother Lionel was living somewhere in London yet to be called up, and my two sisters Lilly and Edna were still in Southend and volunteered for everything they could. Add to this the fact that my mother was coping with it all alone, as was my father. There was nothing I could do about this. They were apart and I didn't know why, though I had my suspicions. The world is not a perfect place and these things happen, relationships break down, just like in war.

On 25th September, I was considering what to do with my day, perhaps another trip to The Scala to see *The Road to Singapore* with Bob Hope and Bing Crosby, when the letter arrived along with another Rail Warrant for travel the following Monday. This time I was heading for the West Country, with my final destination being Torquay in Devon. I was both excited and nervous at what was to come, and I said goodbye to my mother and my Aunt Margaret with a little more trepidation than last time. I really wanted to do what I could, and I was happy to do it, but just like everyone else, in the back of my mind I knew that involvement in the war was not optional and I had no choice.

My journey was uneventful and I was glad to get through London, because by the end of that month the bombing was much worse. There was devastation and rubble everywhere, and I saw a double-decker bus entirely swallowed up by a huge hole in the road. The Hun had mostly abandoned his mass daytime raids because he'd been given such a pasting by the RAF, but now every night the Luftwaffe crossed the Channel, inflicting more carnage and misery on the civilian population.

What kind of people did this to defenceless civilians? What kind of air force took pleasure in such indiscriminate killing? The Hun air force must surely be populated by the worst kind of heartless bastards.

I arrived at Torquay station in the late afternoon of Monday 30th September, and I was met by an officious warrant officer with a clipboard and a huge moustache who directed me to the Sefton Hotel on the seafront. I expected to be taken to an RAF base but was told along with two others that this would happen in the morning, at nine o'clock sharp. Inside I found a state of overcrowded chaos. In the room allocated to me there were two others in the double bed and four RAF camp beds crammed in with little or no floor space remaining. We were fed in a packed dining room, and I then spent almost two hours walking along the seafront alone as night fell, in order to escape the cramped conditions. That night, despite being exhausted, I didn't get much sleep in a noisy, uncomfortable bed under a draughty window. The room was loud with snoring and farting, making the air stale and oppressive. I hadn't expected this at all.

7

AFTER BREAKFAST OF TOAST AND MARMALADE I MADE my way back to the station for nine o'clock. The same warrant officer was checking names and identity cards when I climbed into the back of a brand-new RAF Hillman Tilly, cramming myself in with five others from the hotel for the thankfully short ride to RAF Babbacombe. It had just started raining heavily, and I could hear it pattering loudly on the canvas roof even above the noise of the Hillman's engine. I passed my cigarettes around, but there was only one taker. Everyone looked rather fed up. Our driver must have been very inexperienced because he grated the gears constantly, throwing us around bends with merciless disregard. The rear flaps of canvas came loose and occasionally flew inside, sending rainwater in our faces and causing us to lean into the back of the van on top of one another in what became moments of welcome hilarity. It wasn't until we got out of the vehicle that we saw the driver was a very pretty WAAF undergoing driving instruction. She smiled shyly at us in what was probably meant as an apology.

During a brief pause in the weather I noticed RAF Babbacombe had a wonderful view of the sea, with easy access down to the water, and in my mind the place seemed better located for joining the navy than the air force. In the first hut we were issued with our kit and it was then that someone pointed out that we'd all been promoted to the rank of Aircraftman Second Class. Once in uniform we were marched everywhere, often with no particular destination but just up and down, backwards and forwards, for hours. This was our rather pointless routine for several days, and every now and then we'd have a break for a cup of tea and to be individually inoculated against every known disease. One of these injections, I think it was the one for yellow fever, caused me to lose the use of my left arm for several hours and feel terribly unwell. I wondered if I'd ever feel better, until after a while I realised the nausea had passed.

We were then taken in a huge lorry to an open-air firing range overlooking the sea where we were taught to shoot. There was a cool onshore breeze and the ground was wet, so as I lay on the mat my uniform became damp, and I sensed moisture seeping through at my elbows. I was relieved to see everyone else must have been the same. After the first volley I discovered I was a good shot with a Lee Enfield .303, and I was very pleased with my performance. Waiting for the Range Officer's next order while gazing down the range, a lone seagull I'd been watching for a while came closer, drifting in from the sea, soaring effortlessly on wide outstretched wings, glancing left and right with casual head turns. Every now and again he would rise up a few feet, skilfully mastering a stall turn before drifting back the other way. If they do think, then he must have been thinking about fish, his next meal, or of finding somewhere to land, maybe on the water with the others.

Fifty yards in front of us he turned again, closer still, coming to a virtual stop in the air, hanging there for a moment, poised to resume. Just then I heard the Range Officer shout and the man next to me fired a shot, causing the poor bird to explode in a cloud of red mist, falling to the ground with a lifeless thud. "Got 'im," he said, smirking at me.

I was much less successful with a Webley pistol; I could barely hit the target let alone get a bullseye, but it didn't seem to matter because we were not given an opportunity to improve. Back in the hut we were shown the workings of a Bren gun, the British Army's most popular light machine gun, and how to strip it down and rebuild it. To this day I've never had to use one, and so why on earth I had to strip it and rebuild it while blindfolded I've no idea. There must be some merit in it somewhere! We were taught Morse code and were tested on it a hundred times daily until we all passed. One or two of us, me included, already knew of it as I'd come across it at work so we had a little advantage, which was always helpful. So far I suspected the training I'd received was no different to that experienced by army recruits; I'd been in the RAF for weeks and the only aeroplanes I'd seen were the black silhouettes in aircraft recognition charts covering the classroom walls.

Despite my mixed results at shooting, it seemed I'd passed the initial training and on Monday 2nd December after eight weeks, we were all given a few days' leave. I returned home, already armed with a Rail Warrant for my next destination.

I was shocked when I passed through London again. The Hun had been very busy since my last visit. Worse news was to come. Southend had been bombed several times, on the 12th, 19th and 27th November. They had even dive-bombed our hospital. What utter bastards they were. The estuary had been attacked regularly all summer and they even put the pier out of action with mines, but these latest raids were a new low even for the Hun.

Aunt Margaret was in town when I arrived, after apparently hearing a rumour that Arnold's greengrocers had some onions, and when she returned with one, she looked visibly older and frailer, as did my mother. Hardly surprising, really, with bombs falling all around and invasion imminent. Our street was thankfully still intact, but some were not so lucky, with every third or fourth house missing like gaps in someone's teeth, and a heap of rubble where a family home once stood. I felt guilty that I had escaped and was no longer living among these people. Because of this I didn't enjoy my last few days at home. I wanted to get on with the war, my war, to play my part in it. I felt a deep sense of helplessness as I walked around Southend seeing all the bomb damage. Quite a few people had been killed in the most senseless and brutal way, and though I didn't need any greater antipathy towards the Hun, it was unavoidable now.

At last I was on my way; heading back to the north-east, this time to a transit camp at West Kirby on the Dee Estuary near Liverpool. From here I would be sent to Elementary Flying Training School, wherever this would be. I'd reached a point at which I began to feel more excited as the aeroplanes were getting closer. Not only this, I'd been promoted again, to Leading Aircraftman and my pay had doubled from two shillings a day to four.

This increase in wealth really didn't affect me much, other than the fact I now had more money to spend on my only expenses at that time, namely beer and cigarettes. A couple of the chaps I knew had expensive wives or girlfriends, but not me, so I left a ten bob note on the mantelpiece at home before I left, despite the fact it had been refused earlier. I knew they were all having a tough time without me.

I gazed out the window of the train, contemplating my future. I anticipated Canada; it seemed the logical place to go for flying training well out of the reach of the Hun, and it was where most people were currently being sent. It would be very cold at this time of year and I didn't relish the long sea voyage, but so be it. On my return, if I passed I'd be posted to a fighter squadron in the south-east of England where I'd be flying above familiar countryside close enough to return home every now and again. I'd no doubt be busy, but this is what I thought would happen, and I was prepared for it. You can imagine my surprise when I arrived at West Kirby on 9th December to be informed I was not heading west to Canada but to South Africa, and almost immediately. I was thrilled.

I spent an uncomfortable night in a temporary billet within sight of the sea, and in the morning we all walked carefully up a precarious gangplank that bounced like a trampoline onto the deck of a huge ship, the inside of which had been gutted and was now full of swinging hammocks. I soon learned these were comfortable enough if you slept on your back, mainly because there was no other way. Some couldn't do this and chose to sleep on the floor instead. My immediate neighbour was a pragmatic Yorkshireman called Bob Davis from Barnsley. We connected immediately, and it's odd how this happens, when getting to know someone seems so easy. He was my age and had been working in a string of different jobs before taking the plunge into the air force. Like me he'd seen how the war had touched civilian life, but worse than me he'd had relatives killed in Sheffield during the bombing only a few weeks before.

We were ushered into a dining area fifty at a time and given a meal that was quite good: meat, potatoes, bread, real eggs and as much tea as we could drink; then Bob and I spent hours walking on deck despite the cold in order to escape the stuffy conditions below. At ten o'clock that night we were confined to quarters and all lights were extinguished.

The ship was packed with servicemen of all types, and also some women who were kept separate under lock and key at all times, hidden away like priceless jewellery. We would occasionally hear their laughter echoing around the ship, but we'd never see them, like a ghost in the attic. Even on deck, they had separate areas, fenced off from the rest of us cattle.

Once out of the relative safety of British waters, I had a real fear of being torpedoed. We were told to keep the noise down when below deck, and to avoid any loud banging, particularly metallic sounds, which could be picked up from many miles away.

8

I WAS A REASONABLE SWIMMER, BUT THE ATLANTIC was freezing at that time of year, and so it was with some relief I noticed our small convoy of ships was being shadowed by a Royal Navy frigate which eventually left us once we had crossed the Bay of Biscay, silently disappearing back to Blighty under cover of darkness. We were not left completely alone, though, as from then on every day I noticed a Coastal Command Sunderland buzzing around overhead.

We tried to keep ourselves clean, but it wasn't easy. Fresh water was scarce, and we had to wash and shave in saltwater. We had access to saltwater showers, but it meant leaving our belongings and queuing for an hour. I trusted Bob, and so we took turns as I looked after his things while he went for a shower and vice-versa. There were plus points to this voyage, though: the breakfasts were superb, with plenty of eggs, bacon, sausages and mushrooms, quite exceptional for that time.

After six uneventful days at sea, we arrived in Freetown on the west coast of Africa. We picked up supplies and fuel, and it was so incredibly hot we all just hung around on deck to get some air, as none of us were allowed off the ship. Some locals tried selling us fruit from their little boats and we tossed pennies into the water to watch them dive down to retrieve them. They were bloody good swimmers!

Quite a few qualified pilots disembarked, and I didn't find out why until weeks later. Volunteers were asked to fly freshly un-crated rebuilt Hurricanes all the way from there right across Africa to Cairo. I was astonished because it was such a vast distance. There were staging posts for fuel, of course, but if your navigation was just one degree out, you'd miss everything and end up plunging into the jungle, never to be seen again. There was a common joke about it that went, "Just follow the line of wrecked aircraft." I was very relieved not to be taking part.

Once we were moving again the sea breeze was wonderful, and we spent most nights sleeping on deck. Seven days later we arrived at Cape Town, South Africa very early on a bright, sunny morning. I couldn't believe what I saw. Table Mountain stood in spectacular splendour high above us, and everywhere was lush greenery in a lovely, warm summer breeze. Only a few days before we'd been in the dark wartime austerity of an icy English winter, and now it seemed we had landed on a different planet. The air was sweet and perfumed from the many flowers in bloom all around, and it was easy to forget why we were there. With no time for sightseeing, we were sent straightaway to the nearby railway station and onto the first train we saw.

I settled in a window seat with Bob and it wasn't long before the train lurched forward, very slowly at first until gathering speed as we were soon passing open countryside.

Rattling north in packed carriages I found the heat exhausting and so I slept for most of the journey. We stopped late that night at Pretoria for sandwiches and coffee. It was real coffee too, strong and full of flavour, nothing like the chicory mix I was used to, and I'm sure it was that and my earlier sleep that kept me awake half the night.

The next day Bob and I parted company with the train at Bulawayo Station in Southern Rhodesia and we were taken with quite a few others in a large open truck to an airfield nearby, arriving there just before dark. The sign at the gate read 'Welcome to the RATG', which stood for the Rhodesian Air Training Group, and underneath that: 'No. 27 EFTS – Induna'. As we entered, I saw a line of bright yellow aeroplanes, with the sunset's glow turning their wings to pure gold. Twilight lasted just a few minutes and very soon it was pitch dark. The daytime heat seemed to carry on right into the evening, my clothes were wet where they touched and all around the chatter of insects was deafening. This was unlike anything I'd ever experienced before. It was Christmas Eve, 1940.

We dumped our kit in a wooden barrack hut that smelled of old blankets and boot polish, and we were marched straight into the mess for dinner. There were huge wooden tables laden with fresh fruit – some of which I didn't recognise – piles of bread and butter covered with thin cotton mesh, fresh salad, cooked meats, and as much tea and coffee as we could drink. Compared to the rationing in England, this was paradise.

I slept really well and the next morning we were all woken up at six o'clock to be told because it was Christmas Day we were allowed to spend the entire day doing nothing; officially we were to familiarise ourselves with our new surroundings, as the Warrant Officer phrased it. They would never tell us we could do nothing. We found out there was a swimming pool a mile away which we all made good use of, and just like everyone else I found it hard to grasp what date it was, as we lay in the sun by the pool, smoking and relaxing.

In the morning it was business as usual. We were all scalped by a huge chap with an enormous belly that quivered violently when he laughed, which was often, and arms thicker than the tops of my thighs. His hands and face were dark and creased like old leather, and there was an odd odour about him, a mixture of wet dog and stale cigarettes. I could hardly understand a word he said his accent was so thick, and occasionally he lapsed into Afrikaans, which is similar to Dutch. Then in our brand-new khaki uniforms we were marched across the camp in lines of three for yet more Morse code revision. We were now wearing entirely tropical uniform, and there was serious speculation we would all be sent to the Far East, perhaps to help protect Singapore from the advancing Japanese. To be honest, I wasn't bothered where I was sent; provided I could fly aeroplanes, what did it matter?

Several bright yellow Tiger Moths stood idling, the draught from their propellers hurling dust into the air. One of them moved off onto the strip and took off past the wreck of another Tiger Moth that had up-ended and was lying on its back.

I wondered why it was still there until I found out it had only just happened and the two occupants were in hospital. I also noticed none of the buildings were camouflaged; the walls and roof of each shone brilliant white in the sunshine. I remembered the Hun was nowhere near and after a year of war in England this took some getting used to.

Later that same day we were all issued with a personal flying kit and the single most important item for any pilot: the flying logbook. Every trip in an aeroplane from now on, however short, was to be recorded contemporaneously as evidence of flying experience. We were split into groups of four and were led by a flight lieutenant into the dispersal area. I stood in awe with my small cluster of fellow students in front of a de Havilland DH82A Tiger Moth, gazing at it, hardly listening to the officer introducing us to this wonderful machine. He pointed to the wooden propeller and then at each of us in turn.

"This is the business end of the whole thing, gentlemen, but be warned, it enjoys chopping the heads off the unwary." With this thought in mind, he led us around the aeroplane in a clockwise direction, checking the leading edges of the wings, the wires, struts and control surfaces, looking for dents, rips and other damage. Then, once back at the nose, he opened the cowling to reveal the engine. It was mounted upside down, with the exhausts underneath, apparently to aid visibility. The starting procedure was explained and I was worried sick at this point; it seemed such a lengthy procedure I couldn't remember any of it. Finally the cowling was closed again and we were asked if there were any questions. None of us dare speak up, least of all me, even though I was unsure. We were told these checks were to be conducted before every flight. I wondered how a combat pilot would have time to do this, unaware that much of it would, of course, be done by the ground crew. We then took turns to sit in the front seat, where the student sits, going through the instruments and the effects of the controls. This was far more interesting, and I had little trouble remembering what was said.

"That's it then, gentlemen. You start first thing tomorrow," the officer said, beaming at us. We played cards that night, with most conversations centred on what was to come. There was an air of quiet but excited anticipation among my fellow students. Those who already had some flying experience were listened to intently as they repeatedly described their first moments in the air, but few had done very much.

It was already light at six o'clock in the morning, and I was wide awake. It didn't cool down much overnight and our room was quite breathless by morning with the addition of the mosquito net around the bed and the fact we'd been warned to keep the windows shut, which didn't help. I heard the noisy chatter of house sparrows and when I opened the window I felt a wonderfully scented warm breeze drifting into the room. Then I caught a whiff of high-octane petrol and oil that I would soon learn always comes with the close proximity of aeroplanes. Excitement, nerves, apprehension, all mixed with adrenaline in a powerful cocktail of emotions, though I still managed a decent breakfast!

9

I put on my flying gear and marched off to the dispersal hut, clutching my new logbook. It was a fine, clear morning with hardly any wind, and I was ready to head off into the sky.

Four of us sat in front of a well-used blackboard. We were again told about the altimeter, the rpm gauge, airspeed indicator, cross level (a kind of basic turn and slip indicator), oil pressure gauge and the compass. Today we were going to fly circuits around the airfield: take off, climb up to five hundred feet, then a gentle climbing turn left up to eight hundred feet, and then level out and throttle back into the downwind leg, parallel with the airfield.

Then a left turn onto the base leg over the crossroads, then left again beyond the end of the airstrip for final approach. This was the theory following the diagram on the blackboard. It was the shape of a huge rectangle in the sky around the airfield, and it would always be the same unless the wind changed direction, in which case it would just be the opposite way around. The landmarks were the key, remembering at which point to turn and at what height. I would soon see how I would cope with this.

I met my instructor, Flying Officer Andy Green, for the first time. There were instructors of many nationalities, but Andy was British and was already an RAF veteran. He had clearly been in Africa for a while because despite being just a few years older than me the fair skin of his face was now bronzed and leathery, very much like that of the camp barber. He grabbed my right hand, shaking it firmly.

"Copping?"

"Yes, Sir," I replied, gathering up my flying helmet and logbook. I saw him looking at me, making his initial assessment. I've no doubt I appeared as nervous as I felt.

"You're with me. You don't need your logbook, leave that here, and follow me." Andy was a little taller than me and walked with long, self-assured strides, the side parting of his sun-whitened blond hair flapping like a bird's wing as he moved.

I felt awkward as the rubber speaking tube on my brown leather helmet trailed along the wooden floor before I fumbled along, gathering it up as we walked across the already-warm concrete. I didn't feel as though I needed to impress, I was just terrified of coming across as a blithering idiot.

"Either put your helmet on or leave it on the seat a minute," he said, sounding impatient, dropping his on the rear seat. I immediately did the same and then followed him around the aeroplane. He ran his fingertips along the control surfaces and leading edges of the wings, glancing underneath at the tyres. All seemed fine. A thin chap in khaki overalls appeared from nowhere with a cheery shout of, "Morning, gents!" before grabbing the propeller and turning it clockwise three times.

"In you get then, Copping," Andy said, nodding at the front seat. I climbed onto the wing and into the cockpit to a heady smell of leather, oil and fuel.

I connected the tubes on my helmet and adjusted it on my head before setting my goggles neatly over my eyes. There was an almighty blowing noise in my ears followed by, "Can you hear me alright?" To which I instinctively nodded before shouting a reply into the tube on my right: "Yes, thank you, Sir!"

The thin man in overalls had the cowling open and was checking the fuel. He then shouted, "Throttle open!"

"Throttle open!" Andy replied. The cowling was fastened shut and the propeller was then turned back eight times, as though winding the aeroplane up like clockwork.

"Throttle closed!"

"Throttle closed!" Andy replied from behind, before: "Ignition on, contact!" The propeller was flung once in a clockwise direction by the chap outside and I noticed the throttle lever move back towards me a little on my left as the engine burst into life. There was a brief thumbs up from outside as he walked briskly away, dragging the chocks with him.

I couldn't believe the amount of noise and vibration. I looked at the instrument panel as it rattled, watching what was happening. The rpm gauge and the oil pressure were the only ones moving.

We sat there for a few moments before moving off towards the end of the airstrip, occasionally zig-zagging very slightly because it was impossible to see straight ahead.

"Put your hands and feet very lightly on the controls and follow me through, but I'm in control, alright?"

"Yes, Sir," I replied, as we turned to point the nose down the airfield. The lever on my left moved right back as the propeller responded to full throttle. I felt my left foot move forwards a little, and the control column – or stick, as it's known – was eased back very slightly, and then within seconds we were ever so slightly bouncing along, a little lighter every time until everything was beautifully smooth and we were up. All the instruments were now moving; I watched the altimeter as we passed a hundred feet, then two hundred, three, four, and at five hundred we turned gently left around the airfield.

"Climbing turn, Copping, fifteen degrees, no more!" I heard in my ears as I saw the cross level confirming the angle of bank. I then looked outside. The huge flat-topped hill a few miles to the north-east had gone, or at least didn't look quite so high anymore. Most such features disappeared, and everything now looked flat and shapeless. I had a sudden rush of panic that I'd never find my way around, so I kept my eyes fixed on the airfield below and the reference points we had been told about. As I saw them pass beneath me, I remembered I must also observe the controls and instruments at the same time, and I then saw the throttle was eased forward and the rpm gauge responded. The wings levelled, as did the cross level, one following the other. The nose dropped forward, the airspeed rose and settled at 60 mph. This was all happening in just a few seconds and I was desperately trying to take it in.

"Downwind now, Copping, can you see the airfield down there off the port wing, on the left?"

"Yes, Sir!" I shouted into the mouthpiece.

"Circuit height, eight hundred feet."

"Yes!" I replied, not knowing what else to add, if anything. The roads below seemed to disappear into the distance, and as we flew beside the airfield I was relieved when I recognised the main gate and a few other buildings, but not our accommodation or the mess. I quickly realised that roads were the easiest features to remember, then buildings and clusters of trees. We turned left onto the base leg, a thirty-degree bank this time, I saw the crossroads underneath us, and a minute later we turned left again. The throttle was eased forward, and as the engine noise subsided, I could hear the wing wires singing.

"Fly it right down onto the ground using the throttle, stay in control, keep the same angle of approach with a point on the horizon, and never let the airspeed drop below forty. At the height of a double-decker bus, throttle right back and allow the aeroplane to gently land on the main wheels."

We passed over the edge of the airfield and then floated ten feet over the ground and slowly sank lower, touching down very gently, the earthbound aeroplane, so graceful in the air, suddenly blind and awkward again like an injured bird.

"Got that, Copping?" I heard in my ears.

"Yes, Sir, I think so, Sir!" I shouted back, my head now bursting with information.

"Good, then let's do it again, shall we?" he shouted as the throttle lever came all the way back again and in a few seconds we were up.

My logbook entry for that day stated I spent two hours and ten minutes as second pilot or *pupil under instruction* in my first flight, on exercise one, two, three and four, in a total of four circuits. It was known as 'circuits and bumps' and after lunch we did it all again, but this time Andy was letting me have a go. I'd have the nose too high, or too low, and I'd come in too fast or too high, with him shouting in my ear, "Keep the same point on the horizon and stick to it," as we landed. Nothing else was discussed; just get up into the circuit, turn left three times and get back down safely, over and over again, until it became almost automatic. Finally, at three o'clock that day, we gathered in a large room near the dispersal hut for some ground school. Everything seemed to fit into place now that I'd actually tried it all for real. I knew how and why the instruments did what they did, and that the controls only needed the slightest touch to function. I'd been gripping the stick with both hands and Andy must have guessed because he repeatedly shouted, "Gently, you're overdoing it," until I realised perfect control can be achieved using just the fingertips.

10

For the Tiger Moth, a few important figures were drummed into us: VNE of 150 mph – that's the Velocity Never Exceed, or maximum airspeed the aeroplane could safely handle – manoeuvring speed for aerobatics at around 100 mph, stall speed around 25 mph, but this was the absolute lowest airspeed, and 40 was the preferred minimum. These figures became permanently etched into our brains, until we were to fly another type of aeroplane when the same things had to be re-learned. We brushed up on our maths too, the theory of flight, and aero engines and airframes. We were taught navigation and using a lamp to send Morse code. This was new as we'd only previously used a Morse key. We still had to do drill, of course; parading in full flying gear seemed a bit odd, and very uncomfortable in the heat of the day, though thankfully most of the time this was done in the early morning, probably for that reason.

That night at dinner I learned that two of our number had gone missing. At first I didn't understand, or believe it, but then I realised. It was not well publicised but became common knowledge via the 'bush telegraph' gossip. They hadn't crashed or got lost while flying; they'd just packed their bags and disappeared, both at the same time as though it had been planned. They hadn't failed the training course to be sent home either, and so officially we were told they had gone AWOL, Absent without Leave. Whatever the reason, we never saw them again. I later found out this was surprisingly common.

Some men were understandably tired of war and the bleak austerity back home in Britain. We were losing the war then as we still are, with the unstoppable Hun bombing and smashing and goose-stepping his way right across Europe he was expected to be stomping up Whitehall at any moment. The temptation to stay in the warm sunshine of South Africa or Rhodesia far away from it all was too great for some. I could understand this; it was a lovely place, and we were all young men with our whole lives ahead of us, but the thought of never being able to return home horrified me. That's what would have happened, return would have been impossible, regardless of which direction the war took. I wasn't looking forward to being shot at in combat, but the alternative was unthinkable. I also knew I wouldn't have been able to live with the shame, and besides, I really did want to do my bit, but I know I wasn't alone in thinking about this incident for several days.

Like all trainee pilots, I struggled at first. I had a bad habit of settling the aeroplane at 65 mph in the circuit when it should have been 60.

"If you can keep it nicely at sixty-five, why can't you keep it at sixty?" Andy would repeatedly shout, with obvious frustration in his voice. He was right, of course, why was I doing this? Every time I sat in the cockpit I disciplined myself to get it right until eventually it clicked. I don't remember when, it just did.

We pupils often discussed our flying and it seemed everyone had their own individual problems. Gradually over time these were overcome and I made good progress along with some of the other chaps I knew well, and it seemed we were becoming reasonable pilots. Andy was my instructor throughout most of my Tiger Moth training, apart from a few occasions when I had a couple of others. Learning to fly was an oddly personal business and each instructor had wildly differing ideas about flying. I was always glad to settle back in my seat knowing Andy was sitting behind me.

I tried very hard to get to know Andy but almost every time I offered him a mug of pre-flight tea or a cigarette he refused, at least in the early days. He was shutting me out and I had no idea why. This changed a little towards the end, when he would grudgingly take a cigarette when I offered. On reflection I realise just how incredibly naïve I was, and understand only too well now, but at the time I knew very little about him and I wanted to know much more. Discipline was always maintained between us and to him I was always 'Copping' or when under instruction in the air it was 'For god's sake, Copping', or similar, and to me he was never anything less than 'Sir'. I referred to him as Andy only once, in my latter days at Induna. It was a vain attempt, only too obvious, and even though I know he heard me, he very definitely chose to ignore it. I know this for sure. Of his war background I only heard brief snippets; he'd taken part in the early stages of the war as a Hurricane pilot in Eleven Group over southern England, but that was about all. I asked another instructor about him and all he would tell me was that he'd been through a rough time and that his squadron had 'lost a lot of chaps' before he was sent to South Africa. I rarely saw him smile, but when he did I could see there was still a lot pain in his eyes.

I was unaware that each of us were being scrutinised for suitability on various aircraft types even at this early stage. By now we were often flying at three or four thousand feet learning how to really handle the aeroplane. The Tiger Moth was known to be a forgiving little thing but like most aeroplanes it would turn around and bite you if you were careless. We practiced stalls and spins and even some basic aerobatic manoeuvres, which to me were real flying, and I enjoyed every moment. There's nothing in the world like looking up in an aeroplane to see the Earth above your head. It was during these manoeuvres that I often heard some brief but enthusiastic vocal noises from the seat behind me; these were not shouts of praise or disapproval but expressions of joy.

There was a serious message in most of these handling exercises, of course. Recognising an incipient spin or the onset of a stall could save your life, particularly on approach to landing. You could lose a hundred feet or more in a stall, so if you were approaching at a hundred feet you'd therefore find yourself in serious deficit of sky. An aeroplane stall is not like when you stall the engine of your car; it's connected to the lift over the wings not the engine. If the airflow isn't maintained the wing becomes stalled and useless, causing the aeroplane to fall from the sky. It can happen to any aeroplane in the wrong hands.

By the middle of the third week my logbook was filling up, and I was by now in control of the aeroplane most of the time while training, particularly during take-offs and landings. Andy signed it at the end of every day's flying, and on one occasion after accepting one of my cigarettes I was chuffed when he looked me in the eye and said, "You're doing well, Dennis, really well."

We spent several frustrating days at a time in ground school without any flying at all, but conversations in the mess were lively due to frequent rumours about some of us going solo. We'd accrued the right amount of hours, so what was the delay? As I gazed out the window, I saw Andy leading another pupil to an aeroplane and I noticed him glancing in at us several times. I was unaware of the plans he had in store for me when I returned to flying training. We'd been practising emergency landings at some point during every flight until the procedure for an engine failure or a fire in the air was now instinctive. There had obviously been a reason for this.

At the end of my first full day back, he climbed out of the aeroplane while the engine was idling. I remember it was a particularly warm day and I thought at first that he needed a drink or a pee until he stood on the wing next to me and shouted, "One circuit, then back here, right?" He then walked away as though he hadn't a care in the world, not once looking back.

I wasn't nervous. You might think that taking an aeroplane up on your own for the first time could be a terrifying prospect, but far from it. I suppose it's odd, but the excitement completely overwhelmed every other emotion, every thought, every distraction. There was nothing else now, just me and the aeroplane. Certainly it would be terrifying if you were placed inside an aeroplane and told to fly it without any experience; this would be foolhardy in the extreme. But my training had been superb, and now I was ready.

Everything looked the same to me, as I had been sitting in the front seat all along and so could never see the instructor's presence or therefore his absence. Take-off was fine, the Tiger Moth touching only once in a very slight bounce before it left the ground, and with the help of a gusting 20 mph headwind it gained height quickly like a kite on a string. A gentle fifteen-degree climbing turn left at five hundred feet, then level off at eight hundred feet in the circuit.

During the downwind leg I managed a quick glance behind me at the empty space where Andy's head usually appears. I knew he wasn't there, of course, but it was just something I had to do! I also knew I was smiling broadly like a village idiot, and on the verge of silly laughter before I began singing out loud while alternately scanning the ground and checking my instruments. I had become a curious mix of serious adult and happy little boy all at the same time. I then had a brief but powerful urge to leave the circuit, open the throttle wide and climb high into the sky, but I managed to resist this very real temptation. I turned left again – or to port, as I should say – into final approach over the airfield boundary and the threshold, holding it until ten feet or thereabouts when I cut the power and allowed it to sink gracefully onto the main wheels and solid ground with a gentle bump.

11

I taxied to a standstill near the dispersal hut. I shut down the engine and just after the propeller stopped, I let out a long breath and another wide smile. It was Wednesday 15th January 1941 and I had nine hour's experience.

There was no champagne or smiling handshake from Andy, just a wry smile with a very cynical, "You survived, then?" as he signed my logbook. Under the column *Pilot or 1st Pilot* I'd simply written 'Self' for the first time with no other name present. There were no loud celebrations. That was it. It was wartime, after all, despite the warm sunshine, no blackout and plentiful food. I sometimes forgot the reason I was there, to become a killer in a killer aeroplane. Three others made their first solos that day, and we celebrated over a beer later, with some modest congratulatory handshakes and back-slapping. One of the chaps pranged his aeroplane quite badly after misjudging the landing a little, but luckily he was uninjured.

It was rumoured that he'd be for the chop, but he wasn't, and he managed to stay with us. These were the most dangerous times, when they trusted us alone with so little experience. We had to gain more experience of flying solo by taking the aeroplane up on our own, but when we did so we were most at risk. At least we had the weather on our side with mainly warm sunny days, light fair-weather cumulus clouds and a gentle breeze most of the time. I imagined learning to fly in England in January, or even in Canada, and so I knew how lucky we were.

From then on, we left the circuit immediately after take-off and when we did so Andy would shout loudly in my ear, "Let's get up there, shall we!", opening the throttle and climbing up to three thousand feet or more for general handling exercises, as they were known. Flying with Andy became a real pleasure, and to me at least I forgot he was my senior officer and I was his pupil. Closing the throttle and gently pulling up the nose of the aeroplane, I enjoyed practising stalls and spins. "Now, Copping, now!" came the shout from behind me. "Full left rudder!" with a firm tap on my left shoulder as the aircraft, now almost vertical, came to a near-complete stop in the air, the wing wires silent as I thrust my left foot forwards as hard as I could. With my right hand on the stick and my left on the throttle, the propeller was now turning very slowly like a windmill on a summer's day, my back pressed hard into my seat as the ground disappeared and all I could see was sky.

Over to the left it dropped, nose-heavy like a stone, flipping forwards, the ground three thousand feet below suddenly filling my vision and rushing towards us. The Tiger Moth began turning, settling quite flat at a thirty-degree angle, once, twice, accelerating all the time. On the third rotation there was another shout: "Right, recover, full opposite rudder and full power!" with a very firm tap on my right shoulder for good measure. I pushed hard with my right foot while drawing the throttle lever towards me, the engine easing back into life.

I began pulling on the stick but was corrected: "Not yet, get some airspeed first, don't be too hasty!" As the speed built up and the wing wires began singing again, I gently pulled back on the stick, eventually settling the aircraft in straight and level flight before reducing the throttle to settle at 60 mph. "Well done, Copping, that wasn't too bad. Let's try it again." Close the throttle, pull the nose up gently, watch the speed decrease, *feel* the aircraft slow down in the air, hear the wires fall silent again, pull the stick back as far as it will go, then just before it comes to a stop, kick it over into the spin. I recovered on the third rotation, this time with no shouts of derision from behind me so I assumed it had met with approval. Either that or Andy had fallen from the aircraft, but no, he was still there. I checked.

We did this over and over until my own senses began to merge with the aeroplane; I could feel through my whole body the lift under the wings, the gravity acting upon us, together in unison, as though my blood was merging completely with the oil in the engine as one machine. I was no longer occupying a seat as a mere passenger; I had become part of it. I threw the aeroplane around because the whole of the sky was ours, we could go anywhere in it and do anything, it belonged to us, it was our infinite blue three-dimensional playground, and yet I'd only seen a small part of it.

I was suddenly shaken from my enjoyment by a voice in my ears. I hadn't noticed the sun slipping low over the horizon, casting a golden glow across the earth as far as I could see. There was a shout in my ears: "It's getting dark now, Dennis. Take us home, will you?"

We were all doing well and everyone at least managed their first solo flight, even though some didn't find it easy and were put back for more training after it took them twelve or more flying hours. It was only wise. It wasn't all fun; there was tragedy at Induna that in a way was a foretaste of what was to come on operational duty, or 'ops' as it was known; we lost four pilots to flying accidents before the end of my six weeks' training, two pupils and two instructors. One Tiger Moth had crashed on landing and burst into flames, the two pilots most probably suffering terribly as they were burned alive, trapped in the wreckage. I saw it happen, but there was nothing any of us could do; it was all over in a few ghastly seconds. It was by far the worst thing I'd ever seen in my life at that point. The other one crashed a few miles away, but we were not told the details. We were never warned about this high rate of attrition in the beginning.

Andy had been a great instructor for me, and we had understood each other right from the very beginning. Others weren't so lucky. You know within a few minutes of meeting someone whether you'll get on, there's something in the eye contact and the smile. Towards the end we talked at great length about what we hoped for in life. We just talked, and it was fantastic. He never spoke about his combat experiences other than to give advice on the flying aspects. I'd probably seen him high overhead Southend as one of the many anonymous chalk marks in the summer sky. I didn't want to push it; I could see he didn't want to.

However, he did mention what he described as a particularly hairy scrape with some Me109s one afternoon, and even though he laughed about it, he wouldn't tell me in detail. But he did warn me to look out for the gaping hole in the spinner of the 109, because 'it has a nasty bite in the form of a 20 mm cannon'.

Now my time at Induna was coming to an end, I'd never be able to really know Andy Green. I miss him and I miss flying with him. He was my first introduction to the reality of this damned war as a pilot and he wouldn't be my last. I'm getting used to it now, as he was, a fact that I realise was the cause of such pain for him. He's fading from my memory as all his colleagues faded for him, as he pushed them out of his mind, trying and failing to forget. I remember his smile and the hours we had in the air, and not that dreadful last time when I saw him trapped in the back seat of a burning Tiger Moth. He told me only the night before that a pupil had flipped the aeroplane completely inverted on final approach at a hundred feet and it was only Andy's strength that enabled him to right it just in time. I saw it just by chance as it happened again on that fateful day. I can imagine what was going on in the cockpit as Andy tried and failed to regain control. As it struck the ground, the fuel tanks split, sending gallons of petrol cascading over the hot engine and igniting.

Two days after his death, news came through via *The London Gazette* that Andy had been awarded the DFC for his heroic action against enemy fighters.

We were all informed and I read it for myself that night in the mess. The citation stated that despite his aircraft being badly damaged, he deliberately and selflessly placed his Hurricane in harm's way as a distraction so that injured colleagues could evade a large group of Messerschmitt 109s. Despite being wounded several times and his Hurricane being struck by cannon shells, he pressed on and used up all his ammunition, bailing out just before his aeroplane exploded. That would be the 'hairy scrape' he told me about. They were obviously unaware the award was now posthumous.

I now had the grand total of fifty-four hours flying time, and I could fly aeroplanes, or at least one type, and my time at Elementary Flying Training School was over. I'd passed because my logbook said so with so many of Andy's signatures, all countersigned by our Flight Commander. Finally we took a written exam on everything we'd learned, which I passed. The next part of my training was at another airfield, so now I was on the move again. Some of us were sent to Belvedere, and the others, including me, were sent to Cranborne, both bases near Salisbury. These were for single-engined pilots – fighters, in other words. The remainder were sent to either Heany or Kumolo, not far away from Bulawayo, to fly twin-engined aeroplanes, fighter-bombers or bombers.

Sixty of us began our course at No. 20 Service Flying Training School, Cranborne on Monday 10th February 1941. The vast majority were RAF Volunteer Reserve like me, though as at Induna there were some Greeks, Rhodesians, Australians and South Africans. As we arrived, I saw so many aeroplanes I couldn't count them, despite trying, and all were North American Harvards, modern radial-engined monoplanes glistening bright silver in the afternoon sun, as with the Tiger Moths totally un-camouflaged.

12

I FOUND A BED IN OUR NEW ACCOMMODATION, THIS time only two to a room, rather than a huge barrack block. We were going up in the world. My roommate was Bill Short, one of the chaps I already knew, and thankfully we got on well together. This arrangement was obviously far superior to what we'd been used to, and we had superb showers and toilet facilities too, much of them private rather than communal, which I was very pleased to see. Cranborne was therefore a huge improvement from Induna in every way. It was also more like an active RAF base back in England, though again there was virtually no camouflage on any of the buildings. We were very close to a much bigger town too, Salisbury, perhaps just a couple of miles, and we were to get to know it well in the next few weeks. We also had the advantage of employing a local boy who for a small fee would make sure our kit was cleaned and pressed, and our shoes were immaculately polished. Later on, we had an arrangement where he would brew up our first morning cup of tea and bring it to our rooms all for the price of a shilling a week.

At our first parade the following morning we were all informed we had been promoted to Acting Sergeant, and as such we could therefore use the sergeants' mess as opposed to the airmen's mess. It just kept on getting better!

We first had a week of ground school before we even saw an aeroplane close up, and for these first few weeks we were part of the Junior Flying School.

We were taught advanced navigation, this time over much greater distances, and some of which we were told would eventually have to be done at night. We were also taught how bombs fall from aeroplanes, dependent on your airspeed and the angle of release; there's more to just releasing them when you fly over the target! The Harvard had radio communication and I'd never used an aircraft radio before – or R/T, as it was known – so this was something else new. It all seemed fairly straightforward to me, but then I knew quite a bit about radios already. I'd seen a Link Trainer before, but now we spent a lot of time on them learning advanced instrument flying. The Link is a kind of aeroplane cockpit mock-up made of wood, safer and cheaper than the real thing and surprisingly effective, though without the thrills of being airborne, of course. We were also taken to the edge of the airfield in groups of ten for clay pigeon shooting. I had no idea why at first, until we were told the reason, and of course it soon became obvious. It was a great way to understand the time delay involved in shooting at a moving object. If you aim directly at the target crossing your path at 200 mph, you are bound to miss it as the bullets will pass harmlessly away behind it. You have to aim *ahead* of it by just the right distance, so that by the time it reaches your aiming point your target flies straight into a stream of bullets, unless you are so close behind it you can see the enemy crew inside, frantically trying to shoot you down. At my first encounter with a Harvard IIA, I was taken aback by the sheer size of the beast. To put this into perspective, the Tiger Moth had a 120 hp engine; the Harvard's Pratt & Whitney was 600 hp. I admit, when I climbed into the front seat, my knees were shaking a little; whether this was nerves or excitement or a combination of both, I don't know. A young flight sergeant climbed into the back with a serious expression and little in the way of introductions, and began the formalities immediately. It was a great relief to communicate via radio headset rather than the antiquated rubber sound tube and he began talking me through the instrument panel very quickly. There were twice as many dials as in the Tiger Moth, and the cockpit seemed enormous, smelling just like a new luxury car, with fresh leather and spotlessly clean surfaces. It was, of course, an American aeroplane and I would soon appreciate the differences between these and British-built machines. These Harvards were imported directly from the factory in America in huge crates at the port of Durban, and this one was obviously a recent arrival. I was told to follow through lightly on the controls as we took off and left the circuit, then conducted some basic manoeuvres, such as medium and steep turns, and then returned home for some circuits and bumps. Cruise speed, approach speed and stall speed all had to be learned. Take-offs and landings were further complicated by the use of flaps and a variable pitch propeller, not forgetting the retractable undercarriage! There was also the trim to get used to; smaller control surfaces on the rudder and elevators in the tail to settle the aeroplane in flight or to literally 'trim' it and were operated by hand in the cockpit using small wheels. It was a huge amount to take in, but I could concentrate on these additions because I already knew the basic principles of flying an aeroplane. It was like learning to drive in a Model T Ford, and then suddenly being given a brand-new Rolls Royce; the principles are the same, but nothing else is!

On my second lesson I had a different instructor, a much older sergeant. Apart from the obvious limp in his right leg, I saw a single medal ribbon above his left breast pocket, the unmistakable purple diagonal lines of a DFM. After a brief introduction, when Terry and I took off with him in charge, we'd barely climbed a hundred feet before we levelled off and the engine continued to roar on full power. This was different and I immediately sensed he was up to something. The airspeed increased rapidly and I wondered for a moment what on earth he was doing.

There was a brief crackling in my ears, then his voice:

"What's your low flying like, Copping?"

"Never done any, Sarge, not yet, sorry," I replied.

"Right, we'll see about that, shall we? Follow me through, will you?" As soon as the undercarriage was retracted and the flaps stowed, we turned sharply away from the airfield. We followed a road at a hundred feet and close to 200 mph before reaching the edge of town. We swept low over several busy roads to the astonishment of those on the ground, many of whom had stopped to look up. There were constant adjustments to the power as we then dropped further down in a steep turn that held me firmly in my seat. I looked to my left and the wing tip was almost scraping the ground.

"Get up as close as you can to the target, Copping, and then you won't waste your ammunition," Terry shouted as we dropped further down to about ten feet above a railway line. We caught up with a train and flew overhead so close the passengers would have surely dropped their tea and sandwiches. Another high-speed turn took us over a field, in which we had to pull up sharply to avoid a tree and then back onto the same railway line again, pulling hard round, this time from the other direction. Then a car was targeted as it trundled quietly along a dusty road, the lone occupant – and yes, I was close enough to see he was on his own – probably never knew what had just happened as we thundered overhead and were gone in an instant. We then headed out over the bush and chased some very startled animals for a while, avoiding giraffes for obvious reasons, all the time dodging trees and sometimes flying between them rather than over them. "Get in quick and get out before they know what hit them!" Terry shouted, with remarkable calm in his voice, the engine roaring louder than ever as the ASI never dropped below 150 mph. After twenty minutes of this, we then climbed up to eight hundred feet almost vertically, and rolled over and over in a string of barrel rolls across open fields before the engine quietened and we throttled back.

I suddenly realised we'd returned to the circuit, and the wheels were lowered and then full flap onto final approach. I was busy collecting my thoughts, my stomach and my senses, while still drowning in adrenalin.

This was a truly impressive aeroplane. We touched down gently, the flaps were stowed and we pulled up at the hard standing from where we had started. I let out a deep breath and I'm sure I heard a brief, suppressed giggle from somewhere not far away. We climbed out of the cockpit and Terry stepped up close to within inches of my face. I thought he was going to congratulate me on surviving his aerial display without being sick, but he looked far too serious. With the index finger of his right hand pointing directly at my nose, he said, "Never, ever, play silly buggers like that again, Copping. If they catch you, they'll scrub you off the course, do you understand?" He was deadly serious, but only for a moment as he then winked at me, turned around and walked off towards dispersal. I smiled. I always looked forward to flying with Terry.

After this unbeatable introduction to the Harvard, I enjoyed becoming thoroughly familiar with it and I soon found it a great aeroplane to fly: powerful, fast and very stable, but still responsive when you wanted it to be. With a roomy enclosed cockpit and powerful engine, it was the last stage in our training before flying a modern fighter. After six hours of subduing this mighty beast, I flew it solo for the first time in a few simple circuits, remembering the undercarriage, and the flaps, of course! At the end of the sixth week and many more flying hours, I took written examinations in meteorology and navigation, which I passed. At this point we were told we had earned our wings but would not be formally awarded them for another six weeks. We still had to get through the Advanced Flying School first.

13

THE TONE AMONG SOME OF OUR TUTORS IN THIS
final six weeks was much more serious. There were still times
for enjoying ourselves, but the squadron leader in charge
made it absolutely clear what we were being trained for: to
kill. There was no other reason for our existence. Wherever we
were to be sent it was our job to kill, every day, from morning
until night, and sometimes during the night. It was what we
were being sent to do and everything was geared up for us to
do this one job. We were to become killers. At the same time
the enemy would be in his aeroplane with the same thoughts;
his sole purpose was to kill us. We therefore had to kill him
before he killed us. It was as simple as that, and I remember
the squadron leader's face to this day as he was saying it, quite
expressionless and cold.

I did more low flying, but this time in approved areas such
as the Mias and Myelbo bombing ranges and I practised my

cross-country navigation by landing away at other airfields, such as Parkridge, Nkomo and Marrony. I enjoyed these trips and rarely had a problem navigating. On one occasion when I should have arrived at my destination, I couldn't see it anywhere. Just as I had been gaining confidence, it seemed I wasn't as good as I thought I was. It was the right time and so I should have definitely been there by now. For a few moments, I thought I might have to start the drill for being 'temporarily unsure of my position' (you never actually use the word 'lost'), until a thirty-degree bank revealed Nkomo Airfield two thousand feet below me. My navigation and timing had been bang on.

By now we were also flying in formation with other Harvards, either in 'V' pattern or line astern. We had to guess what enemy ground fire would be like and we were trained to be constantly on the lookout for enemy fighters while always keeping an eye on the movements of the leader and listening out over the R/T for instructions. I found this very tiring and could not at that stage imagine all this going on while being shot at as well. How would I cope with this?

The week beginning Monday 7th April began well when we intercepted an 'Ox-box', a twin-engined Airspeed Oxford trainer that was posing as a hostile bomber. All we were told was that it had just taken off from one of the relief airfields and it was heading for Cranborne with the intention of bombing it. I flew on the starboard side of the leader in a three-ship formation, searching the sky around us while trying to keep my place in the formation. We'd been flying for about twenty minutes when the three of us spotted it at about the same time, flying from right to left ahead and a little below us. As soon as the pilot of the Oxford saw us, he banked hard to starboard and tried to make a run for it. My leader shouted, "Tally-ho!" over the R/T and flew up behind him so close I thought he'd have his rudder off with his propeller before banking away to port.

We each repeated this manoeuvre in turn before the pilot of the Oxford eventually declared that we'd got him with a brief, "Well done!" over the R/T. I really enjoyed this, and we were to do it several times, but never enough, in my opinion. If we were to be employed at shooting down enemy aeroplanes, then surely this was the best practice. The crew of the Oxford were also training, of course, ready for the day when they might find themselves bounced by real enemy fighters. It was a lot of fun but deadly serious at the same time.

I found night flying difficult. It wasn't just the flying but navigating in the dark too, of course. The vast Rhodesian bush was not very well lit, as you can imagine, but we were told this was ideal practice for flying in wartime Europe, where the blackouts created similar or worse conditions. There was just nothing to take from the ground as reference points and it all had to be done by instruments as though flying in thick fog. It takes some getting used to at first, putting your complete trust in a few dials in front of you on the instrument panel.

Taking off in the dark for the first time was very strange, and I was glad Terry was with me until I felt confident enough to try it alone. We flew numerous short hops to nearby airfields and my final night flying navigation test was a three-hour flight landing at two different airfields. Thankfully the landing strips were well lit for my expected arrival each time as they would be in England, if only briefly; even in wartime some concessions are made. It was a hard enough exercise, and though I succeeded, even then I wondered what it would be like to do the same while being shot at from below or behind.

My big day came on Friday 9th May 1941, when I'd accrued 153 flying hours and had passed the course. It was now time for me to be presented with my wings. We all gathered for a formal parade in our best blues and marched up in turn to collect our wings badge from the station commander with a quick salute and handshake. We were all substantive sergeants now too, mainly because I suspect the RAF would never allow anyone below that rank to fly their aeroplanes! The weather was breezy and cool; it was their autumn, after all, though still nothing like the dismal British equivalent. It was a proud moment for all of us and sadly only the Rhodesians and a few South Africans had family members present. They were lucky to spend the entire day with their families; I wrote long letters home instead.

From the replies I eventually had weeks later and from what we managed to find out from elsewhere, the news from Blighty was worse than ever. Southend was still being attacked at least once a month and it seemed this damned war would never end, as everywhere the Hun went he was succeeding. He'd just taken Athens, and Rommel was continuing the siege of Tobruk while pushing east all the time towards Egypt. There'd been no Channel crossing yet, though we knew it could happen at any moment as the Blitz on our cities was worse than ever. The speed of Rommel's advance across North Africa was a serious concern and we now suspected this would be our destination. It was the main topic of conversation in the mess, so when the orders finally came through a week later it was no surprise.

On Wednesday 14th May we were back on the train, this time to Durban, on the east coast. I'd been in Rhodesia for almost six months and I loved every second of it. I think we were all a little sad to leave it behind and frankly I was surprised there weren't many more chaps going AWOL. We didn't yet know exactly where we were going, just that we would end up somewhere in the Middle East. A chap called Rashid Ali had recently taken control in Iraq and was siding with the Hun and so some of us might end up heading there to RAF Shaibah, or even to Syria to fight against the Vichy

French. It would seem very odd indeed to fight Frenchmen but these supported Hitler, and by all accounts were quite determined in their efforts.

If Rommel managed to cross Egypt and join up with German and Vichy forces in Iraq and Syria, then god knows what might happen. The whole of the Mediterranean and the Middle East would be lost and he'd have control of the Suez Canal, so this was unthinkable. I had no detailed knowledge of all this until then, so it's amazing how you become aware when you might be dropped right into the middle of it all. We had long discussions on the train and then on the ship north, with rumour and supposition mixing freely with the facts, but stopping Rommel was clearly the highest priority at that time.

We were on board the ship for a week, playing cards, deck games and generally relaxing before we docked at the top of the Red Sea at Port Tewfik, near the Suez Canal. We'd made it safely and without incident; we were told U-boats were much less of a problem than in the Atlantic, though we were also told not to be too complacent.

It was raining when we stepped ashore for the first time, but as soon as it stopped the sun came out and almost immediately it was scorching hot. It seemed to be a different kind of heat to that of southern Africa; even after the rain this was an intensely dry heat that parched the back of the throat, making it difficult to breathe. We climbed aboard huge Chevrolet lorries for an hour's journey north to a transit camp at Geneifa, where we spent the next two very uncomfortable days as the guests of 107 MU (maintenance unit). I assumed we were now in the middle of the Egyptian desert; it certainly looked like it, but we'd hardly made any impression on it and there was a lake just a few miles east that we didn't even see.

It was clear we'd had it easy until then and our part in the war had been very comfortable indeed, but now we were faced with harsh reality. I was truly shocked by my first sight of what we were to live in and in my naivety I hoped this was not the standard lifestyle we would have in the desert. I really had no idea what to expect, but I should have known when they failed to warn us about it. We were billeted four to a tent, not a very big tent either, sleeping on the ground on what we could make ourselves from ground sheets and very old army blankets that stank of petrol. I was fearful of lighting a cigarette in case the whole lot went up.

14

EVERYTHING ALREADY THERE WAS COVERED IN SAND AND anything you brought in was soon the same, including us. There was no mains electricity, running water or flush toilets. Our first meal consisted of cold bully beef pie on a tin plate with a mug of lukewarm tea. We were told water was in short supply and so there were no showers or baths of any sort, just a very limited quantity restricted for use in shaving and brushing of teeth. I wondered on reflection whether these austere conditions were deliberate in order to toughen us up; it wouldn't surprise me. Looking back on it now, even that Spartan accommodation was first-rate compared to some of the places that were to come. This was my nightmare introduction to life in the Egyptian desert; and we hadn't even been shot at yet.

Early on the morning of the third day, we were up as dawn broke; another huge orange orb rising from the eastern edge of the world into a vast azure sky. It was unlike anything I'd ever seen before and it was the same every morning. I'd handwashed some of my kit with carbolic soap in an inch of second-hand water the night before and hung it out on some guy ropes to dry overnight. To my horror, I noticed it had all gone, along with the kit belonging to several other chaps. When I reported it to the Duty Warrant Officer, he just walked away laughing. We had been warned never to leave anything lying around, so it seemed he had no sympathy, and I had no change of clothes.

After breakfast of more bully beef pie and tea, we were back in the lorries heading south again, very glad to be leaving Geneifa. Within a few minutes, we turned off the road and began heading west towards Cairo. We joined the main Cairo–Suez road, and it was as busy as Piccadilly Circus on a Saturday afternoon, with vehicles of every size dodging huge numbers of locals and their camels. Luckily we reached Cairo before the midday heat and I caught a glimpse of the pyramids as we made our way through the bustling streets and out the other side to Heliopolis Airfield, where we were very relieved to get out the lorries.

We stayed the night in proper wooden huts with decent facilities and as soon as I could, I found a stores department where I spent twenty minutes pleading for some replacement kit. Eventually the Warrant Officer in charge gave me a pair of shorts and full tropical uniform with long trousers and lovely brass buttons, which from then on, I kept well out of sight.

Heliopolis looked like a decent airfield and it would have been good to stay for a while, but we were back on the move again by morning. I saw Beaufighters, Hurricanes and even Wellington bombers taking off and landing, looking like they were in a tearing hurry, so we were obviously getting closer to the war.

We waited for several hours at Cairo station before boarding a train to Luxor. Had we known we were destined to spend so much time hanging around, we would have surely left the confines of the station and seen some of the sights, but we were ordered to stay put. MPs (military police) were on constant watch, not only keeping us in, but also keeping out some very determined locals trying to sell us anything from items of very dubious-looking fruit to assorted clothing, shouting, "*Baksheesh!*" at us repeatedly, as the MPs sent them away with shouts of, "*Imshi!*" meaning 'go away' in Arabic. Then there were the tricksters called *gilli-gilli men* with their 'find the pea' games under walnut shells. I saw a sergeant lose two shillings once, he was so sure that he could follow the pea! In the heat, noise and crowds, it all seemed very chaotic, but it was something we would quickly get used to.

As the train rattled along, we were heading deeper into Egypt, a long way further south for our final training far out of reach of enemy aircraft. We barely had enough time to stretch our legs on the platform at Luxor Station and we were back on again, gathering speed and dust before arriving at Aswan in late afternoon. A rather grand riverboat was already there, so we eagerly carried our kit up the gangplank and into the cabins, four to a room. It was incredibly hot and stuffy below deck, so we wasted no time dumping our things and getting up top.

The two-day boat trip to Wadi Halfa was wonderful. We drifted smoothly along at surprising speed around the many felucca sailing boats, with some of their occupants busy hurling nets into the brown water not giving us a second glance. Lean, barefoot, tanned bodies in white linen, hoping for a good catch. Theirs was a simpler life with no war and I envied them. After disembarking at Wadi Halfa, which was nothing more than a few huts each with a corrugated iron roof, we were ushered back onto a train for a final overnight trip in a very decent two-bed compartment, arriving at No.

71 Operational Training Unit, Khartoum on the morning of Friday 30th May.

No. 71 Operational Training Unit reminded me of Heliopolis and I was impressed. It looked like a proper RAF base that had been dumped in the desert. We were billeted in long wooden huts containing half a dozen rooms with two of us in each, with the luxury of running water and flush toilets in each building. We soon found out the mess was pretty decent too, serving good food with most of it being local fresh fruit and veg that was excellent quality. It was blindingly hot to the extent I'd never experienced before. My clothing became wet on my body almost constantly, only to be dried in the sun and warm breeze when I would sweat profusely again in an endless repeat.

Several Hurricanes were engaged in circuits and bumps as we watched, and before noon all flying stopped for a few hours due to the heat. We were ordered to assemble in the mess for our first briefing by the station commander. As he walked in, we all stood up promptly and the chattering ceased. He only spoke for a few minutes, welcoming us in a very business-like fashion with little ceremony, but I'll never forget his final words to us: "You are urgently needed, gentlemen. We will make sure you are ready, be in no doubt about that, but we must get you up the blue as soon as possible. Good luck to you all." It was the first time I'd heard the Egyptian desert referred to as 'the blue'.

At five o'clock the next morning a young local lad came bounding into our block and into each room in turn shouting, "Tea! Tea! Tea!" It's not the calmest way to be woken up, but I've had much worse. This would be repeated every day for the next five weeks, usually by the same lad, Omar, carrying his sparkling urn of freshly brewed tea. His English was as good as my Arabic, which was non-existent, and there were other tea lads occasionally, all in their early teens with wide smiles and boundless energy. The sun was barely forcing the night sky into retreat, but of course the early start was essential so that the most important tasks could be completed before midday, when it was just too hot to do anything.

After a fantastic breakfast of eggs and bacon I made my way to the dispersal hut with my flying kit, and as I did so I couldn't fail to notice a neat row of Hurricanes sitting proudly nearby.

Further down the airfield, there were other aeroplane shapes similar in size to Hurricanes covered in canvas tarpaulin close to an open hanger, the noise from which revealed ground crew and mechanics already very busy.

Throughout that first morning we were each subjected to a routine physical which included further vaccinations and I eventually sat in the cockpit of my first Hurricane at ten o'clock. This was why I was here and the reason for all my training so far, to sit in this superb machine. I was more than a little in awe at first and was gratified to see the controls and instruments were not that different from the Harvard. I couldn't fail to notice the state of the Hurricane after flying brand-new Harvards. These were Mk Is that had clearly been around for a while and compared to the Harvard, the cockpit was tiny.

My instructor, Sergeant Julian Prendergast, seemed a decent type and he went through the controls with me very patiently, along with the aeroplane's vital statistics: the stall speed, approach speed, cruise speed and so on, and then to my surprise he disappeared, saying, "Take it all in, but don't touch anything. I'll be back in half an hour." I sat there imagining myself up in the air running through the start-up procedure: take off checks, landing drill and so on. When he returned, he was carrying a curious hessian sack which he promptly dropped over my head, blinding me. I could breathe alright, but the inside stank of gun oil and petrol. "Right, Copping, I want you to put a hand on everything I say, right?"

"Yes, Sarge," I replied, guessing what was coming.

"Turn and slip," he said, as I lifted my right hand onto the stick and then just behind it, bottom right, below the climb and descent. "Oil pressure," he said, as my right hand moved just to the right of that. "ASI," as my hand moved to the top left of the main six instruments immediately in front of me, then, "Throttle," and, "Mixture," and then, "Magnetos," and, "Flaps," until we'd gone through them all.

15

He didn't say whether I'd got them all right; in fact he didn't say anything as he pulled the sack off my head. "Watch the flaps and the undercart levers, okay? They take some getting used to. Everything in the Harvard is electrical, a typical Yank thing, but in the Hurricane it's pneumatic, okay? You seem to know where everything is, Copping. Circuits here are a standard pattern at eight hundred feet, left hand today, alright? Bring it back here after the first circuit." With that he climbed off the wing and walked away.

I went through the start-up procedure with the ground crew and the trolley. Fuel cock and booster cut-out on. Throttle to fifteen percent, and ignition. I thought the Harvard was a powerful machine, but the Hurricane's Rolls Royce Merlin was twice the horsepower of the Harvard's Pratt & Whitney. It started with a magnificent roar and I had to check the throttle hadn't slipped further open it was so loud. I set the reflector sight to two hundred yards and a thirty-two-foot wingspan – that of a Messerschmitt 109. I had no reason to do this yet, but I thought I'd start getting into the habit. I waited for the oil temperature to reach forty degrees and then I released the brakes – a handbrake on the stick, different to the footbrakes on the Harvard.

I then taxied to the end of the runway, where I paused and lowered ten degrees of flap. Radiators open and boost cut-out off. Oil pressure and temperature was fine, fuel was sufficient and switched on, and so I gently applied full throttle. The response was immediate and breath-taking. I was airborne in seconds, raising the nose as the aeroplane left the ground. At five hundred feet I couldn't get the damned undercarriage to come up; the lever was stiff, or so I thought. I put it back to neutral and tried again while briefly looking down into the cockpit. When I looked up the aeroplane was nose-high, so I levelled out at eight hundred feet and trimmed it, then banked to the left, remembering to stay in the circuit. I finally managed to get the wheels up, only to set them down again almost immediately for the downwind leg. I struggled a little again, still getting used to the undercarriage lever, as close as it was to the flaps.

I then allowed myself just a few seconds to take in where I was and what I was doing. The huge Merlin engine was merely ticking over in front of me, the smooth vibration from which travelled right up from the rudder pedals and into my legs. I waggled my wings a little, feeling the response, and it was instant. I thought the Harvard had been brilliant, but this was something else.

Because this aeroplane was faster, I gave myself plenty of extra distance on the final approach, lowering flaps and getting used to the throttle, making constant adjustments. I flew it right onto the ground in a pretty good touchdown without any bounce at all. I was really chuffed.

I taxied over to dispersal, coming to a stop when I applied the brakes, the engine idling but not yet shut down. I drew back the canopy as Julian climbed onto the wing to speak to me.

"Any problems?"

"No, it was fine," I replied, grinning like a child. I didn't tell him about the undercarriage lever.

"Then do a few more just to make sure, will you?" he said, jumping off the wing. It was just what I wanted to hear, so I lined up and took off again, and then twice more until I'd completed my first wonderful hour in a Hurricane.

By the end of the first week in June, I'd accrued six hours on the Hurricane and I'd finally mastered the undercarriage lever and the flaps. I was so pleased I even included it in my letter home, though I knew I couldn't be specific or the censors would chop it out. I think I just put 'I finally got the hang of something I was struggling with for a while'. I'd started advanced formation flying and had engaged in some fantastic low flying and ground attack target practice, which I found really interesting. The rattle from the eight machine guns was like nothing I'd heard or felt before, and I hadn't realised that the recoil has a noticeable effect on the aeroplane's speed, slowing it up just a little. I remembered the essentials of trying to hit a moving target while having little problem on some old broken-down vehicles we were using for static strafing practice. The Hurricane was solid and steady, yet very responsive with a rapid turn rate, and it was a real pleasure to fly. At first it felt like it wanted to fly itself, especially in the turns, but this was just something that was different from the Harvard. It was easier to see over the nose and the difference in the controls being pneumatic rather than electric was not an issue. I'd now accrued twenty-five hours in it and felt reasonably confident in the cockpit.

My training at 71 OTU formally ended on Tuesday

8th July 1941. We were told we would not be going up the blue until the weekend at the very earliest, and so we had a wonderful few days to ourselves. Throughout our stay we frequently hitched lifts into Khartoum and Omdurman, where we found local cotton planters very welcoming, not just for tea and cakes in the afternoons, but almost every weekend for cocktail parties at which we were entertained as VIPs. We were used as new dance partners for the daughters of the wealthy but very bored ex-pats, and even some of their mothers. Despite the intense heat, these people were always immaculately dressed; the men wore black ties, white shirts, dinner jackets and black trousers, with their feet crammed into leather shoes specially sent over from Savile Row. The ladies wore spectacular evening gowns with glittering jewellery draped across their very low cleavage which glistened increasingly as the evenings progressed.

On our last night the gin flowed freely and a tall redhead at least twenty years older than me wanted more than I was willing to give her. She persisted for over an hour, bringing me very strong gin and limes with hardly any lime, which didn't cost me a penny, as she quaffed them down like it was the end of the world.

I eventually found myself sprawled across the floor on my back in the darkest room of this enormous house while she took from me exactly what she wanted, her evening dress rolled up tightly around her waist in what was clearly a well-practised procedure. I didn't even get her name. I have little recollection of it other than before the light went out I noticed the room was lined with books, it was incredibly hot and stuffy, and I fell asleep straight afterwards.

We all had far too much to drink. What an odd existence these people had, hundreds of miles away from the war and everything familiar, and in such oppressive heat too.

I had no idea how, or even who, but one of our group drove us back in the early hours and on Monday 14th July, Omar woke us up as usual with his wide smile and clattering of his tea urn. He was never quiet, with all his mashing tackle swinging around and his incessant chatter, his noise was not particularly welcome with the hangover I had, but his tea certainly was. He poured us all a cup and a few of us sat on the wooden veranda at the front of the hut to watch the sun come up, having had barely three or four hours sleep.

We passed around our cigarettes and enjoyed the early-morning peace that surrounded us. I suspect we were all thinking of what was coming. We'd finally reached the end of our training, and the end of our innocent relationship with the aeroplane. Today we'd be on the move again, 'up the blue', where we'd use our flying skills to become proficient at killing.

Our journey north was the reverse of the one we'd taken to reach Khartoum; we boarded the same riverboat at Wadi Halfa and then at Aswan we took the train all the way back up to Cairo via a brief stop at Luxor. There was a more serious atmosphere amongst us as we travelled north, mixed with some genuine impatience. It seemed our lives had been completely dedicated to training and so despite the dangers ahead, we were ready to test ourselves. No-one said otherwise, anyway, how could they? The fear wasn't discussed. On this subject there was no-one to confide in at all.

We arrived at what we were told was RAF Almaza near Cairo very late on 17th July. We were billeted in the same type of accommodation as at Heliopolis, and it wasn't until morning we realised it was Heliopolis, under another name. From before dawn the air was filled with the hum of aero engines. It seemed twice as busy as it was during our last brief visit six weeks before. We saw an array of older aircraft such as Gladiators and Vickers Virginias, as well as more modern types such as Beaufighters, Hurricanes and Blenheim bombers.

We waited for our postings. Every morning we asked, only to be told 'not yet' by the orderlies, while every day we watched more Hurricanes flying off up the blue. Days became weeks as we filled our time playing cards and writing letters. Most of the chaps played cricket or football to kill the time, much to the amusement of watching locals. I was good at neither so I sat in the shade reading and writing; I wondered when I would next get the opportunity to either send or receive letters.

16

I TRIED TO PUT INTO WORDS WHAT MY LIFE WAS LIKE. I'd been living an unreal existence until now, and I'd become thoroughly used to it. I've no doubt I revealed just how much I'd been enjoying myself, and I felt terribly guilty about that, but there really was nothing else to say other than to describe the great food, lovely weather, the great flying and a few good mates. We all knew we couldn't describe the operational side of things in detail, even in training, but I did describe the aeroplanes, up to a point. I asked about the war at home, and when letters arrived for me, I was asked when I would be heading north.

The mail to and from Blighty could take up to six weeks, so in a way it was pointless guessing so I didn't bother, but this was foremost in our minds. What was to come would be exciting and at the same time it would be sad to see some of the chaps disappear.

I wondered why they kept us hanging around like this if we were so desperately needed, and then finally, on Monday 11ᵗʰ August, they arrived, pinned up on the bulletin board in the mess. No-one told us, they just appeared, typed on a very ordinary yet life-changing RAF Memorandum. 'RAF Middle East Command – Egypt' had just been reorganised and all the written orders were now headed 'No. 204 Group', under Air Commodore Collishaw. My name appeared in a list under '233 Wing', followed by '260 Squadron'. Quite a few others had '73 Sqn' and '6 Sqn', though I wondered whether this would be the case, considering these two squadrons were in Tobruk, which was still cut off. Several names were missing, and to the shock of those named, some were listed under 45 Sqn and 14 Sqn, which were currently flying twin-engined aeroplanes, namely Bristol Blenheims. Consequently some of the chaps quickly disappeared to find the CO in order to ask about their postings. There were a few who I'd grown quite attached to, and thankfully some were heading to the same place as me. I'd been particularly close to Bill Short ever since we were roommates at Cranborne, but now, with great sadness, we found out he was being posted to the Far East, possibly Singapore. This was a blow, but we vowed to keep in touch if we could.

I tried to find out where 260 Squadron was based, but no-one seemed to know, or they were unwilling to tell me. I eventually found out later that night that most of them were in Palestine at a place called al-Bassa in the north of the country, having been involved in conflict across the border in Syria fighting the Vichy French. I was also told I wouldn't be going there because they were about to pull out and come to Egypt to a place called Gerawla. Then I was told they would be at a landing ground near Mersa Matruh, which was very confusing. This was only the beginning, of course, as squadrons would move at short notice frequently between landing grounds, as I was to find out. I looked on a map and saw Gerawla was near Mersa Matruh, so that was probably right.

It was quite a way from the front line which was currently holding at Sollum, just inside Egypt, west of Sidi Barrani. The map I was privy to did not have any landing grounds written on it.

The war in North Africa had recently developed into a stalemate; Rommel had insufficient supplies thanks to a lot of his ships being sunk in the Med, and we were busy regrouping, though from the build-up I had seen, it was obvious something big was brewing from our side.

We had one more day at Almaza before we were to be moved out and dispersed. We were all issued booklets about Alexandria, the closest city to where we'd be posted and therefore the most likely place we'd end up spending leave. It included locations of approved bars and hotels and a few words of advice with useful Arabic phrases. I was later to learn other Arabic phrases and find some bars that were very definitely not on this list.

We had some sobering news on the day of our departure. We found out that two of the last group of five sent from here to Gerawla had already been clobbered, killed in their first week in combat. I'm not sure if this had been deliberately kept from us and we only found out from some 'erks', aircraft fitters who had just arrived from Gerawla. It seemed there'd been some bitter fighting and his shortage of supplies didn't stop Rommel's persistent attempts to break through 'the wire' towards Sidi Barrani. The Tobruk garrison was still holding out valiantly against everything he and the Italians could throw at them. We assumed when a chap gets clobbered while flying it was because he wasn't paying attention or he was just very unlucky and that we were sure we wouldn't make the same mistakes. You couldn't allow yourself to think anything else.

We took the train to Alexandria first thing in the morning. It was the height of summer and it was packed with troops and RAF personnel like us, and so it was an unbearable journey. We were glad to get off for a while in Alex, as we were now calling Alexandria. This city had enjoyed almost mythical status amongst British military personnel for decades already and was always referred to fondly like some demanding but irresistible mistress, maybe because it was certainly cooler on the coast and always a place for beer and entertainment. But it was also a staging post for the front line, where we were heading.

The train left Alex just after midday, lolling from side to side on an uneven track as it trundled very slowly westward. Thankfully it was no longer quite so crowded, and we paused briefly for some air at a tiny insignificant place called El-Alamein. It stopped again at a station called Ma'aten Bagush, where to my surprise most of us RAF personnel were told to disembark. We waited in the shade of the station platform for an hour until a lorry took us along a dusty desert track to what I thought was Gerawla, but it wasn't; we had arrived at Ma'aten Bagush transit camp. There were wooden buildings, dozens of tents and lots of vehicles. We were fed bully beef and potatoes on tin plates with hot sweet tea and then we were shown camp beds in one of the tents where eight of us settled in with our kit. We were told not to show any naked flames outside after dark, and we had a can cut in half with a candle in the bottom for light. It wasn't much, but it was just enough to stop us falling over one another. I was exhausted and so it wasn't long before I fell asleep. I didn't dream that night.

My sleep was refreshing but curiously empty. I slept well, there's no doubt, but I had no-one to confide in, no-one I could tell just how alone I felt, even though I was in a crowded tent surround by many other crowded tents.

Two men were coughing, both with a dry, rasping cough, and it was this that woke me up. It wasn't quite light, but I knew I couldn't get back to sleep, so I rolled off my camp bed and out the tent. I'd slept in my uniform, apart from my boots, so I slipped them on and went for a stroll. I found a latrine block, which I used, then a mess tent, and saltwater showers. Then I saw the sea only a hundred yards distant, reminding me of home, the tiny windless waves gently rolling up and stroking the sand as they fell back in retreat. Just for a fleeting moment I had an odd thought that gripped me with panic: *What the hell was I doing here?*

A group of us new arrivals were briefed by a squadron leader shortly after breakfast. We were at a transit camp and the nature of it was such that we would simply have to wait our turn until called. In the meantime, we were virtually non-combatants; we were not allowed to go to Alexandria or leave the camp at all, unless for call-up. That was it. Some were called immediately, others like me spent yet more time waiting for our invitation to the war. I slept for most of my first day in the Egyptian desert; until mid-afternoon when I heard a group in my tent talking about going for a swim in the sea, so I joined them. The water was blood-warm and crystal clear on gently sloping, soft, white sand. We were 150 miles from the front line, and so we assumed we were safe.

I'd been in the water less than a minute when two Ju88s roared overhead at a hundred feet heading west back towards their lines, pursued by three Hurricanes. I can only assume their gunners had run out of ammunition, otherwise we would have been easy pickings. There was a rattle from the leading Hurricane as the Ju88s weaved around low over the water, turning right as they followed the coast towards Mersa Matruh and disappeared.

I waited two weeks until the end of August. I felt like an old hand by the time my name was called, but I was almost thinking I'd been forgotten. I didn't doubt I'd still be able to fly a Hurricane, but the thought that my very next flight might be in combat made me shiver. I wanted to take one up and familiarise myself with it again, at least for an hour or so, and I feared this wouldn't happen. It was the late afternoon of Friday 29th August when I was taken with one other sergeant pilot, Dave Clark, in the back of an open-top Humber to LG115, a landing ground about an hour's careful drive west of Ma'aten Bagush. Mines were a constant threat and so vehicles were only driven over sand that already had fresh tracks on it, so it took a while. The main east/west road was topped with tarmac but was badly pitted and bomb damaged in places, along with sand partially blocking the way like snowdrifts.

17

WE WERE FOLLOWING OTHER VEHICLES AND THE
sand was inevitably blowing in our faces. The driver opened a
battered ammo box beside him and passed back some goggles,
which we gratefully accepted.

I was glad to be leaving Ma'aten Bagush, but I was just
beginning to know some of the chaps quite well, some more
than others. As the lorry pulled up, I wondered why we were
stopping. Was this an airfield? I could see aeroplanes dotted
around – Hurricanes, mainly, and also a Lysander – but it was
unlike anything I'd seen before.

There were no gates, fences or buildings of any kind, just
an assortment of vehicles and tents with sandbags around
them. An unattended Bofors anti-aircraft gun sat nearby
surrounded by waist-high sandbags, the barrel pointing
almost vertically skyward. Several twin Lewis guns were
also dotted around, also unmanned. We stood in the warm

twilight breeze as the Humber disappeared east, wondering what on earth we should do. Moments later we were joined by several men, their faces barely visible in the fading light, and names were exchanged before Clark was ushered away, leaving me standing alone for a few moments. As the natural light faded, I saw no man-made lights anywhere, with a blackout obviously much more strictly observed than at Ma'aten Bagush.

"You must be Copping?" someone said from behind with a hand thrust towards me.

"Yes, Dennis Copping," I replied, hesitating a little, briefly shaking hands.

"I'm Derek, pleased to meet you. This way, follow me; you're with Wrigley and Saunders and that lot." I picked up my kitbag and dutifully followed. We passed a large EPIP tent – European Personnel Indian Pattern – from which there was a very dim light, raucous laughter and loud clunking of tin mugs. "Mess," my escort said, "too bloody loud as usual," he said in a broad South London accent. "We'll have the neighbours complaining again," as we stopped at an area where smooth sand ended and rough ground began, and there was a tent much smaller than the one we'd just passed. "Anyone at home in there? You have a visitor."

"Of course, skipper, but wipe your feet will you, the maid's just been cleaning our room and she's only just finished, bless her," the voice said from inside. The tent flap was opened and shadowy figures were moving around. "Come on in, chaps, make yourselves at home."

"Thanks all the same, but I won't be staying," Derek said. "I'll see you in the morning, Copping," he said as he disappeared into the dark. I bent down a little to get my head inside.

"You met the CO, then?" another voice said from the canvas gloom.

"Derek?" I said, shocked. They laughed. "Squadron Leader DR Walker DFC," another said. "He likes to do the old meet and greet for some of the new chaps."

"I had no idea," I said, genuinely surprised. There was more laughter.

"Don't worry; he's probably just come from the latrine," someone said.

"Was he pulling his shorts up, old chap?" another said.

"Were his hands wet?" someone added, to raucous laughter.

"Shut the door, will you, Copping, so we can put the light back on," the first voice said, as I dragged my kitbag inside, closed the tent flap, and where I could feel them, I buttoned it up. Someone struck a match and a candle was lit inside the bottom half of a large petrol tin. Three faces were beaming at me, each one leaning forward as they introduced themselves, shaking my hand in turn: Sergeants Jimmy Wrigley, Sandy Saunders and Bill Wareham, their dusty, unkempt hair sticking up on their heads like ghostly scarecrows.

"Copping, Dennis Copping," I said, looking around.

"What are you current on, Copping, Hurricanes?" Wrigley said.

"Yes," I replied. "I trained on Harvards after the Tiger Moth," I said, to which there was some nodding of approval all round.

"So you've not had a bash on the Tomahawk yet, then?" Saunders asked.

"No, not yet," I replied, finding somewhere to sit.

"We're mainly Hurricanes at the moment," Wareham said, in an unmistakeable Rhodesian accent. "There are some older types still here, but you'll probably be flying Hurricanes. Some squadrons still have Gladiators. The chaps at 112 have Tomahawks already, so we might be getting them soon, better than the old kites we've got. They've painted teeth all over the bloody front and now they call themselves the shark squadron, for god's sake. They do look impressive, though, I have to admit."

"It depends on the skipper and what's happening, really," Wrigley said.

"It depends on the op," Saunders said, contradicting Wrigley. "Not been doing much other than holding our own until the rest of the squadron arrive. We've been hitting Jerry in the Med, but something's definitely building."

"We need to relieve the chaps at Tobruk," Wareham said. "I've got a brother in there with the Aussies, and I've not heard from him for weeks, the poor sod, it must be pretty grim in there by now."

"I saw masses of men and material coming up through Cairo and Alex, so yes, I think there's something happening," I replied. "I have a brother in the army too, Gordon," I said, anxious to impress, "and as far as I know, he's coming out here, though I'm not sure where," I said, to general silence and more nodding approval.

"Yes, we're going to be busy, that's for sure. We'll need all the help we can get, so welcome aboard. There are two of you, is that right?" Wareham said, now lying down.

"Yes, we came up from Khartoum via a couple of weeks at Ma'aten Bagush," I replied, as the others also appeared to be bedding down. "Good old Martin Bagush! How is the old bugger?" someone shouted. Wareham saw me looking around for somewhere to claim as my own. I saw three bed spaces, two of which appeared to have been slept in.

"Here, Copping, this is your luxury bespoke four-poster bed, beautifully constructed by RAF craftsmen from the very finest local timber, as you can see." He pointed. There was a layer of rough-sawn wood with a mattress barely an inch thick on top of it, with some blankets covering the lower half.

"By the way, the latrine is straight out the door, about thirty yards," he added. "It's the open tent with the bench in it and three holes where you stick your backside, so look out for the splinters. You'll find it, just follow your nose," Wrigley said, laughing. "But there's a spade just outside the door here in case you get caught short. You might get a jippy tummy; everyone does at some point."

I nudged my way over to my bed and prepared it for sleeping. All around me there was a mixed unpleasant odour of old canvas and stale sweat. I didn't feel inclined to strip off. It wasn't very warm, for a start. The others were now lying down and so I lay on my back. I didn't even take my boots off. Saunders was nearest the candle, with a book in his hands, trying to catch what little light there was. I caught a quick glimpse of the cover. It was *Wuthering Heights* by Emily Brontë. There was silence as a gust of wind took hold of the tent and shook it a little, rippling the canvas next to my face and above my head. I was crammed into a tiny space in the desert with these men, and as nice as they seemed to be, I'd never felt so alone in all my life.

I must have been asleep when the entrance flap was pulled open, because it was pitch dark and I wondered what the hell was going on as two more bodies piled inside, noisily rolling onto their beds. Beer breath and cigarette smoke added to the mix, with the occasional burst of flatulence. There was no conversation, and within seconds it seemed they were all asleep.

The wind had strengthened and the rhythmic movement of the canvas sent me into a deep sleep fairly quickly. Suddenly I was dreaming I was no longer in the desert but on a polar expedition, with Scott of the Antarctic, stranded in a tent on an ice shelf with three other men, exhausted, hungry and freezing to death. No-one seemed to know where the expedition was going and everything about it was chaotic and bleak. I was shivering with cold and feeling pretty wretched, and I noticed everyone on the expedition had very untidy hair.

Who knows where my Antarctic adventure would have taken me, I would never find out; the earth shook violently underneath us, followed by two loud bangs that seemed very close. This wasn't part of my dream. I woke up cold, and I was dragged by one arm off my makeshift bed and out under the side of the tent, rolling over several times and into a ditch ten feet away. We were all there, and it seemed at least one of my new friends was still snoring, having successfully rolled into the slit trench while still asleep.

18

"Eighty-eights," a voice said, his body pressed close to mine like a honeymoon couple on their first night. I could even taste his breath on my face. "They're just guessing, they don't know we're here for sure," he said, sticking his head up over the edge a little into the darkness. There were two more bangs before the throbbing of their engines faded as they flew off into the night. "Jerry likes to ruin our sleep every now and again. At least he's regular, bang on eleven o'clock, the same time it was two nights ago." He paused before standing up.

"Carlisle," he said, giving me a hand up. "You can call me 'Cork', or 'Corkie', everyone else does. Sorry about earlier, dragging you out of bed, but you can never be too careful. You must be Copping?"

"Yes, Dennis Copping," I replied.

"Morley and I are not on ops tomorrow, so we've had a few in the mess. Let's get back to sleep, shall we?"

There was no firing back or thoughts of taking off into the darkness in pursuit of the Ju88s, as both were apparently hopeless. Besides, it would only give us away, in case they really were just guessing, so Carlisle said. He was right; it was a pair of Ju88s that usually flew over, more in hope than serious planning, lobbing a few bombs around in one or two passes before disappearing, most of the time without causing any damage, unless they were lucky.

In the morning we were up just before first light, and despite the early interruption to my sleep I felt quite refreshed. Sappers were already gathered around a fresh crater on the airstrip where only one bomb had caused damage, the clanging of their spades on the hard ground echoing across the emptiness.

The latrine was the first priority for most. I needed to go too, and it was a little unnerving sitting down on the cool wooden seat just a few inches away from another man doing the same, while several others were standing nearby waiting. Would it be better when I knew them well? I was glad it wasn't fully light. There's something deeply undignified about such public displays, in my opinion. I knew what I should do in future, if I could. But I noticed no-one seemed to care about their loss of dignity; indeed, the latrine seemed as much of a social gathering as it was a biological function. There were magazines and newspapers lying around, not just for the essential paperwork but for reading too. I needed to get used to it quickly because on that first attempt I couldn't produce anything substantial. There was no sink or even bucket of water for afterwards; merely a small can of petrol next to the latrine, for handwashing purposes. I realised it would not be a good idea to smoke while washing. As soon as it was fully light I took in my surroundings for the first time. A hundred yards from me there were no fewer than eight 'erks', aircraft fitters, already clambering all over a Hurricane; the engine cowlings were off, as was the propeller hub, and all eight .303 machine guns were laid out neatly on the wings. I wondered if it had been damaged, but I couldn't see anything obvious.

"The erks have to strip the engines and the guns regularly, or they seize up," Saunders said, standing next to me. "The bloody sand gets everywhere," he said, "as you'll find out. Come on; let's get some nose-bag and a brew, shall we?" He slapped me on the back and we walked towards another tent wide open at the front, euphemistically called The Canteen.

"Morning, Bill," Saunders said, peering in.

"Morning, Sarge, what's your pleasure this morning?" the orderly said, struggling a little with a rope as he tied back the last of the tent flaps.

"Well, Bill, I'm just sick and tired of lobster and caviar every bloody morning, and all that damned champagne, so could I just have some plain old bully beef straight out the tin, all sloppy and disgusting, a few of your driest dry biscuits, oh, and a cup of tea with plenty of lovely desert sludge in the bottom of the mug to add a bit of texture, if that's alright?" He smiled. I ordered the same. I'd never tasted lobster or caviar anyway, so frankly I didn't fancy it. We gathered our breakfast on tin trays and moved over to the mess tent, which was already busy. I noticed Clark and gave him a nod. He smiled, but he looked as lost as I felt. Behind him at the back of the tent hung the tail fin of a Messerschmitt 109, and obliterating most of the black swastika were the words: '260 Squadron – Celer et Fortis – Swift and Strong!'

"Copping, Clark, the old man wants to see you both at 0800 hours," Wrigley said with his head just visible at the entrance before disappearing. I lit a cigarette and moved over to Clark.

"How are you doing?" I said to him. We'd only talked a

few times at Ma'aten Bagush, but now we had a lot of nervous common ground between us.

"Okay, are you?"

"Alright so far," I replied, offering a cigarette, which he took.

"It's hard to know what to expect, but this is roughly what I suspected," he said, taking a long pull on his Woodbine. "If you expect the worst, it can only get better, can't it?"

I smiled. It was a few minutes before eight.

"We'd better go," I said, standing up.

We found the CO's 'office', a three-ton lorry with wooden steps at the rear. The doors were wide open and held on hooks around each side. We climbed up and with nowhere else to do it, I knocked on the metal floor. There was movement inside. "Climb aboard, chaps," the CO said, briefly scanning our faces in turn before leaning forward, shaking hands and then removing a thin layer of sand from a map desk in front of him with a great sweeping arc of his hand. "Please sit down a minute, will you?" he said, pointing to some folding wooden chairs. We both retrieved one and we sat down feeling like fresh faces at a new school, even if it was a rather chaotic and untidy new school. Maps were pasted all over the walls and to the west of us was a place called Cyrenaica. I wondered where this was until I realised it was the name for eastern Libya, as Tripolitania is for the west.

"Welcome to two-sixty, gentlemen. My name is Walker, and I have the inordinate honour of being the mother hen to all you see around you, except the damned Krauts that fly over now and again, of course. I met you last night, didn't I, Copping? Settled in alright?" he said, eyebrows raised.

I nodded. "Yes, thank you, Sir."

"Good. Sorry about the mess," he continued, "but we are still in the process of moving here and half the squadron haven't arrived yet, as you may have gathered." We hadn't. We assumed the chaos was normal. "It's a long way from al-Bassa and I think some of the chaps think they can spend most of their transit time in the fleshpots of Alex before they get here. Never mind. You are very welcome. I asked for more pilots and now we have them we don't have enough aeroplanes. Sod's law, I'm afraid. At the moment most of our erks are Aussies from 450 Squadron RAAF, and they are all great chaps but our own should be here any day. Mickey's already gone, after he copped a burst appendix in Syria, rotten luck. Sorry, I mean Squadron Leader Chris Mount, my predecessor. Gordon, his oppo, Squadron Leader Steege, is still here, but he'll be off too, as soon as our own erks arrive. It's all a bit complicated at the moment, I'm afraid, so I won't bore you with too many details, but as you probably know, we are part of 262 Fighter Wing, which has three South African units: No. 2, 4 and 5 Squadrons. They are handy chaps to have around because some of them actually learned to fly 109s in East Africa. What a bonus that's been. Suffice to say, it's a great little aeroplane, better than the Mark I Hurricanes we have, I'm sorry to say, so don't tangle with them on your own, that's an order, okay?" We both nodded at him and then at each other before he continued. He sat facing us with his right arm splayed across the table, rubbing the stubble on his chin with his left hand. "We are still flying the old vic formation at the moment, which you were no doubt taught, were you?" We both nodded. "Well, this is likely to change. Harry Bandinell and one or two of the other chaps have already been practising the finger-four. I'll explain it later. Meanwhile, we observe strict R/T procedure here, so don't use it unless you have to, the fewer distractions up there the better. Some of the 109 pilots are pretty hot, but don't underestimate the Ities, some of theirs are very experienced, and one or two of their aeroplanes are first-rate, particularly the new Macchi 202 with the 109 engine. Stick together, watch out for each other, and stay alert. We are all pretty relaxed down here on the ground, but up there you do as you're bloody well told, right?" I nodded, and at the side of me I saw Clark's head moving. "Check the gaggle board at dispersal for daily ops, and make sure you're always prompt at briefings. I don't mind the chaps having a drink, but not when you're down for ops. That's for your own benefit and that of your colleagues." He paused. We both looked rather blank, wondering if he expected us to say something, which we didn't. "Our collective goal, gentlemen, is the destruction of the enemy, by whatever means. Wherever he is, whatever he is doing, we must kill him. Be in no doubt he has the same brief, so we must do it before he does it to us. Is that clear?" At this point his voice softened a little, as though he was about to tell us a secret.

"Your personal goal, however, is to achieve your OTE and go home, your Operational Tour Expired. This is currently two hundred front line combat hours. No-one is close yet, but the hours will soon build up, I can assure you, so keep your logbooks up to date with the adjutant." There was a brief awkward silence until he said something that surprised me; it was a curious thing to say because it seemed more of an emotional and psychological warning. "The war and the people in it are very fluid and liable to change at a moment's notice, and so we should all get used to it." I wasn't sure what he meant at first, but I later realised exactly what he was saying. I think it was his way of telling us not to get too attached to anyone. I already knew the consequences of this, but of course it was only just the beginning. I wondered if he was saying this as much for his own benefit as well as ours because he'd been in the war from the beginning. "While we are on the subject," he said, lightening up a little, "this is my safe." He leaned back, slapping the top surface of a metal cabinet with his right hand. "I never used to insist, but I do now. You put your personal effects in here before every op, gentlemen: wallet, photos, letters, including those French ones you keep meaning to use, that sort of thing, except the Goolie Chit, of course, you keep that with you, otherwise, everything goes in here. We don't want to give Jerry a lot of information about us from what's left of you, and you don't want what little cash you've got and all your photos of Aunt Maud scattered across the desert, do you?" We looked at each other. I nodded. We shook hands again as our briefing was concluded.

As Clark and I descended the wooden steps he looked at me.

"I need a beer," he whispered.

"It's twenty-past eight in the morning," I replied.

"I know," he said.

19

DESPITE THE INFORMAL WAY OF LIFE AT LG115, THE British class system and some traditional customs had followed us into the desert. Six sergeant pilots were crammed into a single tent, whereas the commissioned ranks were two to a tent or even one on their own. It seemed unfair as all pilots flew together and took the same risks, but it was the only such acknowledgment of rank on the ground. I was yet to find out how strictly it was observed in the air, as the CO had told us. Apart from this, the mess tent was an *aircrew* mess, regardless of rank, and I soon found out this classless approach also applied to the latrine.

It was when I was seated at the latrine, having found an opportune moment to use it on my own, that the Equipment Officer, Dick Hickson, found me.

"Copping, isn't it?" he said. I nodded. He then came straight to the point. "Do you want a gun? I mean, I have one for you, a pistol, if you want it. You ought to, just to be safe. You don't have to take it up with you, but you never know."

"Does everyone else have one?" I asked, forgetting for a moment where I was seated, and that he was an officer. I really didn't know what I'd do with a pistol. If I crash-landed or bailed out behind the lines I could hardly imagine shooting my way back against the entire Afrika Korps.

"Oh yes, but not many carry them around, I have to say."

"Okay," I said, "then I will."

"Right, I'll tell the armourer you'll collect it later today?"

"Right," I said, as I sensed my bowels had briefly stopped functioning.

"Do you have one of these yet?" he said, leaning even closer, thrusting a piece of paper into my face. I thought for a moment he was being helpful by passing me toilet paper.

"What is it?"

"A Goolie Chit."

"A what?"

"A Goolie Chit. It saves your balls," he said, adding with a smile. I thought I'd misheard him. He could clearly see I looked puzzled. "Have you not been told yet?"

"No, the CO obviously forgot about this, though he did mention it briefly. What is it?"

"It stops the Arabs from cutting your balls off," he said matter-of-factly. "Here." I held this crisp new sheet of very official-looking paper in my hands. "Don't lose it," he said, "and always keep it with you on ops," he added, turning his back and walking away. I began reading. It was one page of politely worded Arabic and English written beneath a bold Lion and Unicorn crest stating that the holder was 'An Officer of the English Government' requesting safe passage, with the offer of an undisclosed reward if the finder complied.

At the bottom there was an assortment of English words with Arabic translations: English, Flying, Officer, Friend, Water, Food, Day, Night, Half, Near and Far, with some additional cultural advice: "The older Arabs cannot read, write or tell the time. They measure distances by the number of day's journey. 'Near' may mean ten minutes or ten hours. 'Far' probably means over a day's journey. A day's journey is probably about thirty miles. The younger Arabs are more accurate." It concluded with the words 'GOOD LUCK' in capital letters. *This must be a joke*, I thought, so when my bowels reopened and I finished what I was doing I took my Goolie Chit to the mess, where I found Wrigley and Carlisle drinking tea and smoking. They laughed when I showed it to them. "Don't lose it," Carlisle repeated, laughing again. Wrigley smiled and nodded, before eventually telling me. Early on in the desert campaign, two RAF pilots were captured by hostile tribesmen who cut off their testicles before allowing them to return alive, but obviously in a bad way. It was not a joke, or a rumour, but the truth. It seemed the locals could therefore be both hostile and friendly, and were quite likely to render assistance to RAF pilots, or indeed kill them, dependent on their mood at the time. I was horrified, and from that moment I saw the desert as nothing but hostile, and if it ever came to it, it would be better to ditch in the sea. The only good thing about it was they were equally likely to behave the same way towards the Hun. I was glad I'd agreed to have a gun, and I seriously thought about taking it up with me.

I could only see perhaps a dozen aeroplanes, and half of those appeared unserviceable, with erks crawling over them like ants on a drop of treacle. They were now reassembling the Hurricane I saw earlier, with all its guns out on the wings, and three men were leaning into the cockpit. The sun was quickly high in another cloudless sky, and some of the erks had already removed their shirts. Everyone was wearing shorts, and obviously in order to confuse matters some of the officers were not wearing rank insignia, or at least it was crumpled and difficult to see. Some of the pilots didn't even wear their wings. Getting to know who's who wasn't going to be easy.

I called in at the armourer's tent and signed for a Webley Mk VI revolver in a canvas webbing holster and belt, with a small box of bullets. It was heavier than I remembered at the range in Devon. I wrapped it around my waist and it hung low on my thigh like I was a cowboy. I tried wrapping it around my chest to wear under my Mae West life jacket, but I couldn't find a comfortable position. Exasperated, I took it off, rolled it up in the belt and stuffed it under my bed.

Just after breakfast I saw three men in shorts and desert boots gathered around a large homemade timber 'A'-frame coat rack a few yards from the mess tent. I'd already seen this contraption and had assumed it was just washing left out to dry in the sun. They each picked up a few items in an unhurried manner while chatting to one another, before moving over to a blackboard mounted on the back of a chest of drawers. I could tell they were all pilots because they had parachutes slung beneath their backsides and were wearing leather flying helmets.

Another man at the blackboard wasn't wearing any flying kit as he chalked in the last of the names at the bottom. These were the positions in the formation, who would be the flight leader and who would be his wingman. This was the 'gaggle board'. They stood in the mid-morning sun casting short shadows onto the yellow sand, listening in and nodding while making last-minute adjustments to their parachute straps. In the absence of a hut, or even a building of any kind, this open-air gathering was 'dispersal'. It reminded me of the first time I peered through the fence at Southend Flying Club on one particularly hot summer's day as a boy.

I didn't know any of these pilots, though I'd seen their faces in the mess. One by one they climbed into their Hurricanes and started the engines. Hand signals were exchanged between each pilot and the erks, until a final thumbs up caused them to ease the throttle open and move off, the soft wheels and uneven ground causing the aeroplanes to waddle a little as they taxied to the end of the strip. I saw the flaps lowered and heard a brief rise in engine noise before they all began roaring across the desert in line abreast, hurling up great clouds of dust as they went, their wheels retracting as soon as they were up and climbing away. They turned right, heading west towards the enemy, gathering together in a group as the roar from their Merlins faded to a distant hum.

Two army types were standing around the open door of a Lysander when it sprang into life. The overly stuffed map cases around their necks began twirling around in the wash from the propeller. They were shouting and nodding at one another as the CO shook their hands before they climbed aboard. They took off, low and slow, heading east.

Some erks busy with a Hurricane called me over. I think they'd been watching me gazing up at the sky and though they were quite capable of doing it themselves, they asked me if I'd start it up, apparently to check the compression. The battery was low, so a trolley jack was wheeled over and I climbed into the cockpit. Just for a moment I thought I'd forgotten what to do, but my hands were already there before I'd fully engaged my brain. *I may not be able to fly it*, I thought, *but this is the next best thing.* It started perfectly and was running smoothly until the erks waved at me to shut it down again. One of them jumped up onto the wing and stood next to me, cursing the desert in the same way Saunders had done. As the propeller came to a stop, he shouted, "We had to strip it all down yesterday: carburettor, fuel lines and all the guns. It's a real pain in the arse." They did all this in the open and in full sun, and so I quickly acquired a genuine admiration for the erks and wondered if they could fix absolutely anything.

All three Hurricanes returned safely an hour later. In the mess I heard the pilots saying they'd conducted a routine patrol after sightings of 109s heading this way. In the end they hadn't seen any enemy at all. I spent the rest of the afternoon in our tent, hiding from the sun. It was hot in there, but there was nowhere else to go. I must have passed out and slept really well because I woke up just in time for dinner; this was my first day at 260.

On my second day, a Blenheim flew in fast and low from the east, thundering overhead at fifty feet before turning around and lowering its undercarriage to land. It was a good job we had been informed in advance due to the Blenheim's similarity to a Ju88. It was from 14 Squadron and had coincidentally arrived just in time for breakfast carrying fresh supplies from Alex. I introduced myself and struck up a conversation over several mugs of tea with the pilot, Flying Officer Tim Murray, and then assisted with some of the unloading, which was mainly fresh food, mail and what was described as 'miscellaneous', which on closer inspection was in fact gin and whiskey. I wondered where he'd got some of it from, as a lot of it, like the American cigarettes and cheese, weren't the usual NAAFI stuff. I could see Tim was on his own in what should be a three-man crew, and when I asked about it, he simply replied very casually, "Do you want to give me a hand, then?" I looked at him.

"What do you mean?"

"Are you on ops today?"

"No," I replied.

"Then fly back to Alex with me. I'll bring you back this afternoon. Check with your CO but I'm sure it'll be alright."

20

I'd never been in a Blenheim before, and now I was flying one as co-pilot. I wondered if all Blenheims smelled as bad as this one; with what looked like animal faeces trodden into the floor around the bomb bay and a lot of feathers, as though someone had recently had a pillow fight, all accompanied by a very strong latrine-type odour. When I asked him about this, Tim just shrugged and said, "Oh yes, I know, it needs a bloody good clean, doesn't it?" and sat down. Of course it never occurred to me there may well have been roving bands of 109s hunting for easy targets like us, but I couldn't resist the opportunity. I later found out that running supplies and passengers in an unescorted aircraft 'on the milk run' was one of the most hazardous pastimes for a desert pilot.

We took off smoothly and I was immediately impressed. The view ahead, the handling and the speed were remarkable. I could see the coast and began to get my bearings in relation to where LG115 was, and I tried hard to remember. Once we'd settled at two thousand feet on a heading of 080°, Tim suddenly unfastened his harness and stood up, leaving his parachute in his seat. "Just watch the shop for a minute, will you, Copping?" he said as he disappeared into the back, leaving me at the controls. Not only was this my first trip in a Blenheim, it was my very first time at the controls of a twin-engined aeroplane. I resisted the urge to shout him back straightaway and decided to give it a try, mainly because I had no choice.

Like most aeroplanes once trimmed correctly in fine weather, the Blenheim settled in my hands, purring gently like a lap cat on my knee. I glanced around the instrument panel and felt the energy of the aeroplane through my hands and feet. It was unlike anything I'd ever flown before. I tweaked the throttle levers together and then alternately to generate a response and after a few very small movements of the stick I realised I was falling in love with it. She was fast too; the ASI showed we were cruising comfortably at 250 mph. She should be fast; this was a long-nosed Mark IV with 900 hp in each engine.

I assumed Tim had merely gone for a quick toilet break, but the time just went on. I wondered how long my impromptu flying lesson would last, so after ten minutes I shouted into the back, "Everything alright?" I didn't know whether to shout 'Sir' or 'Tim', as I'd only just met the man.

There were some scuffling noises before a response: "I'll be with you in a minute!" A full five minutes later he popped his head into the cockpit with a pencil behind his right ear and a clipboard under his right arm. "Everything okay? You know the heading, don't you? I set it a while ago. Just stick at that and we'll be fine. You're doing terribly well, you know, Dennis, you really are. I'm very grateful," he said as he disappeared again. I don't recall ever giving him my first name at that point, but I must have done.

After twenty minutes I knew we were getting close to our destination. I was just about to throttle back to begin what downwind checks I could think of for a Blenheim and reach for the undercarriage lever and flaps when Tim reappeared and strapped himself in. I'd been flying the aeroplane for almost half an hour. I realised then why he had brought me along!

Tim landed the aeroplane at an airfield just west of Alex, close to the sea. I thought it was Aboukir, but apparently it wasn't; that was the other side of the city. As soon as we'd shut down the engines, a very old civilian lorry pulled up and a local man jumped out. He bounded up to Tim and began shaking his hand vigorously, smiling and patting him on the back. He was an enormous man with a booming voice that had no problem fighting its way through a thick black beard covering his face. He seemed angry but Tim said something to placate him and he returned to his lorry, opening up the back and disappearing inside. "Having trouble with the locals?" I shouted, smiling.

"Oh no, he's not a local," he replied. "Well, he lives locally, but he's not a local, if you see what I mean. That's Aggers, my supplier. He's Greek. He runs a wholesale business in Alex, 'Olympus Minerals' he calls it, imports and exports. I don't quite know how he does it or where he gets his stock from, I don't ask, frankly I'm not bothered. I suspect we're probably one of his best customers." He laughed. When he returned, Tim introduced me. "Agnides, this is Copping, a new chap from two-sixty," he said. The man grabbed my hand and shook it warmly, but not as firmly as I imagined he would. "I can settle my account tomorrow, Aggers, if that's okay?" I heard Tim saying, to which a reply came with some exaggerated nodding and a friendly right arm around Tim's shoulder: "No problem, really, I know you are a good man, this is not a problem."

I hung around for a while, watching the aeroplanes,

occasionally sitting under the Blenheim's wing, leaning against one of the wheels. After an hour or so I'd almost nodded off when Tim reappeared. I helped him load quite a few brand-new boxes, some of which I was surprised to see had the palm tree and swastika of the Afrika Korps painted on them, along with some anonymous heavy sacks that clunked when moved. Was our Greek friend dealing with the Hun too? Finally we picked up a bag of mail from dispersal and two army officers and their luggage. The Blenheim was extremely cramped inside for an aeroplane of its size and I had to sit squashed up in a windowless area for the flight back because Tim also picked up his co-pilot who had been inexplicably delayed in Alex until then.

Two minutes after engine start-up we were off again, and to my surprise we landed after only fifteen minutes at LG017, Fuka Main. This time we stayed longer so that we could have a brew and a bite to eat, as by now it was late morning, it was pretty hot and I was hungry. Tim disappeared again with the army chaps and I sat outside the dispersal tent in the shade of a tall palm tree, smoking. No-one seemed to be in a hurry and I was getting concerned I might not make it back to LG115 that day at all. I wondered if I'd get into trouble because I said I'd be back before dark. Suddenly Tim reappeared and indicated we were ready to go, so I climbed back aboard with my fellow passengers. The Blenheim was now incredibly hot and smelly, full of flies and very uncomfortable, but thankfully the trip from Fuka to LG115 was brief.

On my third night at LG115 the Ju88s came over again. They were lucky this time, badly damaging a Hurricane under repair, the flames from which seemed to set them off on a blind strafing run before they left. We lay in the slit trenches as bullets whizzed around randomly, plopping into soft sand but then thumping into harder ground and spinning away like fireworks into the night. In the morning we could all see the

CO was fuming, stomping around chuntering to himself, and he called some Army Intel chaps into his lorry. Several mugs of tea later, they all emerged. It was generally acknowledged there was a 'lull' at the moment as things continued to build, but the CO wanted to know exactly where 'those damned eighty-eights' were based.

I was beginning to get used to the latrine, along with all the other indignities of desert life. When you really have no choice, it's amazing what you can tolerate. The only personal hygiene ritual that was never missed was shaving, often using very dirty water, but this one simple thing tricked you into feeling cleaner than you really were. We were often forced to wash with petrol, which was not too bad for the skin, but care had to be taken when lighting up immediately after.

Every morning we were woken up by the same clangourous din of the sappers and their spades clearing more flat areas for the aeroplanes. Several of us pilots helped in the digging of slit trenches around our tents; they were for us, after all. It was as though we'd all just arrived in North Africa and the war was beginning all over again.

I'd heard about the local sandstorms, the 'khamsin', and the first time I experienced one was at the end of my first week. It was around midday when the wind began picking up, hot and dry from the south, and the erks, clearly aware of what was coming, ran around like madmen covering cockpit canopies and engine cowlings of every aeroplane they could get to in time. It was obvious the sand was a menace to machine parts, but I was told it could also wreak havoc on the canopy, causing so many tiny scratches that you could hardly see through it. A 109 appears like all aeroplanes as a tiny speck a thousand yards away but could be on you in seconds, so it was vital to keep the canopy as clear as possible.

I could see the rolling cloud of sand approaching like an

enormous wave hundreds of feet high and I found our tent just in time to barge inside and button it up. It was gratifying to know that everyone would be grounded in this weather, even the Hun. As the *khamsin* took hold of the tent and tried to rip it from the ground I took a look through a gap in the tightly buttoned door; the sand was so thick in the air I couldn't see the other tents. I couldn't even see the ground a few inches below. I realised that if you were out there in this, you'd become disorientated immediately and probably choke to death. All we could do was stay inside and wait it out. We played cards and slept on and off for hours until it stopped as quickly as it had begun. When normality returned we found that sand had piled up everywhere like snowdrifts, and much of what had already been cleared needed re-clearing in what seemed a thankless task. Luckily this was just a small *khamsin*. Sometimes they would continue for days at a time.

That night in the mess we crowded around the one wireless set we had. The news from home was bleak. The Hun was driving east across Russia at incredible speed and seemed unstoppable. We wondered how long it would be before Rommel tried to match this success in the desert. If he tried to break through we'd have to do our best, but we were definitely not ready, as our own ground crews and half the aeroplanes had still not arrived. Britain's cities were still being attacked, but now Bomber Command was taking the fight back to the Hun and bombing Berlin, but at heavy cost. At least this was something. At the end of the night, the wireless was tuned to the German Forces Radio and we listed to Marlene Dietrich singing 'Lili Marlene'. The CO took a very dim view of this and so we had to make sure he was safely back in his office, which he also slept in. It was often turned up very loud and in the dead calm of some of those nights he must have heard it.

I returned to our tent and was almost asleep when

Saunders and Morley came in.

"Have you seen the gaggle board, Copping?" Saunders said. I'd forgotten to look. Frankly I'd given up.

"No," I said.

"You're on ops first thing in the morning with Morley and me, briefing at 0800."

Suddenly I was wide awake.

21

I DIDN'T SLEEP MUCH AFTER THAT NEWS. OF COURSE I was excited about flying again, but I was also going into combat for the first time, and I couldn't stop thinking about it. As the tent began to lighten I had an uncontrollable urge to use the latrine. I smiled when I found Clark there before me.

"Flying today?" I asked, as the contents of my bowels fell away like water. The urge remained even after I knew nothing was left.

"Yes, with Alexander and Cartwright. I heard you're up with the CO?" He knew more than me. I'd find out at briefing. We finished together and I dipped my fingertips in the petrol, going through the actions of washing my hands. I went to the mess and sat with a tin mug of sweet tea and a cigarette. I could smell eggs frying, but I wasn't hungry. These were a luxurious rarity and had recently been delivered in one of Tim Murray's Blenheim trips, specifically reserved for those on ops. My stomach was tightening and I felt just like I did on my first day at Induna. Eventually I forced down a slice of dry bread with a fried egg, then more tea and cigarettes before Saunders found me.

"Got any kit yet?" he said, to which I shook my head. He knew I hadn't. "Then come with me," he said as he disappeared, forcing me to abandon my tea. I caught up with him at a tent surrounded by waist-high sandbags that had 'Aladdin's Cave' written above it on a piece of wood. "Copping needs the usual," he said to a tall, thin corporal standing inside the tent. "Get some kit and meet me at dispersal in twenty minutes, alright?" I nodded. "Meanwhile, take this and shove it down your sock or something."

"Thank you," I replied, taking a folded map from him before he strolled away, whistling.

Without speaking, the corporal handed me a battered cardboard box containing what were obviously second-hand leather flying helmets. I took one, along with an oxygen mask that thankfully appeared brand new, and a pair of goggles. I was then directed to the parachute packer, busy outside his tent standing at the longest table I've ever seen. Without having to ask he handed me a parachute he'd only just finished with, which I slung over my shoulder. *What this chap had just folded up could very well save my life later today*, I thought. *I do hope he did a good job.*

Briefing was in the mess, the only tent big enough to hold more than a dozen people. The CO came in with an army chap carrying several maps. The gaggle board had been brought inside. He began straightaway.

"Top cover this morning, gentlemen, Blenheims, Bardia," he said, "our friends those damned eighty-eights." I tried to keep up and opened my map.

Bardia was just the other side of the front line, about a

hundred miles away, probably twenty minutes flying time along the coast or thereabouts. "Copping, you're on my right, Saunders on my left. Keep close, but we're not expecting any trouble."

He glanced at the army chap, who nodded, and there were some murmurings around the tent. "Harry, you take Carlisle and Morley, Sparky you've got Clark on your right, he's another of the newbies, with Cartwright on your left. Sticky, you take Polly and Wrigley, and Pedro, you've got Tregear and Curno, okay? Don't hang about above the target, gentlemen; we know a lot of 109s have moved forward to El Adem and Gambut. Let's get in and get out as quickly as we can. Our job is not to engage the enemy in a scrap if we can help it, but to make sure the bombers do their job. Are there any questions?" No-one spoke. "Very well, take off at 0900 hrs, and good hunting."

I tried to remember the names of the flight commanders: Harry, Sparky, Sticky and Pedro. I assumed these were nicknames, and I'd then have to remember their real names too. I was unaware of the friendly rivalry between them, and their tally of kills was rarely mentioned, but it was clever of the CO to nurture it. I'd never seen so many erks milling around as just about every serviceable aeroplane was being readied for use that morning. I lit up and took a long drag, and noticed my tea was still on the table, so I took a sip. The mug was wobbling a little in my hand and I looked around to see if anyone had noticed. It did nothing to moisten my mouth, which was as dry as the desert. I had an urge to return to the latrines, which I resisted. Saunders came up, smiling. "Are you alright, old chap?" I smiled back. He grabbed my tin mug and tipped a hip flask into it with a generous couple of seconds. "You're with the CO for a reason; you'll be okay with him and me." I took a sip. The whiskey completely smothered the flavour of the lukewarm tea and the dry lining in my throat.

On the second sip I knocked it all back in one. I could have done with several more of those. He winked at me before he turned and walked away.

I took a pee in the sand near the latrine because all three seats were occupied. I picked up my parachute and strapped it on. As usual, the bulk of it hung underneath my backside, making dignified walking very difficult. I saw two colleagues at the back of their aeroplanes peeing on the tailwheel before climbing up onto the wing. I had an overwhelming desire to follow them in this but resisted. I'd only just been, so surely there'd be nothing there? I waddled over towards the Hurricane I'd been allocated, currently in the hands of two erks who were quick to introduce themselves.

"She's ready for you, Sarge, all raring to go," Corporal Dave Morris said, as LAC Ernie Roberts climbed out of the cockpit. They were both English, part of 260's regulars just arrived from al-Bassa. "The fuselage tank is full, the wing tanks are on half, so you should have enough for what Mr Walker wants you to do today," he said, giving me a cheery wink and a smile. I liked them both immediately.

I lowered myself into the seat and plugged into the oxygen supply. I briefly turned it up high to check it was alright, holding the mask against my face, feeling the flow on my skin before turning it back down again to 'off' and removing it. Maybe I wouldn't need it? I had no idea what was in store for me.

It wasn't a new aeroplane. The paint on the gun button was chipped as it was on most of the other controls, so it had seen some life before I arrived. It was a Mark I that seemed older than anything I'd flown before, but it started beautifully without the trolley jack and the engine ran very smoothly. Despite the weeks I'd been away from a Hurricane, I was incredibly relieved when I remembered everything. I tried to set the gun sight to two hundred yards and thirty-two feet, the wingspan of a 109, but it was already there. I then released the brakes when the oil temperature reached forty degrees and could see the CO was already lining up, so I positioned myself a little behind and to his right, and then lowered the flaps. A mini sandstorm began behind his aeroplane as he began his take-off run and so I eased the throttle fully forward to keep up beside him as we swept across the desert. It wasn't until then that I realised in the last few minutes I'd been too busy to be nervous.

Wheels up immediately we were airborne, followed by the flaps and then a crackle over the R/T from the CO: "Stick to my starboard side, Copping, you're my number two, okay? Follow me and watch what I do."

"Yes, Sir!" I shouted back, oddly reassured by his London accent, my concentration levels rising exponentially every second. I was apprehensive, I can't deny it, but I was incredibly busy too, trying to keep up, concentrating hard, desperate not to let myself down, or anyone else for that matter. This wasn't training anymore; it was real, and I couldn't let nerves overwhelm me and affect my performance. I knew what I was doing, I knew how to fly and I knew how to shoot, so this was my first chance to demonstrate what all the training had been for.

We flew straight out on the circuit and maintained an orbital climbing turn up to three thousand feet, and I tried again to remember our exact position relative to the coast. This was the most obvious landmark from which to navigate, because looking south there was only empty, featureless desert. We had no radar cover, no air traffic control of any sort, so navigation was by memory, dead-reckoning and instruments, hardly any further advanced than the first biplanes in the Great War. To the east was Egypt and friendlies, and to the west over 'the wire' were the Hun and their Italian chums.

Six of us continued to climb, while the others six stayed at three thousand feet. After five minutes we'd reached ten thousand feet and were joined from the east by nine Blenheim bombers, the aeroplanes for which we were to provide 'top cover' escort. The Blenheims continued on westwards while we maintained a close watch from above and behind. We made radio contact with them and the CO confirmed all was good before we formed up to keep lookout, and it wasn't long before flak started bursting ahead of us as the bombers turned inland, descending with increasing speed straight into it.

22

It was all I could do to stick on the CO's wing while keeping a constant lookout. I had everything going on in the cockpit to deal with as usual, but now I had to watch the CO and the rest of the sky too. In addition to this, he would occasionally hurl his aeroplane around all over the place, weaving around like a madman: up, down, brief steep turns to the left, then the right, and it was during all this that I lost sight of the Blenheims. Suddenly the CO banked sharp right and threw his aeroplane into a steep dive, so I followed, shoving the throttle open and hitting the trim lever hard as I did so. I wondered what on earth was going on as my ASI quickly passed through 300 mph until I saw a trail of smoke and a stream of empty bullet casings from the CO's wings and realised he was shooting at something. I couldn't even see what it was. I followed as close as I could, banking hard right, and then left, adjusting the throttle constantly as he fired again.

Then I saw the black outline of a twin-engined Me110 two hundred yards ahead against a patch of empty sky, weaving around, obviously aware he was being shot at and desperately trying to get away.

As I worked really hard, concentrating on staying close to the CO, I heard some almighty bangs from my right side, as though someone had just hurled a lorry-load of bricks at my cockpit. I saw a flash of pale blue pass right over my head just a few feet above me as a 109 shot past, the black crosses clearly visible on the wings. Damn and blast, where the hell did he come from? I remember thinking, 'The bastard! and how angry this made me feel. It was odd that I wasn't frightened; I was just so bloody angry. I was also disappointed I'd probably be taking the aeroplane back damaged, although I couldn't see anything obvious yet.

I was still on the right of the CO and I thought the 109 had gone, but to my surprise, a few seconds later, he reappeared below and ahead of me, and if he continued he'd soon be right in front of me. I couldn't believe it; how could he be so careless? I had to get in a position to point the nose of my aeroplane directly at him, so I pushed forward a little on the stick and even though he was probably too far away, I fired at him. My guns rattled, the bullets broke through the paper gun port covers and the airframe juddered before I lost sight of him. He'd flipped over onto his back and dived out of sight, apparently undamaged. Luckily I was still roughly where I should have been, about three hundred yards behind and to the right of the CO. It was then, as I sat up and strained to look right for the 109, that I saw what he had done to my aeroplane; blurred images of the ground were visible through a gaping hole in my starboard wing, just this side of the ammo boxes. After the initial shock, my immediate thoughts were that I was uninjured, the Hurricane was still flying and there had been no fire or explosion, not yet at least.

It then seemed our job was done as I followed the CO towards the coast, dropping right down onto the deck. I could see Saunders forming up on the CO's port side as we roared eastwards over the sea with Sollum on our starboard side and the relative safety of Sidi Barrani and LG115 thirty miles ahead.

Now I had a few moments to think, I was suddenly very worried. What if my controls were damaged? What if there was a fire in the engine and I'd have to bail out? What if the undercarriage wouldn't come down? I performed a few gentle turns as we flew along, and then pulled the nose up and down a little. I made adjustments to the throttle, and everything seemed to be functioning correctly. I decided to put it out of my mind. If there was something terribly wrong with the aeroplane that I didn't know about, then so be it. If it was going to happen, and it was beyond my control, then it would and there's nothing I could do about it. I checked the Ts and Ps, the temperatures and pressures, regularly and everything continued fine with the engine; it obviously hadn't sustained any damage. There was still no smoke anywhere, from either the engine or the damaged wing, so fingers crossed I'd be alright. Saunders and the CO would surely have told me if I had smoke streaming from behind me and I'd see it in my mirror. I tried to relax, but I still had quite a lot of fuel aboard so a belly landing would be dangerous, more so on the flat but stony ground of LG115.

Fresh sweat now mixed with combat sweat; my uniform was sodden, as though I'd just been swimming in it. I unfastened my face mask and reached up to the canopy, drawing it open six inches. Fresh, warm air filled the cockpit and I immediately felt better. I noticed some of the squadron never seemed to close the canopy at all, even when going into combat. There were a lot of scratches on the Perspex and I wondered if this was the main reason. Approaching Sidi Barrani, I throttled back into a cruise approach for landing. Passing just to the east of the town I remember thinking how nice it looked, every undamaged building reflecting white in the sun, and every flat roof with something on it: washing lines, chairs or people gazing up. I wondered what they were doing while they were watching us, whether they had run up onto the roof merely because they'd heard the approach of aero engines. Anyone looking up had to shield their eyes from the afternoon sun and so for a moment it looked as though a few people were saluting us as we passed overhead.

Ten minutes later, with the landing ground in sight and the CO on my port side, I lined up on long finals. I brought the power back and speed down to 100 mph. I took hold of the landing gear control lever, pushed it down and waited. If there was a hydraulic problem, I'd find out now. Nothing happened for a second or two, a pause which was normal but now seemed like hours. Then there were reassuring noises as the gear lowered, followed by the wonderful clunking from underneath as indicators showed the wheels were down and locked. I half expected the hydraulics to have failed, but they didn't. I was immediately relieved and lowered twenty degrees of flap, bringing the power back gradually and the speed down to 80 mph. As I approached the end of the runway at four hundred feet, I lowered full flap and a few seconds later I touched down on the main wheels gently in what was one of my best landings. I paused briefly on the edge of the runway and withdrew the flaps before taxiing over to dispersal.

After shutting down the engine, I sat in the cockpit, totally lathered in sweat like a Derby Day racehorse. I'd fired my guns and I'd been shot at in my first op, but I'd survived. I was glad to be down in one piece, but I was also annoyed I'd brought the Hurricane back damaged. Ernie Roberts couldn't resist putting his fist through the hole in the wing, shaking his head and whistling at the same time. "No problem," he said. Dave Morris had already disappeared underneath and was shouting something unintelligible, but I managed to make out the words, "Bloody krauts," and then, "Did you get one, Sarge?" as I shook my head. When I climbed out, I was shocked to see just how close in to the fuselage the hole was; another couple of feet and the cannon shell from the 109 would have landed right in the middle of the cockpit, with god only knows what consequences for me. I shuddered a little at the thought of it.

I took a slightly damp cigarette from a crumpled packet in my shirt pocket and as it hung limply on my lips, the first match burned out before I could use it, so I tried again. This time Ernie took hold of my right hand firmly to stop the match dancing around at the end of the cigarette. "There you go, Sarge," he said, smiling.

At debrief it seemed the Blenheims had successfully hit their target, Bardia Airfield, and had made it safely back home. We'd kept the 109s busy just long enough for them to do their job, and so my small part in this first op had been a success.

23

So this was it, war, and it was unlike anything I'd done before. I'd thrown an aeroplane around in similar fashion before, but never with a hole in the wing, this was new! There are so many variables already attached to flying that adding to them makes it much more interesting to say the least. An aeroplane is a complex machine, and damage from a cannon shell fired by a Messerschmitt 109 adds a whole new dimension. I was relieved I'd made a start at becoming part of the squadron, and I came in for some modest praise from the CO that night, amidst a general air of unspoken relief that we'd all returned safely.

In the afternoon I was astonished to see the erks working on my Hurricane, Dave and Ernie, had already patched it up. Nothing vital had been damaged, so Ernie informed me, and it would be fully serviceable again in the morning. He could tell I was impressed. "Easy," he said with a cheery grin, wiping his ingrained hands on a filthy oil-soaked rag. "Much better than a Spit." I wondered what he meant. "I worked on Spits before; you couldn't do this with a Spitfire. Stressed skin, you see. This isn't, so it's easier. We'll be finished before dark," he added. The sun was now casting long shadows everywhere, and it was then that I heard the strangest sound yet in the desert. "'Ere we go again," Ernie said, looking towards the mess. "That'll be Sticky." I knew Pilot Officer Norman 'Sticky' Glew had a gramophone, I'd heard it a couple of times, but this was much louder, much more real.

"It could be Harry," Dave said from underneath the wing.

"No, that's not Harry Curno, that's the CO," Ernie said, turning his head. Curiosity immediately drove me towards the mess. I hadn't even noticed the dark bulk sitting at the back of the tent covered with blankets, and I should have realised, but who would have thought it?

The CO was sitting astride a couple of ammo boxes rattling out a song on an upright piano that despite some obvious damage sounded perfectly in tune. He was singing too, and what I thought was a cheery tune was everything but, as I heard the lyrics: "*If your engine cuts out you'll have no balls at all…*" Unlike when someone plays the piano at home when everyone gathers around to join in, this had the opposite effect, as the mess began clearing with hardly anyone remaining. "Copping!" he shouted when he saw me. "Get yourself a beer, on me. You did well today!" he shouted, banging the keys with tremendous enthusiasm. The lack of all-round appreciation didn't seem to bother the pianist as he carried on with added gusto. I sat down with a beer and lit a cigarette. For a few minutes the mess could have been anywhere; one tune after another was rattled out and not until a few beers later was the CO joined in his musical soiree by several others. The singing became so loud it almost drowned out the piano. Perhaps that was the intention. I was astonished to find out the piano had been one of the first things they'd brought with them as the squadron migrated from Palestine after they'd pinched it from the mess at al-Bassa.

Just as I was thinking of leaving, I was surrounded by other pilots insisting on the CO's orders that I drink to the health of everyone present and to the future success of the squadron. I was flattered by the attention and didn't suspect a thing. It was whiskey, after all, and so I drank what they gave me as they chanted, "Welcome to two-sixty," over and again. Then they began chanting, "He's a jolly good fellow," as I quaffed yet more whiskey. This went on for twenty minutes until I could barely stand up. Then they struck. I was lifted up by a gang of them and my shorts were swiftly removed to cheers all round. I had been expertly 'de-bagged' and my shorts ruthlessly paraded around the mess in what I realised was my initiation to the squadron.

In the morning my head was splitting, but luckily I was not down for ops so I spent most of it dozing, in-between wandering around, familiarising myself with my new home. The supply canteen at LG115 was the least functional-looking kitchen I'd ever seen, with no running water, no sink, no power or even a front door. It was merely a large open tent with crates piled high and cans arranged on empty wooden boxes in order to resemble shelves in a corner shop or NAAFI. There wasn't much in the way of choice, but there were plenty of essentials such as cans of bully beef and dry biscuits, so we definitely wouldn't starve. I found out quickly that it was always preferable to keep the cans in the shade and as cool as possible, otherwise whatever they were when they were opened the warm contents would just pour out in a disgusting slushy mess. Because it was almost impossible to keep anything cool, it was much better to disguise it all in pastry or in a big stew, making it less obvious. The cooks did a wonderful job with what they had, but we were all on constant lookout for alternative sources of food, whether it was from other squadrons, the army, locals, or even captured German or Italian rations. Perhaps this was how Agnides obtained his Afrika Korps provisions. Sometimes Arabs would appear near the landing ground selling eggs, which we were obviously happy to buy or barter for, and I wondered as they strolled away with their camels, having seen all our aeroplanes, just how much they knew and what they might then pass on to the Hun. Obtaining decent food became quite an obsession with some in the squadron because it could really boost morale, and I was to take part in the regular acquisition of more interesting supplies later on that was quite frankly bizarre.

In my second week at LG115 I was volunteered by the CO to travel with three others in a Blenheim to LG100 at Wadi Natrun on the Alex–Cairo road where four Hurricanes were ready for collection. This was the location of No. 53 RSU, Repair & Servicing Unit, where damaged aeroplanes were taken, provided they could get there under their own power, and those that were in need of a major overhaul, because it was a safe distance from the front line.

My second trip in a Blenheim passed well, even if it was a bit cramped, and we landed without incident. This time I was not asked to sit up front. After a quick cup of tea and a cigarette I was strapping myself into one of the Hurricanes for the return journey. It was a Mark I but far less worked and in much better condition.

Pilot Officer John Gidman took Patterson while I took off with Ron Cundy, an experienced Aussie sergeant pilot. I had assumed we were all going straight back to LG115, but we weren't. Gidman and Patterson headed for LG013 at Sidi Haneish South to deliver their aeroplanes while Cundy and I were despatched to LG008, the other side of Mersa Matruh. I wondered how we'd get back to our own base after delivery, but I forgot to ask. It seemed these ferry flights were common and so transport was not an issue.

Along with a detailed map of our destination, we had strict instructions not to engage the enemy unless absolutely necessary; we were returning repaired aeroplanes, so the last thing their new owners wanted was more damage. Having said that, Cundy checked with the armourers at LG100 and confirmed with a sly wink to me that all four aeroplanes were fully armed. I didn't query what 'absolutely necessary' meant, but I assumed it was self-defence only.

Cundy and I watched as the first pair took off heading north towards the coast, and we gave them a few minutes before we left. The road was easy to follow and I was really enjoying the flight as we turned west before reaching Alex. The entire trip was around two hundred miles, and so at a moderate cruise speed of 200 mph and five thousand feet, it shouldn't take us more than an hour or so. It was midday when we passed Fuka and then about ten miles east of Mersa Matruh we came across a very odd sight. Gathered in the sky near our destination was what looked like an enormous wasp's nest that someone had just poked with a stick: dozens of aeroplanes whirling around, with some diving up and down through the others, and at least one was trailing smoke behind it. With six RAF LGs around Fuka and two at Sidi Haneish, the Hun was always a frequent visitor, and it was clear a big show of some sort was going on. It reminded me of some of the busiest days of the Battle of Britain that I'd seen over southern England. Suddenly the R/T burst into life.

"Copping, stick to my starboard side and get down to the LG as soon as you can after this, good luck," Cundy said, followed by a loud shout of, "Tally-ho!"

"Okay, will do," I replied, without thinking. We were joining in with whatever was going on because Cundy had made the decision in an instant. I felt a massive surge of adrenaline and could only say one word to myself: '*Shit*'. My heart rose so far up into my throat I thought I'd choke on it. I'd been involved in the scrape with the CO and the 109, but this was the first time I was going in cold. Was this the *absolute necessity* we had been told about? We weren't being attacked, not directly, but some of our colleagues certainly were, and this was all happening right in front of us so how could anyone seriously think we could ignore it, fly around and land as ordered?

24

CUNDY IMMEDIATELY THREW HIS AEROPLANE INTO A shallow dive and I followed, opening the throttle wide. He was the same rank as me but there was clearly seniority with experience, and so that was it, we were now committed. I could always argue later that he had ordered me to do it. My Hurricane was accelerating just as I recognised a large group of Ju87 Stukas below and ahead of us, probably above Gerawla, pursued by other Hurricanes.

We closed in on them incredibly quickly and I had to ease back on the throttle and pull back on the stick to avoid tearing straight past. It was impossible to hang on to Cundy, who had immediately begun the pursuit of the closest Stuka he could find. There was no hesitation; he was just gone, like a terrier after a rabbit. I couldn't believe what I was seeing; as I looked around at the sky filled with aeroplanes, I was spoiled for choice. The Stuka has an unmistakeable profile, so it didn't take me long to find one of my own. I selected one and followed my target in a steep turn to starboard, and then the opposite way in classic evasive manoeuvres. He'd clearly seen me already and suddenly I saw his bombs fall away over empty desert as he ditched them and was now trying to make a run for it. To this extent my actions had already been successful in stopping their use on my colleagues.

There were flashes from the rear gunner but luckily none of the bullets had yet made contact. I fired and missed, and he weaved again. He pushed his aeroplane into a very odd negative G dive before another steep turn to port and I could see the rear gunner was still firing up at me constantly, most of the bullets hopelessly off target. I began to wonder if he knew what he was doing, and that like me, both crew members were young and inexperienced. Even so, I knew I had to be quick or they might get lucky and hit me. I couldn't afford any sympathy; would they for me? I closed in to just a few hundred yards and fired a long burst of several seconds, the stream of bullets weaving around ahead of me towards the target like water from a garden hose on a summer's day. I paused briefly for a readjustment to keep him in my sights, and then gave him another quick burst for good measure. I didn't see any smoke, but I saw bits fly off the fuselage and suddenly the rear gunner stopped firing. As I drew near, I was surprised to see the roundels of the Regia Aeronautica, as the Stuka was clearly Italian and not German. He dropped down in a tearing hurry and it was then I noticed wisps of smoke and flame from the rear of the fuselage. *Blimey, I've hit him*, I thought, surprised. I wanted to follow him down, to see what happened to the crew, but I pulled away, conscious there may be 109s nearby.

I'd lost four thousand feet, so I converted my speed into height in order to take a better look around. Back up at two thousand feet, I was shocked to see I was alone in the sky. The great melee had gone and everywhere was quiet.

I turned a three-sixty but couldn't see anyone at all, so with nothing else to do I quickly laid the map out on my knee and headed north, where I was bound to reach the sea, my own lines and my destination. We are always told it's too dangerous to fly alone in the combat area, so I eased the throttle forward, dropped down onto the deck and began weaving a little, just in case. I could see the coast up ahead and so I turned north-east, and within a few minutes I recognised the dog-leg coastline a few miles east of Mersa.

I then saw another Hurricane circling above with its wheels down, so I gratefully tagged along. LG08 was closer to the town than LG07, which was further west on the map, so I brought the speed right down and lowered the gear for the downwind checks.

My approach was good, but then I bumped hard onto the LG08 strip in such a clumsy manner that I wanted to go around again to show them I could do better but decided against it. I pulled off the runway and stowed the flaps before taxiing over to a gathering of tents that looked most like a dispersal area. Once I'd stopped and shut down the engine, an erk jumped up onto the wing with a clipboard, asking me to sign for delivery of the aeroplane. You just can't escape the paperwork. The manifest had been pre-ticked as 'full' for everything apart from fuel but including ammunition.

"Excuse me, corp," I said to the rather tired-looking corporal. "I can't sign for this part, I've used up quite a few bullets, I'm afraid. Sorry about that."

He looked at me and then at the open gun ports in the wings and smiled. "Stopped off for a bit of target practice in the desert, did we, Sarge? That's alright. I'm sure you knew what you were doing," he replied, and I smiled back. I removed my flying helmet and let out a great sigh of relief. My right arm was resting on the edge of the open canopy as though I'd been on a Sunday morning spin in a sports car. Quite suddenly I felt like a veteran fighter pilot.

I wondered whether I would get into trouble for my part in the melee over Gerawla the day before. Some of the other chaps were quite congratulatory when Cundy and I arrived back at LG115 in the early morning, cold and hungry, slumped in the back of an army Humber. I thought I was in the clear, until the CO called me into his office. I climbed the steps into the back of his lorry with great trepidation, alone, and was told to, "Come in!" with clear abruptness.

"What happened yesterday, Copping?" he said, getting straight to the point and looking rather stern as he sat down. I was just inside the door and I suddenly felt extremely under-dressed, standing in the squadron commander's office wearing desert boots, khaki shorts, a crumpled open-neck khaki shirt and no headgear. To my horror, I also realised I still had a cigarette in my right hand. It was too late for that, so I just stood there holding it, hoping he wouldn't notice as the smoke curled up my arm. As it passed over my face, I dearly wanted to take a drag on it, but I knew this would have been just a little too much. Just then he passed me a tin can, half-full of cigarette ends, with a nod to a chair for me to sit.

I stubbed out the cigarette and perched my bottom on the leading edge of the wooden seat before proceeding to tell him that Cundy and I had been *forced* into action, with no choice in the matter. I also told him that I had a few good squirts at an Italian Stuka and that I was pretty sure I'd damaged it, so it wasn't a complete waste of time. He leaned forward in his chair and lit a cigarette. He dropped the match into the tin can on his desk in a carefully aimed lob that plinked with a direct hit, and then drew me over to his map on the table.

"Can you show me where you think this happened?" I leaned in and found the area where I thought I'd lost Cundy and had pursued the Stuka. He alternately scanned the map and some papers that I saw were marked: 'Army Intel: Confidential'.

As he did this, I reassured him that both our aeroplanes had been delivered undamaged and fully serviceable, and so we had actually achieved our objective. He was still scanning the map and I detected a very brief nod of the head, but throughout this he maintained a painfully straight face and I suspected the worst. Did he not believe me? I was preparing a further defence in my head, about to tell him that it was all Cundy's fault because as senior man he had led me astray, in the same way two errant schoolboys caught scrumping apples would blame each other, but he then stood up and threw his right hand towards me and we shook hands. "It seems you've bagged yourself a Stuka, congratulations, well done," he said. "Army Intel state four went down altogether and there was just one that had been unaccounted for, exploded on impact along with both crew, here," he said, with his right index finger pressed onto the map, "and it seems to be the one you got, so well done." Blimey. What a relief. I wasn't in trouble after all. I'd just made my first kill.

That night the sound of aero engines woke us up, passing high overhead. It was becoming instinctive now; a brief pause waiting for exploding munitions prompting a wholesale tip into the slit trenches, but whoever it was this time they didn't drop any bombs anywhere near us, and so no-one moved. In the quiet darkness I began thinking about recent events and my first kill. I wondered if any of the others ever thought about such things. I don't know. No-one seemed to discuss it, anyway. I know you can't afford sympathy for your enemy, I realise that, and I'd seen what the Hun had been doing to London and my hometown, but that's not the issue. I'd destroyed an Italian aeroplane, a machine, not the two men inside it, brothers, sons or fathers of someone, crashed and burned in the Egyptian desert after I shot them down. Their relatives would eventually receive news that they'd gone, killed in action, as just another wartime statistic. I was oddly relieved they would never know my name.

The initial flurry of activity at my new squadron was tempered by several days of inactivity on my part as I wasn't chosen for another op until the following week. The squadron was still amalgamating, more pilots had now arrived and we were sharing aeroplanes two or even three to one until more appeared, and even then my next trip was an uneventful ferry flight.

25

MORE MEN AND MATERIAL WERE BEING DRAWN UP towards the front line for something that we all knew was coming; we just didn't know exactly when or where. During these few days of rest I knew I had reached a point where I could no longer delay the inevitable. I just didn't want to do it, but I finally realised I had no choice in the matter. I felt more apprehensive about this than flying into combat, but it had to be done, however distasteful. My own body odour was making me heave and so I knew I had to do something. The familiarity of the latrine procedure had finally eroded any remnants of dignity I had left anyway, so it no longer mattered. I kept washing my clothes as best I could in second-hand water and even in petrol, but putting them straight back onto a filthy body every time was becoming pointless and downright stupid. I was terrified of getting body lice too, which was a real possibility if I continued like this. I'd been putting it off, but now, what the hell, I may as well get on with it. I put my name down for a bath.

The 'bath' consists of a tiny area of open desert about three inches deep and eighteen inches across. This is lined with waterproof tarpaulin and filled with whatever water can be found. You then strip off and sit in it, and so this is where the added indignity comes in. There is insufficient water to wash on your own, so by necessity it becomes a group effort. There's the ladler and the jug man who pour the water over you, and with the soap in their hands, they reach the parts you cannot reach alone. All the water must then be collected in the tarpaulin and re-used; none is wasted. We were allowed a four-gallon jerry can of water for bath time, which sounds a lot, but it was just once a week, and for the *whole squadron*. The last man ends up sitting in a brown, scummy soup of everything that has been washed off his colleagues, and so that's why names are drawn out of a hat, to see who gets the clean water first.

When my name was called, I stripped off and sat down, focussing my gaze into the far distant desert. Because I was only halfway down the list, the water was still quite reasonable and Sergeant Tom 'Polly' Parrott used the jug to pour it over my head, after which I rubbed the bar of NAAFI carbolic soap into my hair. Sergeant Bill Wareham then took it from me and rubbed my back before using the ladle to wash it off. It was definitely a three-man operation, and it worked well, as I sat there being pampered. It was the first time in my life I'd been touched by anyone else in this way as an adult while still sober.

"You didn't rub *my* back like that," Polly commented.

"You didn't ask me to, darling," Wareham replied, still rubbing, after which all three of us burst out laughing. "Where are you going for your holidays this year, Copping?" Wareham said. "Not St Tropez again, surely?"

"Of course not," I replied, smiling. "I was thinking more of the West Indies, what do you think?"

"What a good idea, I think I'll join you," Wareham said.

"A bit pricey, but at least you can guarantee the weather," Polly added, rinsing my hair.

"I'll write to Uncle Adolf and ask him to keep his U-boats at home for a few weeks," Wareham said, adding, "A final rinse and you should be done, Sir." I rubbed my eyes and shook my head, tapping water from my ears with a finger.

"Be sure to leave a tip in the jar on the counter before you leave, won't you, Copping? We're saving up for the staff Christmas party," to which we all laughed again. I felt cleaner immediately, even though by now the water resembled brown porridge with a foamy crust on the top. But at least it was a sweet-smelling foamy crust. Sadly there was no time to lie back and relax; it wasn't that sort of bath, but the familiarity of it all had completely destroyed any last remaining traces of personal dignity.

I wouldn't say I'd look forward to bath time in future, but there was definitely something inexplicable about sharing such an experience. The finale was a couple of ladles of fresh water direct from the jerry can for the last rinse. When I opened my eyes, a naked man was standing right in front of me just a few feet away. "Have you finished, Copping?" he said. The CO was all ready and impatient for his turn. I helped lift the bath up and we poured the water back into an urn for him. He then sat down and the process was repeated.

I should have done my bit by washing the CO's back for him, but I was excused because it was my first time. He specifically asked Wareham to do it for him anyway. Despite living in generally squalid and unsanitary conditions, this bath time ritual seemed to work; as far as I know, no-one at 260 Squadron had lice, not yet anyway.

The August heat was insufferable; with the only consolation being the enemy was enduring the same conditions. It was at least 104 degrees in the shade on most days, apparently, and the warm breeze from the south-east was known locally as 'the date-ripening wind'. Everything liquid boiled and everything solid melted, including the people. Extra efforts were made by the cooks to disguise the bully beef because it was an inedible slush, and the chlorinated drinking water was very warm, almost hot, made more palatable by a shot of whiskey or gin whenever we could. Tea was the main drink, with powdered milk or no milk at all, but with plenty of sweetener or sugar when we could get it.

On Thursday 21st August two of us were taken in a Lysander to Fuka, and throughout the entire twenty-five-minute flight I felt terribly vulnerable in such a slow low-flying aeroplane. Any passing 109 could have easily clobbered us very quickly, but then it's such a small and inconspicuous little shape that it would probably be missed. Perhaps this is its secret. From there Polly and I returned in refurbished Hurricanes to LG115 completely without incident. The Hun must have been asleep, away on holiday that day, or perhaps it was bath time for the Luftwaffe? At the end of August most of 260 Squadron had assembled at LG115 and we were almost up to full strength. One morning after breakfast all available pilots were called into the mess for a briefing by Harry Bandinell and the CO. Flight Lieutenant James 'Harry' Bandinell was quietly spoken and typically modest, and I found out from others that he was a veteran of the Battle of Britain. Like others who'd fought the Hun above southern England, he brought with him the idea for the 'finger-four' formation that Douglas Bader had introduced and argued endlessly with the CO about it, who was at that time sticking to the official 'V' formation of three aeroplanes.

The gaggle board had been wiped clean and was now displaying the finger-four formations with red, blue, yellow and green flights, in four groups of four. The individual formation of four looked like a finger bent over at the end, hence the name. The flight leader was at the front, with a wingman on his left as usual, and on his right, or starboard side the other wingman, now known as the element leader. This was where it changed. To his right and just behind him was the fourth man, the element wingman.

"No more Vic formations, gentlemen, we have modernised," Harry said, smiling. The CO was standing at the side with his hands in the pockets of his shorts, traces of a grudging smile spreading across his face. "We now have two aircraft ready to open fire, with the other two keeping lookout. It works well, believe me. So remember your positions and stick to them. We'll always be flying in fours from now on, so it shouldn't be too difficult."

The squadron began using the new formation in bomber escort duties further along the coast aimed primarily at enemy shipping. Both sides were building up supplies and it was a game of logistics to see who could get hold of the most and stop the other first. We still had the advantage of Malta as a staging post for our supplies from Blighty, supremely useful as it was right in the middle of the Med, whereas the Hun had to cross all the way from Italy. They were still trying to take Malta from us, of course, and their situation was precarious at best. Tobruk was still holding out too, despite the ongoing siege and the Hun's repeated attempts to break in through the defensive perimeter and take it.

In the next few days I flew in the new formation several times as the fourth man without incident and found it a little easier, but I'd yet to experience it in combat. We were involved in helping to escort supply ships into the besieged city of Tobruk and it was on the last of these ops that I had my first tangle with an Italian Macchi C200 fighter of the Regia Aeronautica.

I'd taken off mid-morning following Harry Bandinell with Saunders on his port wing, Cartwright on his starboard side and with me behind him. Two other sets of four were following on behind us. We climbed up to five thousand feet intending to follow the coast towards Tobruk where a supply ship was due in at around eleven o'clock. They had been unavoidably delayed and they would usually have tried docking at night, but now they were stuck. If they sat out at sea they'd be seen, so it was decided to make a run in and hope for the best.

26

It wasn't ideal, but hopefully with our help it would be okay. We knew that if the Hun spotted it then it would become a prime target. The Royal Navy had so far successfully managed to get it this far and so we didn't want to let anyone down at the last moment. It was a calm day when we flew out to sea to avoid unwanted attention near Sollum and the Mediterranean was a beautiful deep blue, gently rippling onto golden sandy beaches. It wasn't until then, while I was daydreaming, that I realised I'd forgotten to put on my Mae West. This was stupid, and I swore it would never happen again. I'd just have to avoid ditching in the sea. Some of us, me included, were flying with the cockpit canopy half-open to let in the air, but even thousands of feet up it was still hot. Another important thing I'd started doing was loosening my top shoulder straps a little after take-off; I noticed when I was pursuing the Italian Stuka I couldn't lean forwards or look to my rear very easily because the straps had pinned me into the seat. The Hurricane has a great view from the cockpit, so it would be a shame to ruin it.

It was about eighty miles to Sollum and enemy territory, and from there another fifty or so to Tobruk, in all about half an hour's flying time. We saw nothing until we were ten miles from Tobruk and about the same distance over the sea. Contact had been made with the supply vessel and it was still fifteen miles out. Saunders saw the enemy first, coming in fast and low from just south of the besieged city: three Savoia-Marchetti SM 79 Sparviero tri-motor bombers escorted by three Macchi C200s. They must have found out the ship was there. It would have been fine for the twelve of us to handle this lot, but high above and providing them with their top cover were six 109s. Why did the bloody Hun have to get involved?

"Concentrate on the SM 79s; they'll be using them as torpedo bombers. Let's clobber them and get out quick," Harry said over the R/T, followed by the usual shout of, "Tally-ho!" as he pushed his aeroplane forwards into a shallow dive. I kept pace with them just off Cartwright's starboard wing and could see we were heading straight towards the formation. As soon as they saw us they split up. Harry was aiming for the leader in the middle, so with Cartwright I went for his wingman, now banking off to the west. I fired a quick burst as I passed, but it was then I saw a Macchi C200 coming straight for me head on.

My first thoughts were that it looked like a Hurricane with a radial engine and about the same size and profile, but these were my last idle thoughts on the matter; the pilot seemed very determined to kill me. I flew underneath him and banked to starboard, intending to find the bomber, but the Macchi had already turned around and was in pursuit. It was as though he had immediately taken our encounter as a personal issue and whenever I looked back he was there, lining up for a shot at me. It was all I could do to keep out of his sights.

I pulled a steep turn to port with full power that almost made me pass out and cause a high-speed stall, but he was still with me. I tried something different with another sharp turn to port and thought I'd lost him, so I then went after the bomber again. He was now a hundred feet off the water heading out to sea, probably lining up for a torpedo run at the ship, so as soon as I could, and aware I may still have the Macchi peering over my shoulder, from about three hundred yards I fired a long burst, most of which flew right past and around him, breaking the water ahead in huge great plumes. I doubt any of these hit him, but the effect was extremely dramatic. I was about to turn and press ahead with another attack, when to my astonishment he ditched his torpedo and banked off to port, nose down, throttles forward, heading back for land. Whatever the effect the result was acceptable; he'd called off his attack.

I then heard a series of loud rattling noises as though a bag of marbles had come loose under the floor of my cockpit and immediately realised my friend was back, and he was onto me. Was my aeroplane hit? I couldn't tell, but something had happened. With no height to speak of, and very little speed, I had nothing to work with, just the aeroplane's manoeuvrability, which I hoped was better than the Macchi. I rammed the throttle as far forward as I could, trimmed it, and settled into a fight with Franco, as I had named him.

I stayed on the deck; there was no point climbing any higher, I'd be far too slow, so I went even lower. I was now down to fifty feet. I pulled a tight turn to port, so low that the surface of the water shimmered in the wash from my propeller. I saw Franco 180 degrees behind me, just entering the turn, so I kept it up, hoping to see him eventually fill my sights. Once, twice, three times around in a sixty degree bank and we remained 180 degrees apart; there was nothing in it, the performance of our aeroplanes was too similar. Our 360s over the sea were so clean I felt the buffet from the airflow following us, but still I couldn't get rid of him. I wondered what the Macchi was like in a straight out drag race, so I broke away and, still at fifty feet, held the throttle fully forward and just to be on the safe side, headed east along the coast. My Merlin engine was all that was keeping me alive with everything set to max; mixture full rich and throttle fully open. Now in a straight line behind me, Franco fired several long bursts, the fountains of water in front of me evidence of his misses. I weaved around from side to side, up and down as he continued firing and missing. He seemed to have a limitless supply of ammunition as I counted over ten seconds, until silence. He'd run out. There couldn't be any other reason why he would stop, so now it was my turn. I pulled up to starboard and rolled off the top at five hundred feet. I hauled my aeroplane around to confront him with my right thumb already on the gun button. I looked around, but he was gone.

Further towards Tobruk, I saw my colleagues involved in a scrap with the 109s. There was actually very little head-to-head combat with the Macchis for the same reason Franco and I couldn't get at one another: the machines were so evenly matched, but the 109 was different. It was faster and could turn quicker than a Hurricane. The bombers had abandoned their run at the ship and were heading home, which was the main thing, and so if we could hang around for a while until the 109s left, the supply ship would stand a better chance of getting into port safely. I joined in with some occasional bursts at the remaining Macchis and 109s, until after ten minutes or so I too had run out of ammunition, as, it seemed, had everyone else present. By this time the ship was almost home safe, so we decided to call it a day. Franco had been right; there really is no point hanging around making a target of yourself for no reason.

Returning along the coast with the others, I eased the canopy back and suddenly remembered my aeroplane had been hit. It seemed a passing insignificance, as there was apparently no damage, and outside I couldn't see any obvious gaping holes anywhere. Everything was working fine, the Ts and Ps were alright, and so, with LG115 in sight, I lowered the undercarriage and flaps on final approach as usual. Almost as an afterthought, I tightened my straps, just in case. I was very glad I did. The wheels showed fully down and locked as I landed in what seemed a normal touchdown.

Just as I throttled right back and applied pressure to the brakes there was the most almighty bang and I thought the whole world had turned upside down. My port wing tip struck the ground and the end of the prop began wildly threshing up the sand like farm machinery, causing great clouds of dust and debris to fly around everywhere, including into the cockpit. I thought the aeroplane would flip over in a ground loop at any moment and I'd be trapped inside, so I held on and hoped for the best, wrestling the controls with all my strength to keep it level. With what little control I still had left, I managed to get it off the centre of the landing strip and immediately shut down the engine before it finally heaved to a stop in a hissing wreck.

In desperate fear of an explosion, I turned off the fuel and electrics just as a group of erks came running up, one hauling a fire extinguisher, pointing it at the engine, ready. As others arrived, the fire extinguisher was then abandoned on the sand while they began peering underneath. I was still strapped in, dazed but apparently uninjured. Just as I was about to release myself, I heard loud footsteps on the wing and a gin bottle was thrust into my face. "Bad luck, Copping. Hairy business, eh?" Gidman said, forcing me to take a swig, looking down at me as though checking to see if I was still in one piece. It was very welcome anyway as it seared down my parched throat. He took a quick gulp himself before forcing me to take another. My erks, Ernie and Dave, unstrapped me, hauling me out by the armpits. I had no clue as to what had caused this, thinking at first I'd hit a previously undiscovered landmine until I was carried a few yards away and could see the problem: the left undercarriage leg, with wheel still attached, had broken away and was lying fifty yards behind.

27

Doc Craib sat me down in his tent just as one of the cooks came in with two mugs of tea, into which the doc splashed liberal amounts of whiskey before handing mine over.

"Any pain anywhere?" he said, shining his torch into my eyes causing an initial squint.

"No, not really. Neck aches a bit, but that's all," I said, nursing my tea, moving it off my bare leg and onto my shorts. He paused, allowing me to take a sip; it tasted and smelled of Christmas.

"Any dizziness?" he said, looking again, standing so close his warm pipe breath wafted across my face.

"No," I said, lying. The gin and now the whiskey were making my head spin. As though he could tell I was lying, he looked in my eyes a third time. His shirt was open three buttons down from the neck and I noticed despite being only in his mid-thirties, some of the hairs on his chest were already grey, his open shirt the only concession to the desert in an otherwise smart appearance. He never took off his hat even inside, his socks were always neatly pulled up to just below the knee and not at half-mast like the rest of us. His moustache was finely trimmed and it had turned a vivid yellow under his nose from years of pipe smoke.

"Nevertheless," he said, now standing upright in front of me, "I'm going to have a chat with the CO," he said, turning his back and putting away his torch. I had no idea what he meant by that, and I left with some tablets and instructions to rest.

I did as I was told and slept all afternoon. When I woke up just after four, I heard music drifting into the tent on a hot breeze. I looked around and I was alone, feeling fine apart from a pounding headache and terrible stiff neck. I drifted over to the latrine, treading carefully on the hard ground like a ghostly ballerina, then, after pulling down my shorts, I lit up. Sitting upright on the wooden latrine hurt my back, which in turn hurt my neck even more, but then I was distracted when Gene Autry began singing 'South of the Border' somewhere behind me in a very crackly recording. Sticky Glew was obviously in the mess with his gramophone, which he guarded jealously. He wouldn't normally allow anyone else to use it, unless he himself had consumed a few drinks which then caused a slight relaxation in the operating regulations. As Gene Autry finished there was a pause before the Jimmy Dorsey Orchestra began playing 'Amapola'. The Saturday morning matinee at Southend's Scala Cinema seemed a million miles away. An hour later, after dinner, I went back to the tent and slept soundly all night.

It wasn't until I saw my aeroplane up on jacks the next day that I realised how lucky I'd been. Ernie took a break to show me a dozen glancing bullet marks in long streaks under the port wing, mainly around the undercarriage, a present from my Italian friend Franco. A few inches higher and I could have lost my wing altogether. But I wasn't the only pilot to have brought back a damaged aeroplane, as five were now in for repairs or stripping down for the effects of sand. These repairs would take at least a few days, so with more pilots than aeroplanes the CO decided to give some of us leave. The CO told me directly that I was one of the lucky ones after a conversation he'd apparently had with Doc Craib. I was given a 'forty-eighter,' a forty-eight-hour weekend pass that would start on the coming Saturday morning at 0900 hours and end promptly at 0900 hours on Monday. After that we would be AWOL.

This would be my first weekend trip to Alex and I had no idea what to expect. It was 150 miles from LG115 and so the generous offer of a space on a hardwood bench in an open top three-ton army lorry was politely declined. Even with no back problems it didn't seem a good idea. Air transport was the only viable option and we found out a Blenheim was apparently calling in on Saturday morning and flying directly to Alex, so this was our ticket.

When Friday afternoon arrived and we were officially off ops, it really did feel like I was going away, almost like any other job when an exciting weekend lay ahead. It was odd, I know, but I had my pass in my shirt pocket and was preparing my best khaki drill uniform, the one I called my Heliopolis kit with the shiny brass buttons. I only had two uniforms: the one I flew in and the one I didn't, so there wasn't much choice.

We had our full allocation of beer in the mess that night, as Sergeant Pilot Harry Curno, our other piano player, entertained us with a singalong, which we were happy to join in with. I slept quite well and we were not disturbed by the Hun or anyone else.

Our transport touched down at seven o'clock in the morning and two army types jumped out laden with map cases to be met by the CO. There were serious faces all round as they walked towards the CO's office deep in conversation. Four of us were in high spirits, two officers and two sergeant pilots: Harry Bandinell and Andy Gidman, then me and Frank Tregear. We were impatient to climb aboard, but first we had breakfast: bully beef, biscuits and tea, the usual. I wondered if the food would be any better in Alex. *It must be*, I thought. Mail, whiskey and cigarettes were unloaded, and our latest letters home, with the ink still wet, handed to us by our adjutant in a mail sack to take aboard. The Blenheim crew were eating in our mess, and we were all dropping enormous hints for them to hurry up. Harry even lied outrageously by saying a *khamsin* was on its way and we'd all be grounded for a week if we didn't take off right this minute, but they didn't fall for it. I asked them about Tim Murray and they told me he was also on leave in Alex. Eventually at 0900 hours and when our leave officially began, they got the message and we each found our space in the belly of the aeroplane. After Frank slammed the door behind him, we were airborne in a few minutes. I caught a glimpse of the emerald sea on our left and wondered if after the war, in some indeterminate future, these shores would be crowded with European tourists lazing around in deckchairs. I knew flying boats had frequently carried wealthy travellers to Alex before the war, and so maybe this would all resume one day. It all depended on who would win this damned war, of course.

There was no conversation between us after we took off, mainly because it was unfeasibly loud in the back of the Blenheim. I climbed around mixed items of cargo and my colleagues' legs in search of a more comfortable seating position because my neck and back were causing a lot of pain.

I swallowed down a couple of Doc Craib's tablets and lay flat on my back with my legs on a box.

This aeroplane was cleaner and more orderly, a real contrast to Tim Murray's Blenheim and after a smooth but uncomfortable trip, we landed at Aboukir, a few miles east of Alex. After engine shutdown we strolled into dispersal to find a lift into town. We all smoked several cigarettes as we waited impatiently for over an hour. I forgot to bring my official guide to Alexandria, very kindly supplied to us by the RAF, but all three of the others had been before, so I suspected I didn't need it. They had something arranged anyway, so they told me, and I'd heard rumours.

The short trip into the centre of Alex in the back of an open-top RAF lorry after the cramped conditions of the Blenheim was quite pleasant, with the sea on our right and a lovely refreshing breeze on our faces, at least while we were moving. The hard bench was surprisingly comfortable and I was relieved to be able to sit upright in order to ease my neck. We passed a racecourse and a huge sign saying 'The Alexandria Sporting Club' as we drove into the city on the El Sultan Hussein Kamid Road.

We then turned onto a wonderful curved esplanade with a magnificent harbour view to our right and the lorry stopped without any prompting at the end of a side street called Adib Bek Ashak. We climbed down, thanked the driver, and I began following the others, who seemed to know exactly where they were going. Harry and Andy paused at a pair of green double doors, the paint on which was cracked and faded from years of neglect. They didn't knock but simply turned the enormous handle in the centre and pushed it open. There was a sign above the door in a similar condition – 'Pension Crillon' – and without hesitation I followed them, shutting the heavy door behind me.

It was refreshingly cool inside, our footsteps echoing loudly on the churchy floor. Through the initial gloom we stepped towards bright light reflecting on terracotta tiles into a garden kitchen where a wireless standing alone on a table was gushing French accordion music, the reception drifting eerily in and out as though caught in a strong crosswind. A feast of wonderful smells devoured us: firstly a strong whiff of French cigarettes, followed by memories of home from the aroma of freshly baked bread. A middle-aged woman was standing at a sink in the corner and she turned around to see us.

28

"Ah! Monsieur Harry, how nice to see you again," she said, walking towards us, drying her hands and wrapping a flowery cotton tea towel around her left forearm. She took hold of Harry's shoulders and kissed him sweetly on each cheek before turning to the rest of us. "Monsieur Gidman, *et* Monsieur Tregear, so nice, so nice," she said, kissing them all.

"This is Copping, our new chap," Frank said, smiling at me. "Copping, this is Flo, Madame Florence Pericand," he said proudly, as she was already pouncing on me like a cat, taking hold of my shoulders, priming me for a kiss. I leaned my face forward and it was kissed not twice, but three times.

"Pleased to meet you, Madame," I said in reply, beginning to wonder who she was and what I was doing there, but then also aware that I wasn't really bothered anyway. The place was obviously well-known to my colleagues, so I thought I'd just go with it.

"We have not seen you for a while," she said, still looking at me, but clearly referring to Frank and the others.

"We've been very busy, Madame," he said, moving to the wide open French doors framed by enormous climbing plants, the huge leaves of which hung around the opening like elephant's ears. Harry and Andy followed as Frank stood with his hands on his hips releasing a long sigh as though relieved to be home.

"Busy, busy..." she said, turning towards me and reaching for a bottle of red wine from a sideboard on the back wall. "Gabbi!" she shouted, and then, "Cherie!", leaning her head slightly towards the door and placing the bottle on the table. "I cannot open this, my hands, you know, too painful, my husband will do it," she said. There was a corkscrew on the sideboard, so I picked it up. The white ceramic handle was covered in hairline cracks and inlaid in red with the word 'Marseille'.

"Here, let me," I said as I pushed the end into the cork and began twisting, the bottle now firmly wedged between my knees. It was tough and I wasn't making any progress until it began rising very slowly, then just as it popped, a man appeared from the stairs, thick set, all grey, with leathery olive skin.

"*Bonjour, Monsieur, je m'apelle Gabriel,*" he said, squeezing my right hand in a vice.

"Copping," I said, reciprocating, my hand deeply buried in his like a child's lost in its father's.

He smiled.

"Sit down outside with the others, *Copping,*" he said, with great emphasis on my name. "You RAF don't have first names, then? So formal," he said in near-perfect English, laughing. He was unshaven, maybe a couple of days, with a combined odour of garlic, stale sweat and Gitanes that was deeply masculine and not altogether unpleasant. I tried to pinpoint exactly what it was. It was French. He took the bottle from my left hand in a polite but business-like grip as though disarming a prisoner of war, and ushered me outside, the bottle so small in his hand that just the neck was visible.

He didn't immediately shake hands with Harry, Andy and Frank; he kissed them first before giving them each a fatherly pat on the back, until finally grabbing their hands. He poured the wine equally into six glasses, with quick flips as though preparing cocktails, before passing them around. We stood together in a circle as the afternoon sun lit one wall of their courtyard garden. "*Salut!*" Gabriel said, raising his glass, and then, "*La guerre!*" before drinking half of his in one. There were beads of sweat on his forehead that glistened like pearls before being absorbed into the deep furrows of his brow. I looked around. I was having a good time already.

We all sat in wicker chairs with green and white striped cushions as Frank entertained our hosts with tales of the desert – innocent, light-hearted stuff about men in tents – and I noticed the wine had rather quickly reached my legs and then my head. I took out my cigarettes and passed them around. In polite exchange, I took one of Gabriel's Gitanes and we all lit up together. Frank smiled at me. He knew what I was thinking. *Who the hell are these people?*

"Your rooms are all ready," Florence said, pulling on her cigarette. "Are there any others today?"

"No, this is it, Madame," Frank said, tapping his cigarette into a tin ashtray at his feet.

"Good, then there are four rooms as usual, it would be a shame for them to be empty and unused," Florence said.

"There's no risk of that, Madame," Frank said, laughing. "I think we're in for a good weekend, aren't we, Copping?" he said, looking at me directly. I smiled. It would seem so, though I still didn't quite know what to expect yet. "I have this month's payment for you, by the way, Madame," he said, handing her a roll of banknotes. His Australian accent was broadening the more relaxed he became.

"*Merci, Monsieur, merci beaucoup,*" she said, not counting it but leaving it on the table, obviously very trusting. It looked like a substantial wedge of cash, all neatly bound together with a large RAF paper clip, like the ones I'd seen in the CO's office.

"Must keep up with our dues, eh, Copping?" he said, laughing loudly again. Gabriel followed this with a deep, raucous chuckle, and I found myself joining in, I don't know why. Was it the wine, or the nicotine rush from Gabriel's cigarette, Doc Craib's tablets, or a combination of all three? Or was it our surroundings and the shock of normality? Before long we were all laughing. Gabriel then stood up, still chuckling, empty glass in hand, and was gone less than a minute before returning with another bottle, not wine this time, but some sort of clear spirit with Arabic on the label. He half-filled our glasses, topping them up with water from a glass jug which turned the liquid milky-grey.

We raised a toast to General de Gaulle. Following the others, I knocked it back in one. My throat burned as the aniseed spirit dropped into the pit of my stomach. We repeated this for Winston Churchill and Franklin D Roosevelt. I then managed to grab Frank's attention.

"What is this wonderful place?" I said, suddenly realising my neck ache and back pain had gone. "Who are these wonderful people?" He leaned forward and put his glass down. He then stood up, opened his arms wide and embraced the blue sky.

"Copping, old chap, this is our home from home, our little escape from this bloody awful war, this is two-sixty's pied-à-terre!" Everyone cheered.

I must have slept all afternoon because when I woke up I was starving hungry and I had no idea where I was. Clearly it wasn't Southend and definitely not the desert. I was staring at a high ceiling in a room on my own, on a wonderful soft-sprung mattress and sweet-smelling blankets. I dropped my legs to the floor from the high bed and moved over to the Juliette balcony. The wide sweeping bay of Alex's Eastern Harbour stretched out below me to the left and right, a calm, opal sea sparkling in the late afternoon sun. The war had gone. There were no sandbags anywhere or scrim tape over any of the windows. Below me a couple were strolling along the wide promenade, arm in arm as a white lorry passed them, and then a car, briefly obscuring them from view. I heard their laughter as it was carried up to my window and dropped into my room on a refreshingly cool sea breeze.

Looking for a toilet, I discovered a bathroom at the end of the corridor with fresh running water, both hot and cold, and so, without any prompting, I turned the bath taps on full and undressed. There were fresh brown tide marks around the bath and I could have the water as deep as I wanted, and so I did. I lay back, up to my neck, cradling an ashtray floating above my chest, the smoke from one of Gabriel's Gitanes filling the room like incense. Like all the windows, the one in the bathroom was wide open and I could hear voices from the busy street below: English, Arabic and French. Madame passed by the bathroom door, shouting loudly to her husband in French. I was in Paris now, or Marseille, long before the war when we took all of this for granted, this thing we were all now fighting and dying for, this thing we called peace.

My head was fuzzy from the earlier drinking, despite a few hours' sleep, but was soon kicked into clarity by the strength of the Gitanes. Frank bounded in, wearing his best uniform with razor-sharp creases in the trousers.

"We'll leave in twenty minutes, if that's alright with you?"

"Of course," I replied, surprised, stubbing out my cigarette in the ashtray on the floor as he disappeared, singing some Australian folk tune about taking Matilda to a waltz. I finished washing and stepped out the bath, wrapping a towel around my midriff. It seemed odd to be so modest again, but it was just in case Madame Pericand came wandering around the corridors. As the water drained away, half an inch of sand had to be washed down the plughole. It was good to smell like a human being again and not like an old goat soaked in petrol.

29

THE WALLS OF MY DUAL-ASPECT ROOM WERE NOW A deep orange from the early-evening sun setting low across the city. House sparrows were busy roosting in the gables above both windows and in the near distance the call to prayer from a tall minaret echoed around every building. The thin cotton curtains breathed rhythmically over the wide open louvre shutters drawing in the cooler evening air. An enormous wardrobe stood facing me. It was as wide as it was tall, and I wondered how on earth it was originally brought into the room. Perhaps the entire building was constructed around it. I pulled open the heavy dark wood doors that were covered in ornate engravings and inside was an assortment of RAF uniforms, cleaned and pressed, marked with their owner's names on brown paper labels like those on evacuee children. I saw the CO's name abbreviated incorrectly as 'Sq Lr Walker' and on a shirt underneath just one word: 'David'. I saw Polly

Parrott's and Wrigley's names, amongst others from the squadron. Madame had clearly been very busy.

There was a knock at my door and I heard her voice. I opened it and she was cradling my uniform, now also cleaned and pressed. How did she do that? I'd only given it to her a few hours before. It wasn't mine, of course, but that of a colleague of a similar size. She could tell; she had the eye, like a tailor. They know what size you are just by looking at you. She had an ever-increasing number of unclaimed uniforms; something that never occurred to me when I first looked into the wardrobe. I was grateful for it, and thanked her profusely, to which she just shrugged and walked away, waving her arms. It fitted perfectly. I wondered whose it was. It seemed any unused uniform was left for a while in the wardrobe as a matter of respect until the memory of the owner had subsided long enough for it to be reissued.

Frank and I strolled along the '26th July Avenue' around the harbour past the narrow streets of the Manshiya district, at the end of which a Royal Navy frigate lay at anchor in the Inner Harbour. Sailors were milling around everywhere, looking for a place of entertainment. I asked about Harry and Andy. "They have their own place to go. I'll tell you later," he said, shaking his head.

It was almost dark and there was supposed to be a blackout, but it wasn't as rigorously enforced as in England. Ever since the Hun had bombed the city earlier in the year it was assumed he would carry on, but he didn't, not yet anyway. Residential areas were hit, causing hundreds of casualties among the local population, which was a great tragedy but an obvious propaganda coup for us by revealing to the Egyptians the true nature of the Hun. They had previously tried dropping leaflets promising 'liberation' from British rule, which at first had been quite well received, but not after that. Maybe this is why he hadn't repeated it; perhaps he was considering the long-term consequences.

It had been months since it happened and no-one seemed concerned any more, apart from a few very keen MPs wandering around shouting at people to shut the door or put that light out and so on, but they were wasting their time.

I followed Frank into the Carlton Hotel where we stood at the bar smoking, waiting for our first drink of the evening. When I picked up my Rheingold beer, my fingers became so wet from the condensation on the glass I instinctively wiped them on my shorts while switching hands. It was the first cold beer I'd had in weeks and it was well worth waiting for. There were a lot of other service personnel around but not a lot was happening, so after the first one we left. A short while later, we walked into the Cecil Hotel and this was much livelier. A jazz band was playing at the far end of the bar; the three black musicians had the whole room transfixed. They were clearly not local because one of them revealed a very broad American accent when he spoke into the microphone. They were excellent musicians and had everyone tapping their feet, nodding their heads to the infectious rhythm, with some men and women dancing between tables.

We ordered more beer and ten minutes after our arrival, a man in his late twenties entered the stage between songs, carrying a saxophone, wearing a Desert Air Force uniform of khaki shorts and shirt. There were cheers and huge applause as he raised the instrument to his lips and began playing. He had a moustache and goatee beard covering his chin and appeared to be a Sikh or a local. He couldn't be one of ours because beards were officially banned. "Good old Imshi!" Frank shouted in my ear, clapping furiously. I clearly looked bemused, having never seen him before. "That's Imshi Mason, he's a pilot with one-one-two," he shouted, smiling. "He's bloody good on that thing, you'll see," he said. He was right. Just like the other band members, he was excellent, and for the next hour he played virtually non-stop.

Squadron Leader Ernest 'Imshi' Mason eventually descended the stage to someone thrusting a beer into his hand as he disappeared into a throng of back-slapping service personnel, both male and female. He made his way along the bar and Frank introduced us after shaking his hand and calling him 'Sir'. Mason smiled at me, saying, "Just call me Imshi," as he continued moving on, clearly enjoying the attention like a movie star. I wished I'd taken the time and trouble to learn an instrument if it meant this much acclaim, but even then I doubt I would have been anywhere near as good as him.

Frank finished his beer and suggested we move on, and so I agreed. We walked around the corner past several streets and down some well-lit steps, most of which were beautifully shiny, into a club that was clearly more upmarket than anything we'd seen so far. There were numerous small café tables that were all taken and an extensive bar in a room already choking with cigarette smoke. At the far end was a low stage where four musicians were struggling, barely audible above the chatter. These were all local: a man plucking a double-bass, his left hand running up and down the neck of the instrument like a drunken spider; a middle-aged piano player on a very glossy black upright piano; and a clarinet player, tapping his feet and pursing his lips ready for his next blast.

They were nowhere near as good as the musicians in the Cecil Hotel, but their energy certainly made up for it. We ordered two whiskies and stood at the bar, taking it all in. Frank mentioned there were a few pilots from Imshi's squadron that he recognised and when our drinks arrived, we were shocked at the price: twenty piastres each, about four shillings for a single shot.

There was a tap on my shoulder and I turned around to see Blenheim pilot Tim Murray with a woman on his arm; she was as tall as him, with long, jet-black hair and a wide smile made twice its size by the thickness of the scarlet lipstick and the constant pouting like a goldfish. She wasn't British, but she didn't look typically Egyptian either. The black dress that stuck to her body as though painted on showed her figure very well; she was painfully thin. I thought she was ill. "Copping!" he shouted, winking at me. "This is…" he hesitated, looking at her, and then back at me. He was swaying as though the wood floor was the deck of a ship in a rough sea. "Never mind," he said, throwing his right arm tightly around her tiny waist, drawing her closer before kissing her on her pale, veiny neck. She giggled and threw her head back in fake surprise. He smiled, pulling her uncomfortably by the arm. This was a different Tim Murray to the one I'd seen before. As they passed me, he paused and shouted in my ear, "Welcome to the flesh pots, Copping!" They both disappeared behind heavy velvet curtains at the end of the bar as she did her best to keep him upright.

Frank was gone, or at least not with me anymore. When I came back from the toilet, I saw him standing in a group near the stage and so I stood alone for what seemed hours and drank another beer, followed by a whiskey chaser. The war had comfortably faded away along with the desert, and I no longer cared about anything at all. I contemplated returning to the Cecil for a while to see if Imshi was still there but realised I may not find it in my increasingly drunken state. I edged along the bar, closer to the stage so I could hear the music a little better and began to enjoy myself again. The band seemed to be improving, and my right foot began tapping along, occasionally sticking to the beer-soaked floor. I stayed off the whiskey now and ordered another beer, at ten piastres, around two shillings; it was expensive, but a lot cheaper than whiskey, and it lasted longer. I thought about Tim and his lady friend. Maybe he knew her, or just knew how to appear as a willing participant. I suspected I didn't, and that was my problem. If indeed it was a problem, which it wasn't. I knew I'd soon reach my capacity for drink, which was where I wanted to be, but it was difficult to stop. Oblivion was beckoning and I was more than happy to fall in, feet first.

30

I WAS HALFWAY DOWN MY LATEST BEER OF HOW MANY I'd lost count when I was bumped quite heavily from behind. "Sorry," I barely heard her shout and almost didn't bother to turn around. She was very slim but definitely not thin; her curves were well-defined in her white dress, she was quite tall and didn't look like a local. Her thick, shoulder-length, mousy brown hair appeared lighter in parts, as though dyed or bleached by the sun; it was difficult to tell in the dim light. She ordered a gin and lime in perfect English and at first ignored me, even though she must have been aware I was looking at her. It was unavoidable; we were pressed together at the shoulders facing the bar. She was an off-duty WREN or a member of some other British forces, I thought, or the spouse of someone here, lost elsewhere in the crowd. I was about to resume my beer and turn back towards the band when she apologised again. This time she smiled, a wide, radiant smile to which I returned the same because it was polite to do so, and for no other reason, adding a cursory nod of the head. She threw her gin back in one and I instinctively offered to buy her another.

"Thank you," she said, "I will," as she began fiddling with the cocktail stick in her empty glass, releasing the slice of lime into the bottom with her left hand.

"My pleasure," I replied, looking over the bar. I signalled the barman and within seconds, before I could even tell him what I wanted, he brought her another. I paid, dropping the change into my pocket, and then picked up my beer. "Cheers," I said, clinking her glass with mine, and, "bottoms up." I was trying and failing to appear sober and not quite so English, but I could hardly stand up without leaning against the woodwork. She raised her glass and, without pausing, drained it completely. The waiter brought another, which I paid for again after they conversed briefly in Arabic. She picked up her glass and took hold of my left hand, drawing it closer to her.

"Do you want to go somewhere quiet?" she said, smiling again. I looked at my beer, and then back at her. I was fine where I was, but I didn't want to sound rude, so I replied,

"Maybe," leaving it suitably vague. I could see Frank was still engrossed in conversation with the other chaps and when I put my glass to my lips she tugged at my arm, almost spilling my beer. I pulled back my hand and she let go.

In the next moment I heard a man shouting loudly in Arabic very close to where I was standing. There were people milling around us and it took me a few seconds to realise she was the subject of it all from a swarthy, well-built man in his thirties who was now holding her right arm just above the elbow. He took her drink and slammed it onto the bar, spilling it and very nearly breaking the glass. She was clearly in some distress, trying to pull away, shaking her head. She shouted back in fluent Arabic, instantly destroying my WREN theory. He appeared to be about to strike her but when he saw me looking, he released his grip and stormed off towards the door, cursing. I saw him push his way through the crowded room and up the steps towards the street and out of sight.

She was immediately given another gin by the barman, without payment. "Are you alright?" I said to her, genuinely concerned, touching her right shoulder with my left palm, my beer now standing on the bar. She didn't answer immediately but turned her head towards me, smiling. It was the first time she'd looked deeply into my eyes for more than a few seconds and I felt a certain sweetness that was totally absorbing and which disarmed me in an instant.

"I'm fine," she said, obviously lying, her hand trembling terribly as she swallowed the entire contents of her fresh drink, before the remnants of the first. I wasn't too bothered about her hand being in mine before when I had pulled it away, but now I wanted it back. I wanted to take hold of it again but didn't feel as though I could.

"Thank you," she said with a deep sigh. Suddenly feeling a little more clear-headed, I decided I'd take her up on her initial request.

"I'll take you out of here if you like," I said, offering my hand. She took it without hesitation and we made our way through the club and up the steps into the street.

She looked around at the doorway, but there were only a group of sailors and some women laughing. The fresh night air was invigorating and was a welcome tonic to us both. We walked straight across the esplanade towards the sea and as we did so I realised I was still holding her hand. There were plain wooden benches every fifty yards, so we sat on the closest, facing the sea, with our backs on the city. She took her hand from mine to dab her eyes with a handkerchief. "Boyfriend?"

I said, to which she made no reply. "I have to say on first impression he doesn't seem a particularly nice chap," I said, staring out into the darkness, "and if I'm right then you are well rid of him."

"He's not," she said, blowing her nose. "I'm sorry, I shouldn't behave like this. I apologise."

"No need," I said, rolling a little on the bench before correcting myself, a reminder if I needed it that I was still drunk after all. "I'd be happy to walk you home if you like," I said, tentatively placing my left arm on her shoulder. She laughed. I had no idea why.

"I'm finished for tonight, sorry," she said, as she shook her head, rising to her feet. I stood up, wobbling. "But you look like you need some help," she said, smiling at last. I took her hand. I thought I was escorting her, but it was more like she was holding me up as I told her where I was staying; she found it without any problem because in just a few minutes we were there. By now we were arm in arm and I began to feel rather unwell. The door was unlocked and we opened it and entered, shutting it behind us with the utmost care but banging loudly when it slipped from my grasp. I have a vague memory of her helping me up the stairs, but after that, nothing.

When I woke up it was to the calling from a minaret – "*Allah-u-Akbar!*" – across the city. The sun had just risen and my head felt as though someone had lodged an axe into the top of it. I was desperately thirsty and very hungry. I could feel my clothes on my skin and discovered I was lying on top of the bed and not in it, fully clothed, though my boots were on the floor. To my total astonishment there was a woman lying next to me, but she was inside the bed, fast asleep.

I needed a pee urgently. When I returned, she was stirring, so I sat on the bed next to her. She opened her eyes and looked at me, smiling. "I need tea," she said sweetly, sitting up. "Do you have a cigarette?" I patted my shirt but there were none. I turned to reach my other uniform and found a fresh packet at the foot of the bed. When I looked back she was sitting up, naked and uncovered. I was astonished by this woman. I sat back down on the bed next to her and we lit up together. Noise was increasing outside with shouting, and the sound of vehicle engines, and an aeroplane roaring low overhead. She blew her cigarette smoke high into the room as though trying to reach the ceiling, then before any conversation she jumped out of bed, her cigarette still dangling from her mouth. She stepped across the room in three strides, naked, to retrieve a towel from a brown wicker chair in the corner and then went over to the door, taking hold of the handle. "I'm going for a bath. Do you want to come?" she asked, opening the door. Before waiting for an answer, she disappeared, whistling 'La Marseillaise'.

It doesn't often happen, but when it does it hits you completely by surprise. When someone like this comes into your life, it feels like they've always been there, and yet I didn't even know her name, and she didn't know mine, but it didn't seem to matter. She had the taps running before I reached the bathroom. When it was full, she climbed in, insisting I join her. Yesterday it never occurred to me that this old cast iron roll top bath was easily big enough for two and now I was sitting at the tap end with someone else.

She sank down under the deep water to wet her hair, her legs rising up to compensate, her ankles settling on the bath either side of me. There was no lock on the door and I wondered what on earth would happen if someone came in – Madame, perhaps, or even Frank. When her head re-surfaced, I decided it was time for introductions.

"My name is Copping, by the way," I said, almost as an aside, as though standing in a bus queue.

"Copping?" she said, throwing her hair off her face and pushing it back with both hands, raising both elbows and forcing her breasts towards me, probably unintentionally. "Is that all?"

31

"Sorry, it's Dennis, Dennis Copping," I replied.

"Is that your full name, Dennis Copping?"

"No. There's more," I said, as she rubbed soap onto the brown skin of her shoulders and then further down her front, beyond her breasts to where it was pale. "Do you want it all?"

"Yes, tell me," she said, teasing.

"Dennis Charles Hughmore Copping," I said, as she laughed so much I thought she was about to choke. She then raised her right arm in mock salute.

"Yes, Sir!" she shouted. I smiled as I watched her push her hair into a bun on top of her head mixing it with the lather from the soap. Then she slid under the water again, this time throwing her legs right up around my neck. She was pulling on my neck and it hurt, but I remained motionless. Perhaps I should have taken hold of those long legs and done something with them. I couldn't fail to notice everything that distinguished her as a woman was now just a few inches from my face. She sat up again and was rubbing her hair with both hands, loosening it, pulling it apart with her fingers. "That will do," she said, shaking her head.

"So what's yours?" I said, as she rose to her feet, water cascading from her body.

"My name is Ayesha," she said, stepping out the bath, picking up a towel from the floor. "Ayesha Marie, Egyptian and French," she said, proudly.

"It's a lovely name," I said, the bathwater now lower, revealing more of me as it settled, which didn't seem to concern her. I pulled the plug out, forgetting I hadn't washed myself. I'd been a little distracted, after all. She wrapped the towel around herself and picked up her clothes.

"See you in a minute," she said as she left the bathroom.

I followed after a shave at the sink and found her sitting on the bed, drawing my comb through her hair. She'd dressed in the same clothes, as I then did, forgetting as I stood momentarily naked that she was in the room. I felt incredibly refreshed after the best night's sleep in months, despite a fading headache, and just for a while it really did seem like the war had been a dreadful nightmare and I would soon be strolling back down Kents Hill Road to catch the number fifty bus to work. But then there was Ayesha, standing in front of me, and the bright sunshine and blue sky and unfamiliar noises from the street below. This was definitely not South Benfleet; it was too peaceful. This woman, this room, and this place were all perfect, though, and the price I had to pay for it was flying an aeroplane into combat. The war had brought both of them to me; there wouldn't have been one without the other.

I heard aero engines approach, so I opened the shutters wide to see twin-engined Wellington bombers, undercarriage down, preparing for landing, followed by Hurricanes weaving around behind them like hungry wasps. Suddenly a dreadful nausea engulfed me from deep in my stomach, rising up through my entire body like a tidal wave. It was the first time I had ever felt like this on seeing an aeroplane and I was shocked, standing there quivering, my knees about to give way. I took hold of the steel railing on the Juliette balcony and looked down at the street. Another pair of Hurricanes flew low overhead and my heart was now pounding in my chest. What the hell was wrong with me?

I shook myself and stood back from the window. Ayesha took my right hand firmly and lifted it to her lips, kissing it sweetly before giving it back. "Try not to worry," was all she said. It was the first time she'd kissed me. She had the same serious expression she had when the man was pulling her arm in the club. *Leave it*, I thought. *Forget it.* I had one more day here before I would return to it all, so just leave it. Whatever it was, I had no idea. *Don't let it spoil what you're doing.* I stepped back and sat down on the bed. I'd slept really well, but now I was exhausted again. I just wanted to lie down, curl up and sleep for a year.

A few minutes later it passed as quickly as it came, whatever it was. I lit a cigarette. Ayesha was at the balcony looking down. She waved at someone. "I have to go," she said as she moved over to the bed. She bent forward and, holding my head in both hands, she kissed my forehead, a long, lingering kiss. Then she crossed the room to the door and was gone.

I saw her leave the room and it was a few seconds until I protested, but it was too late. I opened the door to an empty corridor. The smell of eggs and bacon then wafted over me and I thought I must be dreaming. I ran down the stairs to the kitchen. Madame had indeed been cooking. "*Bonjour*," she said to me, pointing to the wicker table outside as she prepared coffee and bread. I stood in the doorway, lost for a moment until Frank appeared, and then Harry and Andy, who ushered me over to the table. They briefly chatted with Madame before Andy pulled up a chair close to me. He was wearing a red silk dressing gown and his cigarette was perched in the end of a long, black cigarette holder, obviously his weekend clothes. I wondered if he knew he looked like Noel Coward.

"Good night?" he said to me, smiling.

"Yes, thank you," I replied, without specifics.

"Did you get your rocks off, old man?" Harry shouted, smiling. "That's the main thing."

"That would be telling, wouldn't it?" I said, smiling, leading them on. "She had mousy brown hair, I know that much," I said, laughing. It was enough.

"I can vouch for that, I saw him leaving with her," Frank said, winking at me.

"Good man," Harry said, giving me a thumbs up.

"Where were you two, anyway?" I said, changing the subject, looking at Harry and Andy.

"They're officers, don't you know?" Frank interjected sarcastically in a dreadful fake upper-class English accent. "They are allowed into The Sporting Club, but we're not, it's for commissioned ranks only, I'm afraid." He saw the frown on my face. "I know, it's bloody unfair, isn't it? We fly the same aeroplanes on the same ops taking all the same damned risks, yet they get the better treatment. Not that it stopped me. I went in there for a swim once before I was ejected, and I can tell you it's worth getting a bloody commission for or bunking in just the once. They threatened to court martial me for that, the bastards, impersonating an officer. There's a nicer class of skirt in there, not like the dross we have to make do with, eh, Copping?" I nodded. We ate our wonderful breakfast, Madame brought us more coffee and we all lit up.

We sat for an hour drinking coffee, the real stuff with genuine cow's milk too, and then we dressed in our standard kit and left the hotel. We strolled along the full length of the '26 July Avenue' promenade, Harry with his camera taking a few shots of us draped across various statues and steps. We then walked through the El Gumruk district and into the Inner Harbour and eventually to a beach called Stanley Bay where we had a wonderful swim. We had no towels or change of clothes; we simply swam in our shorts. After we'd dried off in the sun, we passed the Cecil and Carlton Hotels and then the last club we'd visited. I was glad to see these places in sober daylight, so I could now find them again. I noticed the name written in an arch above the door, 'The Monseigneur'. The doors were shut and I was about to ask if it was open when Frank turned to face me. "It opens at about six o'clock," he said with a wry smile. I carried on, and it was then that Ayesha filled my head to the exclusion of everything else. I wondered where she was now.

We sat on a low wall eating ice cream like schoolboys, watching the Royal Navy frigate. It looked as though they might be preparing to leave; there was a lot of activity on deck. I wondered if they would try to get into Tobruk. If they did, our combined paths might cross again as we would probably be the ones to provide them with cover. I suddenly thought if they stayed put or disappeared down through the canal we wouldn't be needed. Then if Rommel said he was leaving North Africa and Hitler announced to the world that he was giving it all up, the war would end and we could all go home.

32

I SLEPT ALL AFTERNOON AND THEN I HAD ANOTHER wonderful bath, this time alone. By desert standards I wasn't in need of any kind of wash, so this was pure pleasure because I had no idea when I'd get another. Just before I was planning to get out, Frank came in and sat on the edge of the bath. He took a sip from a hip flask and then offered it to me. "Just refilled it, ready for this evening," he said, as I took it from him and tipped it into my mouth. I expected whiskey, but undiluted aniseed liquor burned all the way down my throat. I coughed and passed it back. He laughed and lit a cigarette before offering me one. I indicated my hands were wet, so he passed it over the bath, pushing it straight into my mouth. I could tell he'd already had a few sips from his flask because he missed my mouth on the first attempt. "Was she good last night?" he said, with a knowing smile as he lit me up, expecting a certain answer.

"Who?" I said, being evasive.

"Ayesha," he said, her name hitting me like a cannon shell, his smile broadening to a grin, and not a pleasant one but more of an evil knowingness that was testing and sarcastic. I don't remember introducing her to him. As far as I know I didn't, so how did he know her? I said nothing, and he laughed, taking another swig on his flask. He offered me a drink, which I declined. I took a last pull on the cigarette before I flicked it down into the water, staring ahead. It sizzled as it hit the surface and drifted in a gentle spin to the end of the bath. I still didn't say a word. He got the message and left, saying, "Be ready in ten minutes, will you?"

We walked in silence along the promenade, occasionally falling in step with one another in long, purposeful strides in the direction of the Cecil Hotel. Frank was already on the way to getting drunk again, and I couldn't find a reason why I shouldn't join him. It was Sunday night and we were returning to the war in the morning. We drank several beers in quick succession before moving to the Carlton and finally on to the Monseigneur, with all our drinks supplemented by chasers from his hip flask until it was drained. I'd be lying if I said I didn't look out for Ayesha because I did, but nothing seemed the same, even the crowds were different, and she was nowhere in sight.

After a while I gave up looking and contented myself with listening to Frank's life story, of growing up in Australia, watching aeroplanes since he was a boy with an ever-increasing desire to fly, all pretty similar to my own life. We were not that different, really, even if we grew up thousands of miles apart. We talked a lot about home, but the immediate future wasn't discussed. We both knew there were tough times ahead and an uncertain future, so why dwell on it? We drank more beer and whiskey and forgot about everything. I vaguely remember singing on the way back, arm in arm with Frank, but very little else. It was after that night that I realised I knew all the words to 'Waltzing Matilda' and I couldn't get the damned thing out of my head for days. An RAF lorry picked the four of us up at six o'clock in the morning from the end of the street. We said our goodbyes to Florence and Gabriel and climbed aboard. Harry and Andy looked with interest at The Sporting Club as we drove by as though straining to see someone, but it was all very quiet at that time of day, and there was nobody around. They leaned back on the bench and resigned themselves to being away from it again. We were returning to the war, and faces and attitudes visibly changed the closer we came to the airfield. The pain in my back and neck, which I'd completely forgotten about, had returned.

There was a Blenheim, with its pilot already there, tinkering around in the cockpit, but it was quite badly shot up and was undergoing a basic airworthiness check simply to be flown down to 53 RSU for repairs. There were some Beaufighters from 252 Squadron looking fierce and ready to go, but we were refused a trip in these too, even though two of us could have easily crammed into one of them. They were preparing for an op anyway, so I suppose it might have been the wrong kind of trip. Other aeroplanes were parked unattended but with no apparent crews. We were offered a lift in the back of a lorry full of very loud New Zealanders, but the thought of several hours sitting on a bench seat was easy to turn down. It wasn't looking very good and we'd been there nearly an hour when good old Tim Murray arrived in a jeep with his crew and offered us a lift back in one hop. His only fee was that we help him load some supplies and check his aeroplane. He'd been shot at by some Italians, so he said, as he took off from Mersa on Friday and was a little concerned.

The four of us took a look around before loading a few boxes of tinned food, bread, beer and cigarettes, most of which had stickers on them: 'Olympus Minerals'. The aeroplane seemed alright, if in need of a thorough clean, both inside and out. There were minor oil streaks under both wings from each engine, but this was normal. Tim emerged from the dispersal room all smiles and keen to go. I asked him about Saturday night and he stated he had no memory of it, or of even seeing me, which wasn't surprising. Ten minutes later we took off and turned straight out to sea, heading directly for Mersa rather than following the coastline. I was lying down between boxes in what I assumed was the bomb bay. I just hoped Tim didn't pull the bomb doors open.

This route shaved ten minutes off the flight time and we landed at LG08 less than thirty minutes later to make a collection. We were back in the air very soon and made the quick hop to LG115 without incident. We had returned from our weekend leave with an hour in hand.

After dinner I was summoned to see the CO. I wondered what I'd done wrong. It's just the way my mind works. Perhaps they'd caught up with me for something, and I began racking my brains for anything I might have done wrong.

I couldn't fail to notice a rather grand soft-top car parked next to the CO's lorry with the roof folded down, and decided I'd ask him about it if I could. As I stood in his office, Harry Curno and Ron Cundy, both sergeants like me, walked in up the ladder. They looked as mystified as I did.

"Relax, gentlemen, I have some good news," the CO smiled. He was fiddling with a canvas bag under his desk. "The blasted things are here somewhere," he said, most probably to himself. "I'm sure I have enough," he added, standing up. "Here we are!" He stepped towards the three of us and handed me two small brass crowns with split pins at the back, and the same to Curno and Cundy. "Congratulations, you are all promoted!" With that, he shook our hands in turn and said, "Right, now bugger off, I'm busy."

I found it strange we three had been promoted to Flight Sergeant at exactly the same time, as though it had been decided alphabetically, but I didn't ask. I didn't ask about the car either; I forgot. Cundy was delighted. It was another step nearer a commission, and access to The Sporting Club in Alex. He and Frank were the only Aussies in the squadron at that time and he had told him all about it. I was pleased, of course, but for me it didn't make much difference, other than a few bob extra every week. But what use was that, stuck out here in the desert? I'd sent money home to Aunt Margaret quite a few times, and I now had my regular contribution to the *Pension Crillon* in Alex at thirty shillings a night, but I had no idea when I'd ever see it again. I made sure most of my riches remained in the CO's safe from now on.

That night the CO entertained us on the piano again. I picked an opportune moment to ask about the car when he'd just finished his rendition of 'Here's to the next man to die'. This was not his most popular song, but he played it relentlessly. I wondered if the car was available for general use. The coast wasn't far away and when not on ops it wouldn't take long to get there and back in a day. "Do you like it?" he said, as he started playing another of his favourites: 'Salome'. I wondered for a moment whether he was talking about the car or his playing. "I may let you all use it, if you promise to bring it back in one piece," he said, laughing. His accent, along with the not-quite-perfect piano playing and dim light at the back of the tent, had turned the mess into a dusty East End pub in the blackout, and I felt guilty interrupting him. I kept the topic of the car going because I wanted to know what it was, so I asked him. "It's not a Humber or anything quite so boring," he said proudly, shouting above his playing. "It's an Italian staff car, and bloody marvellous it is too. It's a bit thirsty, but it reminds me of an old Rover I once had. They are leaving this stuff all over the desert; it's just a case of finding it and bringing it all back."

I never did find out where it came from, but I seriously wondered when we might be able to use it, and indeed when I'd be on ops again after seeing my name absent from the gaggle board that night. I didn't have long to wait. Just after breakfast the next morning, when eight had left on a pre-planned op I was one of four pilots scrambled to check out a sighting of 109s prowling around on our side of the lines and heading this way along the coast. I made sure I was wearing my Mae West this time.

33

The Hurricane I lowered myself into had a new smell about it, and Dave Morris confirmed my suspicions as it had arrived over the weekend, having been delivered by a pilot from 274 Squadron at LG010. It wasn't brand new; it's just that it was new to the desert and so it still had to acquire the layers of dust and sand all the others had. I taxied to the end of the runway and checked the Ts and Ps were exactly as they should be. It was a nice aeroplane.

Just before I applied full throttle, I had a brief but powerful sense of foreboding come over me like a dead weight. My mouth was so dry I had difficulty swallowing and my heart was thumping in my chest. Thankfully it only lasted a few seconds but was similar to the experience I had in Alex when looking up at the Hurricanes. I busied myself in the cockpit with pre-take-off checks, and in a few seconds it had gone.

I was wingman to Harry Bandinell, with Polly on his starboard side and Clark behind him. We took off and banked to port, heading for the coast, climbing to three thousand feet. Yes, it was nice to be back in the air in control of an aeroplane again, feeling the lift on my wings, the power and the speed. I thought I would never tire of this, but it somehow felt different. We climbed higher, to five thousand feet as we crossed the coastline in a gentle turn before levelling out, scanning all around us. Polly spotted them first; four 109s at the same height as us several miles out to sea, now heading in a westerly direction. There's no doubt they saw us as they suddenly dropped down a thousand feet and accelerated. They didn't change course to engage with us, however, but carried on towards their own lines. It was becoming increasingly pointless engaging in a one-to-one in dog fights just for the sake of it. It wasn't a case of scarpering through fear, it's just an operational decision, and it was the same for both sides. We didn't pursue them, but they'd clearly got the message that we were around, and so we may have prevented them attacking our landing grounds; who knows? This was what it was all about for much of the time.

There was sadly no opportunity to take this aeroplane up to ten thousand feet and have a play with it, as I would have liked to have done. Wandering off alone was asking for trouble. So I had to stay in formation and follow the leader. We made a few orbits just to make sure the 109s had gone before turning back for home. I followed the others inland and touched down with a gentle bump before taxiing over to dispersal. Dave jumped up onto the wing and seemed relieved it was still in the same condition. The first thing he noticed was the gun ports were still covered, meaning they hadn't been fired, meaning less work for them. This was the pattern of life for the next few weeks throughout September; occasionally racing up to five thousand feet a couple of times a day when I was down for ops, which was not every day. I was involved in quite a few simple ops like this, but no serious engagements. But then on September 14th there was a truly bizarre incident which would have been unbelievable had I not been there and seen it for myself.

The day began as normal with the majority of our Hurricanes departing on a pre-planned op. After breakfast the remaining two airworthy aeroplanes took off for LG100 and a major overhaul. Two Hurricanes were left, both of which were in pieces while being cannibalised for parts lying spread out around the LG, with most of the erks all over them like ants. I was one of four pilots not on ops and was chatting to Doc Craib at the latrines.

"How's the back these days?" he asked idly, flipping through a copy of *Picture Post*. You had to engage in conversation at the latrines because there was no hiding the job in hand.

"Fine, thanks, Doc," I replied, as he passed me the magazine, standing and leaning forward to finish the job with a few strips of newspaper. He suddenly sat back down when we both heard aero engines. Your ear becomes tuned to the familiar, and we both knew these were not Merlins. There was more than one, so it wasn't a Lysander; the slow approach didn't fit a Blenheim or even a Ju88, and 109s would be screaming overhead shooting everything in sight, so it wasn't them.

I couldn't see down the LG, but I heard an aeroplane on final approach, with what sounded like several others following. The first one had obviously touched down when the usual cloud of dust began billowing up against the blue as the pilot made adjustments to the throttle. The engine was now much louder as it began taxiing towards us at a leisurely pace and I still couldn't see what it was but Doc Craib, now standing again, obviously could.

"Jesus Christ!" he said, frantically pulling up his shorts, repeating, "Jesus Christ," and then, "Shit," before running at full pelt towards the armoury. I stood up, my shorts still around my ankles. I couldn't believe it. *Bloody hell*, I thought, pulling them up, fastening the top button while still running. I caught up with Doc Craib, who was now screaming at the poor corporal in the armoury. He in turn peered down the LG in obvious disbelief and repeated, "Shit," before disappearing into his tent. He re-emerged ten seconds later with an armful of Lee Enfield rifles and began fixing bayonets to the ends. Doc Craib ripped open a box of .303 rifle bullets and started filling magazines. His hands were shaking and he was chuntering something under his breath. I think he said, "We're being overrun."

"Copping, get to the mess," he said, becoming a little calmer, "raise everyone you can, and get them all back here quick, alright?" As I ran, I was aware I was bending forward slightly, ready to dodge flying bullets. I had an odd thought while doing this: *I'm a pilot, not a bloody soldier.*

The mess was empty. I found three startled cooks in the cookhouse tent and told them where to go. No-one was in our tent, but I found Stebbings and Clark in theirs and they ran back with me. I returned to our tent and fumbled around under my bed for the Webley. Where the hell was it? The first time I needed the damned thing and it wasn't where it should be. At last I felt the hard steel hexagon barrel and grabbed hold of it and filled it with bullets, clicking it shut before running back to the others. We then put on as many tin hats as we could find to make ourselves look more soldierly and prepared ourselves for battle. Gidman joined us having seen them already, and then one by one the erks working on the Hurricanes appeared too, running quickly between the tents as though on an exercise. Everyone was asking for a weapon and within a couple of minutes we had a small army at our disposal. One of the cooks ran into the closest AA pit and took hold of the twin Lewis guns, pulling back the slide on both. We were ready.

The first aeroplane taxied right up to us, less than fifty yards away, the pilot skilfully revving the engine and spinning it around very neatly to face the landing strip before shutting down the engine. A second lined up by its side and did the same, followed by another, and then another, until there were no less than eight Ju87 Stukas lined up in our dispersal.

"As soon as they get out and start walking this way, shoot them," Gidman said, raising a Lee Enfield to his shoulder and sliding the bolt forwards. The cooks and erks nodded and there was a thumbs up from the AA pit. I looked at Clark and Doc Craib through the thronging mass of shoulders and rifles and I could see they were as alarmed as I was.

"All of them?" Clark said, holding his rifle vertically. If he wasn't careful, the tip of the bayonet would soon be ripping a hole in the roof of the tent.

"Of course," Gidman replied, looking puzzled. "Before they kill us," he added matter-of-factly. "I don't want to get put in the bag, do you?" They still couldn't see us as we were hiding behind and inside various tents, with most of us still crammed into the armoury. The first two crewmen jumped down off the peculiar gull wing and began strolling towards us, chatting, obviously completely unaware.

"In cold blood?" I said, having quickly given it some thought, rifle at the ready, with my Webley hanging on my thigh like Errol Flynn in *Dodge City*. Gidman was looking down the sights and muttered something which he then repeated.

"It's not cold blood, it's war," he said, finger poised on the trigger.

34

"Wait," Doc Craib interjected with some urgency, now pointing a finger rather than a rifle at the Stukas. "Look, they're Italian," he said. He was right. There wasn't a swastika in sight.

"So what," Gidman said. "They are still the enemy, Doc," he said, his finger still on the trigger, just about to fire.

"It's hardly sporting, though, is it, old man?" Stebbings added. Even though Neil Stebbings was a sergeant he was good friends with Pilot Officer John Gidman. Gidman's face was flushed as he turned from looking down the sights of the Lee Enfield, glaring at Stebbings.

"Sporting? What the hell are you talking about?" he said, clearly incensed. "They're the bloody enemy, for Christ's sake!"

"He's right," I added tentatively. "Stebbs is right," I affirmed again. I could see the doc approved, but was he only thinking of all the work we'd create for him if we wounded them all? I thought Gidman would explode.

"You've tangled with the Ities," he said, looking at me. "It might even have been some of these," he said, in a muffled shout. "Did he fly alongside you, smiling, offering to take you to out dinner?" He had a point. I needed a good reply to this.

"That was a Macchi 200, not a Stuka," I said, not meaning to sound sarcastic. "I shot down an Italian Stuka." I'd won the argument, but I didn't feel any better for it, and I clearly hadn't changed his mind. He raised his rifle again, and this time I was sure this was it and waited for the bang.

"Yes, but think about it," Doc Craib said, not giving up. "Eight aeroplanes means there'll be sixteen of them at the most, and with all the erks there's more than fifty of us, look around you. We're not being overrun as I first thought, listen, there are no vehicles anywhere, they're not driving tanks at us, are they?" He was right; it might not be as bad as we first thought. "This must be a cock up on their part. We don't even know if they're armed, and let's not forget the intel we could get from them. Let's try and get them to surrender first," he said, looking at Gidman. There was a pause of no more than a few seconds, but it was enough.

"Right," Gidman said, suddenly more conciliatory and conceding a nod of acceptance, "but if they start shooting, then we'll have no choice, will we?"

"Okay, agreed," Doc Craib said, taking a deep breath. A few tense moments passed until all the crews could be seen walking towards us and then he said, "Follow me," stepping out of the armoury tent and into full view.

I have to say, we looked quite formidable in our tin hats and fixed bayonets, and as we began walking and spreading out, I was prepared to dive to the ground and start firing, as I think we all were. Perhaps they could see this. If they started shooting at us now it wouldn't be cold blood at all, and no different from shooting a man in an aeroplane.

To our utmost relief, and I have to say surprise, all sixteen crewmen raised their hands immediately. For a few very awkward moments we all stood facing one another wondering what to do until Gidman took a pistol from the front one and we did the same to the others. Some but not all were carrying rather nice Beretta semi-automatic pistols, one of which I slipped carefully into my pocket. A couple of them spoke to us in Italian, until the chap in front stepped forward and introduced himself with a salute and in near-perfect English said, "Regia Aeronautica, at your service, Sir," immediately defusing the tension. Oddly enough, they didn't seem the least surprised or disappointed to have been captured.

We moved them all into the mess and sat them down. The cooks made them tea and asked them if they were hungry. Bully beef and biscuits were then served. Our guests behaved like gentlemen and were no trouble at all. Just one erk remained with them while they ate, with his Lee Enfield lying on the table in front of him. To be honest they all seemed quite happy, smiling and laughing amongst themselves. I suddenly remembered I'd recently killed two of their colleagues in a burning aeroplane and it all seemed rather absurd.

We now had a bigger problem. Any Allied aircraft flying overhead would come to an obvious conclusion. Not only that, but our own squadron would see the Stukas when they returned and think the same. There were no Army Intel chaps on site, but our adjutant, Bob Simmonds, quickly used their transmitter to send an urgent message to all neighbouring LGs and to our own chaps before they returned. "Be aware we have some unexpected guests, but everything is under control here," he said.

There was a pause before the CO replied with the briefest acknowledgement: "Roger that, message understood."

Within half an hour, several Hurricanes from other squadrons arrived and parked near the Stukas, the curious pilots desperately interested in having a look. Who can blame them? It doesn't happen every day. None of us had ever seen one close up and intact so quite a few of us climbed up onto the wing of one of them and jumped inside. We knew these were safe and not booby-trapped in any way, so it was absolutely ideal. The flight controls were basically the same as any other aeroplane, but anything written down was obviously in German or Italian. Astonishingly, in the one we had a look in, there was a photograph of a woman and two young children fixed to the instrument panel. One of the erks retrieved it and took it to the mess to find a grateful owner.

When the squadron returned a short time later, thankfully all safely intact, I saw the CO take one of the Italians into his office, both men emerging after an hour smiling like two old mates stepping out of a pub. He later told us some 109s were supposed to have been providing them with top cover, but they had abandoned them long before reaching the target, leaving them disorientated.

The Italian never disclosed the identity of their target, but they ditched their bombs over the desert and thought Mersa Matruh was Bardia, so decided to land here. I know the CO didn't believe this story. Who knows what the truth was? We'll never know.

Luckily for us this incident seemed to be a typical reflection of the relationship between the Regia Aeronautica and the Luftwaffe. Just before dark, three trucks arrived and the MPs took all our guests away.

"What's going to happen to them now?" Stebbings asked the CO in the mess.

"Prison camp, maybe near Cairo," the CO replied.

"No, I mean the Stukas," Stebbings said, with some interest from the rest of us present.

"Why?" the CO said with a suspicious grin on his face.

"Just wondering, skipper," Stebbings said, as several of us were smiling. He knew what was coming.

"One of them will no doubt be taken for intel evaluation, and the others destroyed. You know that, Stebbs."

"We could evaluate one of them ourselves, skipper, for important intelligence purposes, you know, getting to know the enemy and so on. It would be vital for the war effort." The CO looked at him, took a deep breath, and shook his head.

"What an absolute load of old balls," he said, looking around at a gathering of his pilots, as though he really was the mother hen. Mother hens look after their offspring; provide them with sustenance, security, and also entertainment. He knew what we were all thinking. We must have looked like pleading schoolboys. Finally he gave in. "Right, I'll have a word with the intel chaps, so pick which one you want, okay?"

"You could take one up too, skipper," Stebbings said, smiling.

"I can't think of anything more stupid than flying around here in a bloody Stuka," the CO replied, shaking his head again. "You must all be bloody mad," he continued, now with just a hint of a wry smile. "What the hell are you going to do with it?" There was some nervous excitement building, I could feel it.

"It will be worthwhile, skipper," Harry said, "and we could use it to ferry pilots around too, save tying up one of our own aircraft."

"I suppose so," the CO replied, "but if you leave this LG in it make sure Army Intel knows all about it or they'll shoot you down. I want nothing to do with it, though; it's entirely your responsibility, Harry. I'll put you in charge; you are now our Stuka Liaison Officer, right?"

"Thank you, Sir," Harry replied with an enormous grin on his face as the CO spun around in the direction of his office. He stopped momentarily before looking back.

"It doesn't mean I don't want to know what the bloody thing is like, though, from a pilot's point of view, I mean, but if you prang it and kill yourselves, don't come running to me, okay?" he said, and with that he disappeared.

35

WE SELECTED THE FIRST ONE, THE FLIGHT LEADER'S aeroplane, and told the erks to look after it. First thing in the morning, another one was selected by some chaps who flew in via Lysander and back out with a Hurricane escort, heading east. The other six were taxied or towed to the bottom end of the LG and into the rough until they could go no further. They were stripped of anything of use such as fuel, guns, ammunition and some miscellaneous parts including engine oil before being doused with petrol and set alight. Our own Stuka now sat amongst a gaggle of Hurricanes looking particularly odd. We asked the erks for a favour and they began painting over the Regia Aeronautica markings, replacing them with RAF roundels. It was given the squadron letters HS on the fuselage and then a large question mark, because we didn't know what else to put! A huge wooden sign now leaned against it that read 'Under new management!'

Stebbings sat in the pilot's seat with Polly in the back as I took a look inside. There was a lot that looked familiar, but worryingly, a lot that didn't. We guessed at the throttle, flaps, trim and most of the switches. We'd only find out if we were right when we tried them. I jumped down and stood back a safe distance. Eventually they started it up, but it took them almost twenty minutes. I saw the controls waggling around and the flaps going up and down a few times, obviously testing everything. At least they wouldn't have to search for an undercarriage lever. They taxied carefully to the end of the runway and applied full throttle. It certainly was a curious sight as they flew around in a single circuit before landing again. It was war booty, and it turned out to be very popular, but we had no idea that quite soon we'd be adding some other enemy aeroplanes to our collection.

We were all aware something was building and we were flying a lot of ops just to make the Hun think there were more of us than there really was, and this tactic seemed to increase after the first week in October. We weren't always tangling with them; we just kept letting them know we were there, keeping them distracted, and keeping them busy. But our numbers were actually increasing too, and because of this I was hoping for more leave and another trip to Alex, but it didn't happen.

When I wasn't called on for ops I played cards and wrote more letters home. I had an increasing desire to write to Ayesha, but of course I had no idea of her address or even if she'd be bothered. I dismissed this as being rather stupid and forgot about it. The chances of seeing her again were remote anyway. I washed some of my kit on organised wash days at the laundry near the mess tent. The laundry, or 'dhobi' as we called it, was a couple of small barrels, one containing a few inches of hot water and soap flakes, the other with an inch of plain water for rinsing. We didn't have much to wash, and so it didn't take long, and most of the time it dried very quickly in the sun and warm breeze.

During October we received some new pilots: Joe Bernier, also known as 'Stan', a very quiet French Canadian originally from 94 Squadron; John Colley, an immediately likable Englishman; another Canadian, Dick Dunbar; and Tom Hindle, a Flight Lieutenant. We now had more pilots than aeroplanes again.

On my next op, I took off as Harry's wingman, with Saunders on his starboard side and Wareham as fourth man, heading south-west. We were to see how far over the wire we could get before we were challenged by the Hun, in order to test how active they were and to keep them busy. I was surprised at how deep we were before we ran into a large group of 109s about ten miles south of Gambut and we had to scarper quickly. We dropped down to low level turning south, still behind their lines and passing over quite a bit of their armour and MTs, motor transports, but they were stationary in the middle of nowhere around Sidi Rezegh, which seemed a bit odd. It looked as though they were dug in, trying to hide, and I admit they were difficult to see at first. One pass was all we could risk as it looked like they had quite a lot of heavy anti-aircraft stuff with them, but what we saw was useful information. They say never fly low over the same place twice; the first time you catch them by surprise, the second time they are ready for you. When we landed, we passed all this information to a lanky South African captain called Jan Vanderkamp who was now our permanent Army Intel Officer.

We provided escort a few times for 45 Squadron Blenheims from Fuka and 55 Squadron at Zimla, attacking the Hun at his airfields near Tmimi, Gazala and Bardia around Tobruk. The hornet's nest for us was Gambut, where most of their fighters were based at that time and we did our best to avoid it if we could, unless helping to bomb it, of course. Our visits had become so regular that the Hun now had to maintain a permanent standing air patrol during daylight hours, which was a pain to us but more so for him because it meant he had to burn precious fuel unnecessarily along with pilot's time and energy. We were now supposedly enjoying near-equal numbers in the air after always being the underdog and more Hurricanes were arriving all the time. Pretty soon we'd have parity for the first time and the Hun would become even more reluctant to engage us directly. Vanderkamp and the CO were regularly seen having long conflabs in the CO's office with other army types arriving and joining them. Whatever had been building was now imminent.

In the third week of October, my logbook states I had one hour as 'air experience flying' in a Stuka. I sat in the rear gunner's seat as Stebbings took me up for a spin. I positioned myself to watch him flying it and I could do so easily because the cockpit was remarkably open and roomy inside. We flew circuits and bumps, and I have to say, I wasn't impressed at first, mainly because I was sitting sideways in my seat and felt every bump. There was a lot of noise for not much performance, even though the ASI showed it could reach an astonishing 600 kph in a dive, which we estimated was about 350 mph. I still wanted to fly it myself, though, as did many others, so we put our names down on a rota and waited our turn. Saunders and Polly were designated Stuka instructors and loved it, as did Harry and a few others, but I had yet to experience the controls so I couldn't pass judgement.

I checked the gaggle board for my name and position as usual every night and most days I was flying, but didn't always see the enemy, let alone make contact. On one particular op later in October when providing top cover for Blenheims I had a nasty scrape with two 109s that seemed to be working in unison to kill me. It all started when I thought I saw the first 109 take a pot shot at a man in a parachute. I'd heard the Hun was capable of this and seeing it for myself incensed me. There's something different in shooting a fellow pilot when he's hanging there defenceless, even if he was the enemy, and for me it crossed a line. He must have seen the pilot bail out because it was usually impossible to tell who was who in these circumstances. I didn't even know if he hit the poor unfortunate chap, but I decided I'd get that bastard if it was the last thing I did.

I was at three thousand feet and opened the throttle wide in pursuit. I caught up with him in a dive much too quickly and almost flew right past him; consequently he managed to swing around towards me, which was my mistake. I then noticed a second 109 on my tail. The only thing I could do was roll over between them, pulling back on the stick hard at the same time, conscious of the fact I only had a thousand feet left. I managed to keep one of them off me for a moment but the other was already firing at me; I could see the cannon flashes from his spinner. I heard a few bangs from my aeroplane somewhere out of view and suspected the worst. I was supposed to be providing cover for the Blenheims with everyone else and I'd allowed myself to be distracted like this and I immediately regretted it. One of the golden rules was never to go off anywhere on your own like this.

I pushed the Hurricane into a dive and at two hundred feet and close to 400 mph they were still with me so I pulled into a sixty-degree turn east still at full throttle, which would have torn the wings off any other aeroplane. I levelled out a few seconds later to see them still behind me and both firing. It was as though they were tied to the tail of my aeroplane with rope. I heard another couple of bangs and I could have sworn I heard cannon shells whizz past my cockpit; for the first time in an aeroplane I was terrified. I think some of this was because I'd been an idiot allowing myself to be taken over by emotion and not sticking to what I should have been doing. Even at that moment when it looked like I might have been clobbered at any moment, I had an odd thought that the CO was sure to give me a bollocking when he found out.

36

THIS WAS THE LEAST OF MY WORRIES BECAUSE MY windscreen suddenly became obscured by what looked like oil and was probably glycol. The engine must have been hit so I checked the Ts and Ps and was relieved to see everything appeared okay. I levelled out and took a moment to have a quick look around. To my astonishment the 109s were still in my mirror, and I was now quite close to the sea, so I dropped even lower, following the coast and hoping for the best.

I dragged the canopy open and stuck my head outside to see where I was going. My goggles fogged up with glycol almost immediately, so I tore them off my head. I weaved a little to check the controls and the altimeter confirmed I was just a hundred feet above the desert. If I so much as sneezed I'd go in. I saw flashes from behind and at any moment I expected another hit that would surely be the end of me. Thinking I had nothing to lose, I dropped even lower to just two notches on the altimeter, forty feet, and hung on. I don't know how long I sat like this, probably five minutes, but it felt like an hour. Eventually I passed Mersa Matruh on my starboard side and turned inland. Looking back, I was incredibly relieved to see the 109s had broken off their attack and were heading west. But then I felt a wave of panic as I realised I was trailing smoke.

I throttled back and pulled the nose up a little to two hundred feet, and it was then that the engine began rough-running terribly, sounding more like an old tractor than a V12 Merlin. I had to make a decision immediately whether to try and gain some height and bail out or to put the aeroplane down as quickly as possible before flames and smoke filled the cockpit.

Seconds later I found LG115 and so I decided I'd stay with it, just as I noticed the Ts and Ps were dropping through the floor. There was something seriously wrong with the engine; it didn't just sound awful. It was now clear that my trusty Merlin would either seize up or explode at any moment. I didn't expect the undercarriage to come down, but thankfully it did. I flew over the end of the LG, touching down with a bump and taxied at running speed to the first safe area I could find where I quickly shut down the engine and unstrapped. An awful smell of burning was now drifting up around my feet and several erks ran up with fire extinguishers, shouting at me and one another. When I jumped off the wing, I saw long streaks of oil from holes in the engine cowling and bullet holes everywhere, including a neat line of them in the fuselage that stopped just behind the cockpit.

Wednesday 12th November ended with a little less drinking in the mess than usual because on Thursday 13th, after being forewarned, we were all woken up in the middle of the night by the deep rumbling of heavy vehicles and lots of shouting as a dozen huge lorries arrived. We gathered our things together in readiness, and despite the warning the upheaval was still unwelcome. Most of the Aussie erks had already gone and now our own were climbing aboard to leave under cover of darkness, heading west. Tents were dismantled and packed aboard, departing like a secret nocturnal travelling circus and even though it was planned, it all felt rather sudden. Perhaps it was because we were leaving our own little patch of tame desert we'd called home for so long.

There was an air of tentative excitement as I packed my belongings to move house for the first time. A few hours later by mid-morning, we took off, heading the same way. Every pilot now had his own aeroplane and we were told we could use the same one every op if we wished. I still had the same erks looking after me, and so I stuck with them and the same machine. It was with huge regret that we had to leave our Stuka behind, and worse still, because it could fall back into enemy hands, we had to set it alight. I never thought I'd be sorry to see one burn so well.

The CO was leading and we followed the coast to Sidi Barrani where we turned inland for about ten miles until we began circling a patch of desert that had no distinguishing features at all. I wondered what the CO was doing until I saw movement below and a closer look revealed vehicles and the beginnings of an airstrip. We followed him in and landed at what became LG109, only thirty miles from the front line. Dozens of sappers were busy clearing more space with mine detectors and shovels in some very tough ground.

There really was nothing at LG109. We put up our tents and dug a few slit trenches, but the CO told us not to do too much, which we took to mean we probably weren't staying.

We were right. Only four days later on the 17th and before I'd flown another op, we were ordered to pack up again. This time we were apparently heading south. I'd heard of Fort Maddalena, and knew it was somewhere south of us, but that was all. When I checked on a map, I wondered why on earth we were going there, seeing as it was at least fifty miles south-west of Sidi Barrani. The Hun was west not south. There must be a logical reason for it, but obviously we weren't told. A contingent of sappers had apparently been there for a week already, preparing the ground as usual, and now they were ready for us and our aeroplanes. The lorries were loaded with the tents and all our food and equipment again, and by three o'clock that afternoon we were ready to leave. A couple of aeroplanes had become unserviceable due to the usual problems with sand and so they were disassembled and loaded onto the lorries. We left some old tents up, and several unserviceable vehicles dotted around because we weren't sure whether we'd be back, but mainly because it would confuse the hell out of enemy reconnaissance pilots.

In late afternoon we took off and left en masse for LG124, five miles west of Fort Maddalena, following the CO. As we left we could see a huge build-up of our armour, both near the coast and further inland. We were told that once it was dark, the rest of 260 Squadron would follow in the lorries.

Lamps lined the runway at LG124 as the last Hurricane touched down just after dark. As soon as we were all safely down, the lamps were extinguished and light was restricted again, though not entirely. We were a reasonable distance from the Hun and it was believed they didn't know we were there, at least not in such numbers. Sappers had pitched some tents for us, but there was no mess tent or even a formal latrine yet. For that first night at LG124, such matters were catered for by a man alone with his spade under cover of darkness, provided it was remembered where the deposit was made.

We spent an uncomfortable night initially crammed ten to a tent on nothing more than folded blankets and at around nine o'clock, the lorries arrived amid scenes of organised chaos. In the morning there was more of the same as we were enrolled in some digging around the tents, and most importantly, a proper latrine tent was constructed. We couldn't really complain as we needed to use these facilities, but it was still hard work. This latrine was designed so the entrance was facing away from everything else and into the prevailing wind, for obvious reasons.

We then settled back into our own tent and the six of us made it look exactly the same as it always had been, with each man occupying his usual space: Wrigley, Morley, Wareham, Carlisle, Saunders and myself. We weren't superstitious; we just wanted it to stay the same, just in case.

The CO was keen to get up and have a look around the area, and I was flattered when he asked me to come along, with just Frank Tregear as one other wingman. I had the same aeroplane I arrived in and found it a joy to fly. You do get to know a particular aeroplane and there are advantages in using the same one because even identical types can be different to fly. One aeroplane becomes familiar, like the family car, with certain catches and levers, either stiff or loose in a particular way, which then provides a kind of reassurance to the pilot. It might sound odd but getting to know the same aeroplane makes it feel comfortable, like an old friend.

The CO took us up to ten thousand feet, circling above LG124 in a fifteen-degree climbing turn. It was a fabulous day and visibility was superb. The coast was still visible in the north and in the east I saw clouds of dust from masses of vehicle movements. If we could see this, then so could the Hun and

I wondered if this was what the CO was doing, and why we were up there. We dropped back down and followed the CO into LG122, the new temporary home of 112 Squadron, ten miles east of LG124. We shut down our engines and strolled into their mess tent for some tea.

37

THE 'SHARK SQUADRON' ALREADY HAD THE P40 Tomahawk and their aeroplanes certainly looked impressive with their angry shark teeth under the nose. It was rumoured we would be getting the P40 soon, and it certainly seemed a fearsome aeroplane.

My suspicions about the intel were confirmed when I saw the CO leaning over a table in the mess with Imshi Mason, their skipper, and some army types with their maps. I didn't realise at the time, but Fort Maddalena was on the border with Libya, not that anyone could tell, and even though LG122 was in Egypt, both LG123 and 124 were the other side of the border. After three cups of tea courtesy of 112 Squadron we took off and returned to LG124, this time at low level, skimming the desert at a hundred feet, chasing one another's tails just for fun, arriving back before the engines had properly warmed up.

Tuesday 18th November 1941 began differently to any other day I'd so far experienced in the desert. Firstly it started raining in the night so heavily I thought we'd be completely flooded out, as water poured into our tents and everywhere else, turning the sand into treacle, and it didn't stop. But the main thing about this date was that it was the start of everything we had been building towards for at least the last three months.

The CO called us into the mess for a briefing. I thought it was the middle of the night, but it was just after five o'clock and before the sun appeared. We dressed quickly without shaving and all stood crammed into the tent. There wasn't room for everyone to sit, so we were told to stand where we could. There was an air of tense excitement as we could hear a huge number of heavy vehicles rumbling past heading north-west. We sat around drinking tea and smoking until the CO arrived. He stood at the gaggle board with Vanderkamp. Behind them the piano had migrated with us and now occupied its usual position at the back of the mess, hiding under a mass of blankets.

"Gentlemen, the Hun has been taking the bloody piss for too long," the CO began, as early dawn finally began to brighten the tent. "We are going to help relieve the garrison at Tobruk." There were gasps and some ripples of applause above the sound of rain on the canvas roof. "They've lasted since April and now we are going to kick Jerry's arse right back to Tripoli. Operation Crusader begins now, and we have a very important part to play in it. We will be undertaking the usual bomber escort and so on, but we also want some of Jerry's airfields if we can get hold of them while still usable. It would speed things up a lot if we can do this. In the meantime, usual rules apply; we must make life as difficult as possible for the Hun and his Italian friends so that they quickly form the idea that they want to clear off out of Libya altogether. So we start now. This morning I will lead one flight; the other flight commanders will be Harry, Sparky, Gidman and Wylie. You four stay behind with me, the rest of you get some grub and be ready for 0700 hours." It was the end of a four-month stalemate where the wire at the front line had stayed virtually static. I had breakfast of hot bully beef, potatoes and peas followed by fruit, two mugs of sweet tea and several cigarettes. I was hungry, but my appetite wasn't as great as usual. There were a lot of animated discussions while shaving and preparing for the op. General consensus was that we were all glad something was finally happening. We hoped it might end the desert war altogether and we'd be back in Blighty for Christmas. If only we knew.

After breakfast I sat next to Colley at the latrines, on dawn patrol over the thunder box, as it was now known, with one hand occasionally pulling the tarpaulin over my head to keep the rain off. This was always the daily ritual after breakfast and there was often a queue. Vanderkamp, the Army Liaison Officer, was on my left with his shorts around his ankles, engrossed in a tattered copy of *Life* magazine appearing relaxed as though sitting in his own living room. I'd not spoken much to Colley yet and it was certainly an unconventional way to have a first proper conversation with someone, both naked from the waist down, only two feet apart and with nothing between us but the sounds and smells we both produced.

"What did you do before the war, Copping?" he asked.

"I worked at Cable & Wireless," I said, my reply probably as unenthusiastic as my memories of the place.

"Quite handy, then," he said, "knowing about things like that?"

"I suppose so," I replied. "They seemed to like it when I joined up," I said, looking straight out into the desert. I could hear that he was busy, as I was, so I didn't like to look directly at what he was doing, it didn't seem right. "What about you?" I asked.

"I had a really boring clerical job before the war," Colley said as he finished and stood up. "It was in a solicitor's office and every day I felt like I was drowning in paper." I could see in my peripheral vision that he had ripped a piece of newspaper into a strip, folded it over once and then wiped his backside with it. "So I do hope this is the *only* bloody paperwork I have to do here!" he shouted, pulling up his shorts. I laughed and immediately wondered what the grunting noise was at the other side of me until I realised it was Vanderkamp laughing. He'd dropped his magazine and almost fell off his throne he was laughing so much. It wasn't particularly funny, but some circumstances make the oddest things hilarious, and if you're going to lose your dignity you may as well laugh about it. You have to, there's no other option. You can immediately warm to someone who has a gift of humour at times of tension, and Colley was one of these people.

I was chosen to fly with Harry, Saunders and Carlisle. I joined the queue to surrender my wallet at the CO's safe, keeping my Goolie Chit, fags and a bit of Egyptian cash in my breast pocket just in case. Despite the distance from the sea, I still put on my Mae West. Our first job in Operation Crusader was ground attack, something I'd not done before, shooting at vehicles, and I imagined in my naivety it would be no different to shooting at aeroplanes.

I spent five more minutes on the latrine and after putting on all my kit I needed a pre-flight pee, so I doused the tailwheel of my Hurricane, as others were doing. Not a lot came out, but the urge was irresistible. We took off at seven-thirty, heading north-west. The rain had eased but it was a first for me, climbing up into a leaden grey sky above the desert to a low cloud base of about fifteen hundred feet. It wouldn't matter today anyway.

What we'd seen a few days before were concentrations of Hun armour and troops around Gabr Saleh, west of Sidi Omar, and instead of engaging these, our troops had bypassed them along the coast and in the south around Fort Maddalena. We were to provide cover for these forces and it wasn't long before we found plenty of the enemy, an armoured division with a large number of MTs south of Sidi Rezegh. The place was as busy as Piccadilly Circus on a Saturday afternoon and it wouldn't be difficult to find our targets.

We dropped down to a hundred feet from just below cloud base, converting our height into speed. We flew side by side as a column of vehicles split up when they saw us approaching and I filled my sights with MTs and tanks, and fired several long bursts when I was as close as I dared.

As I flashed overhead, I saw black dots on legs dispersing in all directions. I turned around for another run just as I saw some 109s in the distance coming down towards us. I passed back over the MTs for a second and final run and fired again. I was close now, slower, with more time to see what I was shooting at as hundreds of bullets from my eight .303 machine guns ripped into the earth. The anonymous black dots became dozens of terrified men running from their vehicles. A lorry would explode if the petrol tank was hit, hurling debris high into the air and several were doing just this all around me. It was a truly terrifying situation and nothing like air-to-air combat. We were hurtling over the ground at fifty feet and so there would be no chance of bailing out if we were hit. As I pulled up and small arms fire began pinging on my airframe I realised what I'd just been doing; I'd shot down running men, fleeing in desperation, most of them not even carrying weapons of any sort, shot in the back as they ran away. They had nowhere to hide and so we smashed them up, clobbered them, slaughtering every single one of them, killing everything that moved.

My hands were shaking wildly. I couldn't control them, so I grabbed hold of the stick as firmly as I could. I pulled the aeroplane around and I could see 109s already engaging some of the others. I broke away and shoved the throttle wide open. I just kept the nose up and my hand tight on the throttle, flying almost vertically towards the blue. This was a stupid thing to do because I knew a 109 has a superior rate of climb to a Hurricane; in fact we knew it was superior to the Hurricane in most things, but I wasn't thinking, my mind was suddenly elsewhere.

38

I WAS GETTING CLOSE TO A STALL, SO I FINALLY CAME out of it at seven thousand feet, and to my surprise I wasn't being pursued. In fact, I was totally alone and far away from the op I was supposed to be involved in, staring at the sea in the distance and then at the carnage far below.

The whole area around Sidi Rezegh was now dotted with a multitude of burning MTs, the choking black smoke rising hundreds of feet up. I heard the CO ask if I was okay and where I was. I think I told him I'd just pulled away from some 109s and would be back straightaway. He then told everyone to head back to LG124, mission accomplished.

We all landed back safely and when I shut down the engine I sat in the cockpit, drowning in sweat. My eyes were stinging with salt, I suddenly felt desperately claustrophobic and I thought I was going to pass out. I unbuckled and climbed onto the wing and then jumped onto the hard ground of the LG, collapsing momentarily onto all fours before hauling myself back up. I tried lighting a cigarette, but the match burned out before I could use it. Ernie rescued me again, lighting the end, smiling, without saying a word. I wandered over to the mess in a trance and sat down. Someone gave me a mug of whiskey disguised as tea and less than an hour later, after re-arming and refuelling, we were scrambled again.

I was in the same formation when we attacked more MT and armour, this time near Gabr Saleh, which our ground forces had bypassed. We approached at ground level again and where I could I concentrated on hitting the vehicles after their occupants had abandoned them, but this was just about impossible. At least two vehicles I hit exploded ahead of me, sending flames and debris high into the air which I only just avoided. Small arms fire began streaking up towards us and so on our second approach we came in from a different angle and I just kept on firing until my guns went silent. By this time the Hun was sending up 20 mm from Breda's and a couple of Bofors with the familiar pom-pom shells exploding all around us, so it was time to leave.

I didn't know it at the time, but we were protecting one of our fuel dumps south-west of Gabr Saleh that our MT was relying on. It seemed whoever had the most fuel in the desert had the advantage. This was close support of our ground forces and it was working very well.

We landed back at LG124 and as I jumped down, Dave and Ernie pointed out an enormous blackened rip in the fabric under the elevators in the tail of my aeroplane. I didn't notice any difference in handling, and it must have happened as I flew over the exploding MT. The pinging noises I heard were a few glancing hits from small arms that hadn't caused any significant damage. These were bullet hits on my aeroplane that had now become insignificant enough to ignore.

We were told there might not be any more ops that day and so we took advantage of this to eat and rest. I collapsed onto my bed and passed out. The tailplane was repaired immediately, and my aeroplane rearmed and refuelled. Just before three o'clock we were scrambled again. This time I was with Viesey, Morley and Gidman, as Gidman's starboard wingman, for bomber escort. The worst of the weather had now gone, so we climbed up to five thousand feet and headed due north towards the coast. We joined six Blenheims and eight Tomahawks from 112 Squadron as the Blenheims pounded the Hun west of Gabr Saleh. There was no low-level flying this time; the bombs were dropped quickly from two thousand feet across a line of MT about half a mile long before the Blenheims turned and headed back east. Three 109s came up for a look but when they saw us they turned and ran. We landed without firing a shot. I was very glad our services were not called upon again for the remainder of the day.

That night I was utterly exhausted despite sleeping for most of the day and I slept from just after dark until I woke up some time in the night and couldn't get back to sleep. The luminous face on my watch said four o'clock. Most of the others were asleep, but I could just about see the dark mass that should have been Saunders was missing. I stepped outside into a clear night with not a breath of wind and an unusual chill. All clouds had disappeared and it was the first time I'd known such cold in the desert. I wandered around for no reason and with no purpose, only vaguely wondering where Saunders was, inevitably drifting towards the aeroplanes.

I saw two legs in silhouette that I first thought were those of a fitter's jack propping up the port wing of a Hurricane. It wasn't a jack, but a figure draped across the leading edge, arms outstretched and head resting on it, mumbling something incomprehensible. Two erks on sentry duty were standing together nearby with fixed bayonets, smoking. They ignored me and continued talking. Saunders was barely awake, mumbling, occasionally stroking the aeroplane with the flat palm of his right hand. I took hold of him by the shoulder and he revived immediately. There was a clunk from his left hand somewhere over the wing, which at first for some reason I thought might be a gun. He looked at me and in the starlight darkness I'm not sure he knew who I was. "Want a quick wet?" he said, shoving a bottle in my face. It was whiskey, and there wasn't much left. *Why not?* I thought, raising it to my lips, taking a long gulp. It burned down my throat, crashing in flames into an empty stomach, but it was very welcome. I took out my Chesterfields and lit two, handing him one.

We leaned on the wing together, drinking and smoking like two old pals in a pub. I wished we were. A shooting star streaked across the full length of the sky from right to left quite low down as though the Hun had launched it at us as a new secret weapon. If it was, he missed.

"There was a hell of a lot of twitch yesterday, wasn't there, Copping?" he said before drawing on his cigarette. A few seconds later he let out a long sigh and was shrouded in cigarette smoke.

"Twitch?" I said, questioning; though I'd heard the expression many times before, it was never discussed at length, at least not by anyone who wasn't drunk.

"Sidi Rezegh. The bloody twitch was bad, you were there." He was staring at me now. "I don't mind admitting it, bloody strafing. I hate it, don't you?"

"Yes, it was bad," I said, understanding exactly what he meant. "There was a lot of twitch," I replied in confirmation. Twitching of the ring occurred in particularly high-stress situations, and Sidi Rezegh was certainly one of them. We didn't discuss fear; the word was never spoken. No-one mentioned the sheer terror of low flying into flak and ground fire. But there was 'twitch'.

"Wouldn't mind a spot of leave, would you, Copping?" he said, changing the subject and turning to face the dark emptiness of the desert. I think he smiled, but I wasn't sure.

"It would be nice," I replied, handing the bottle back.

"Yes, about a month should do it," he said, "Alex first, and then a week or so down in Cairo in a nice room overlooking the Nile. Or even further afield, Lebanon, maybe, or Palestine. They say the climate's much better there, and there's skiing up in the hills at this time of year." He took a long gulp, almost finishing it off. "Ever done any?" he said, turning to me.

"Skiing? No, can't say that I have, never had the opportunity."

"Then we'll go, next time we get some decent leave." He reached forward and slapped me on the back. "We can fly to Ramleh or Lydda in Palestine and get a taxi the rest of the way. I know someone who's done it, they had a fantastic time." He finished the bottle and took a long last pull on his cigarette before dropping it into the sand and twisting the toe of his boot over it. I wondered if this suggestion would be remembered in the morning; I doubted it somehow. I knew it would never happen. He put an arm around my shoulders and pulled me away from the aeroplane. He wasn't drunk, but he certainly wasn't sober. "We'll sort the buggers out first, though, eh?" he said, slurring a little, dropping some of his weight on my shoulders as we walked. We found our tent quickly and I helped him inside. He collapsed on his bed, almost destroying it. I lay back on mine, the whiskey now swirling around giving a wonderful sense of well-being, as the first drink usually does. I closed my eyes and passed out.

39

WE WERE ALL UP AT SEVEN IN THE MORNING TO A clear sky, queuing at the thunder box as usual. A two-month-old copy of the London *Times* newspaper was being read and reread as it was torn into strips for the essential paperwork. Colley was reading out some of the classified ads: "Gentile Home Counties widow, fifty-five, requires live-in gentleman for driving, gardening, and any other *miscellaneous duties* as requested, rates of pay on application." There was a roar of laughter.

"There's one for you, Harry," Gidman shouted while bent forward, busy with his paperwork.

"Give me her number and I'll look her up when I get back to Blighty," Harry said to more laughter.

"Fifty-five?" Colley said mockingly.

"What's wrong with that?" Gidman replied. "Just hold your nose and jump in, I'm sure she'd be very grateful," he said, to shrieks of derision as he was bombarded with rolled-up newspaper, one piece of which contained the widow's advert.

Polly appeared at the corner, all his hair standing vertical on his head as though he'd just stuck his fingers in a plug socket. "Morning prayers with the old man in ten minutes, chaps," he said before disappearing again.

Vanderkamp was standing next to the CO in the mess, where all large briefings were held. A map stood on a board behind them, at the centre of which was Tobruk. We sat where we could, on fold-up chairs, small barrels and jerry cans. Copies of *Picture Post* were being passed around, and Polly was reading a tattered copy of *Teach Yourself Arabic*, practising the phrases quietly to himself. Across the airfield the erks were starting the engines of the Hurricanes, testing them, running them up, and then closing the throttle, checking idling speed and both magnetos. Despite the aeroplanes facing inwards and being some distance away, more dust and sand inevitably made its way into the tents and on everything.

"Good morning, gentlemen," the CO began, straight to business, "there are large concentrations of Jerry armour still around Sidi Rezegh, and I've no doubt we will be called upon to assist in breaking this up, but our main task today is Gambut airfield, here," he said, tapping the map close to the sea, east of Tobruk. "It's Rommel's forward HQ, and while it would be very nice to catch him at home, I doubt he will still be there," he said, to some chuckling around the tent.

"We could ask him whether he's going to his mother-in-law's for Christmas or staying at home this year," Harry said to general laughter.

"Yes, quite," the CO said, smiling. "It's a wing op, so 112 and 94 squadrons will be with us as well as 45 and 55 squadrons with their Blenheims."

"We don't want to damage the airfield too much because

I'd like us to use the bloody thing ourselves soon, hopefully, so we don't want to make it difficult for the sappers. The weather could get a bit hairy, there's a lot of rain forecast, but we'll see if that materialises. Take a look at the map and update your own. Are there any questions?" Nobody spoke. "Right then, flight leaders Harry, Sticky, Waddy, Wylie and Gidman stay behind, and we'll see the rest of you at dispersal at 0900. Good hunting." The CO had turned, but then paused and spoke up above the increasing chatter. "By the way, the adj has asked me to make a request of you all." Everyone stopped and listened. "Can you please refrain from pissing on the tailwheels; it's corroding the bloody rubber."

We filed out, back to our own tents, across to the kitchen, or to the latrines. I called on Dave and Ernie at my Hurricane. It was fully armed, fuelled and ready for battle. "No problems, Flight," Ernie said. "I thought she was running a little low on oil pressure earlier when I started her up, but she's okay," he said. I waited until the flight leader's briefing was over then took my wallet to the CO's safe. I needed another trip to the thunder box too, as I found I couldn't keep anything in. I had griping stomach pains and as soon as my bottom touched the timber it came away like water. I wondered if I'd eaten something that disagreed with me. Food poisoning was rare; we hardly ate anything exotic other than bully beef and biscuits, so I couldn't understand why this was happening.

I lowered myself into the aeroplane and Ernie helped strap me in. I'd flown this same one for a while now and it was beginning to feel like a part of me. I was strapping those wings onto my own body as I was being absorbed into the machine. I kept all the straps tight for now; I'd hopefully remember to loosen the top ones after take-off. I checked the controls had full and free movement, selected the throttle setting to one finger width and primed it only twice, seeing as it had been running a few minutes earlier. Flaps to neutral, rudder trim a couple of degrees to the right, prop neutral, fuel on fuselage tanks, carb heat to cold, mags to both, and the Merlin started first time. The power still set my pulse racing because this had now become my heart, the huge V12 three feet in front of me that thundered and shook everything. I primed it a little more and turned the booster pump on. Dave removed the chocks. Out of habit I still conducted a brief engine check as we moved off, then as I neared the threshold Ernie waved with a smile and a thumbs up.

Full throttle sent the aeroplane tearing along the runway and I reached for the undercarriage lever at two hundred feet, and then the trim lever, following Gidman on his starboard side climbing gently away to the north-west. We were joined briefly by eight Tomahawks from 112 Squadron led by Squadron Leader Imshi Mason, who then headed due north. We climbed as we flew; passing four thousand feet we levelled off at five, just as we reached the coast. There were large clouds to avoid, an unusual problem for us, but still nothing on the scale of England in late November, not yet at least. There were masses of vehicle movements all around and tracks were being churned up in the sand as far as I could see in the east, and we soon made contact with a dozen Blenheims two thousand feet below us. They'd also attracted the attention of some 109s, so there were shouts of, "Tally-ho!" as we pushed our noses lower and engaged full throttle. The 109s, probably seven or eight in all, scattered when they saw us and left the Blenheims alone. I tried to follow one, but he was hurling his aeroplane around the sky like he was drunk. I fired a couple of quick bursts, but I was pretty sure I didn't hit him. Another Hurricane then shot past me and engaged him with a long burst and the 109 flipped over with smoke streaming from the tail and fell into a vertical dive, eventually hitting the ground hard and exploding.

I didn't see anyone get out.

We stayed with the bombers until they'd done their job, seeing them safely back over our lines, then I heard the CO on the R/T. "Right, let's hit the deck and sort out this airfield," as we then began a rapid descent towards Gambut Airfield. Strafing an aeroplane on the ground doesn't count as a victory, which was sad because as we passed over I must have hit a dozen or more Macchis and 109s lined up on the ground. You can't tell whether they are serviceable aircraft, of course, or even decoys, but smashing them up like this was hugely satisfying and a lot of fun. I wondered why they were still on the ground, until much later I saw Gambut had had so much rain, parts of the airfield were unusable. We were then bounced ourselves by eight 109s, obviously very upset we were damaging their airfield. The sky above Gambut became a swarming mass of aeroplanes, all vying to gain a good position to attack the other, banking sharply in steep turns, the air filled with the rattle of machine guns from aeroplanes and small arms from the ground. It was a very dangerous place. Bofors rounds were added to the lethal mix and I heard some familiar noises from the rear of my cockpit and after a few quick bursts at two 109s ahead of me, I left the fray, following Gidman heading south.

It took me a few minutes to realise I'd lost radio contact with everyone as I must have copped some damage, so I just stuck by Gidman all the way. The 109s didn't follow as we stayed at low level heading south-east. We gave some Hun MTs a few quick bursts near Gabr Saleh before we had to call an end to the op. I for one had run out of ammunition, so, I suspect, had everyone else.

Sure enough, a bullet had smashed through my radio, making it irreparable. It was an ancient TR9 set and wasn't much good anyway and I watched as Ernie removed it in what appeared to be a fairly simple process. We didn't as yet have a replacement, so annoyingly the aeroplane was unserviceable. Two others had received flak damage so three were out of action for the rest of that day. Two-sixty made three more sorties that day, all up around Sidi Rezegh and Gambut. I didn't fly again until the next day when we were scrambled very early to counter a threat from some roaming Ju88s seen heading our way by the army. They were probably out for revenge at what we'd been doing to Gambut. I was relieved to find a new radio had been fitted to my Hurricane and I took off with Wrigley, Polly and Clark. I didn't want to fly a different aeroplane.

40

THIS PARTICULAR OP WAS A MOMENTOUS EVENT FOR me; I was flight leader for the first time. It wasn't common for non-commissioned ranks to undertake this role and it gave us valuable experience, but it wasn't generally approved of by the higher-ups. Ironically life is actually easier because I didn't have to keep looking out to form up on anyone else; they had to do it on me instead! At two thousand feet and ten miles north of LG124, we found our targets: three Ju88s heading straight for us. With one gun in the nose compared to my eight, I pressed on into a head-on attack. I chose the one in the centre and it seemed he wasn't going to flinch until I was just a couple of hundred yards in front of him at a combined closing speed in excess of 500 mph. I let him have a four-second burst, which must have been a terrifying sight. I could see he was firing at me in return, but I rated my chances as greater than his, and I was right. I pulled up a little and flew over the top of him as I was still firing, to see the front of his aeroplane in a terrible mess. It continued on in a straight line and in level flight, so I turned around and pursued him, lining up for another burst. The gun in the rear of his cockpit was silent and at two hundred yards I gave him another long burst, raking the fuselage. The aeroplane began losing height gradually and then wallowed along in a shallow dive. Ten seconds later it hit the ground and exploded. Polly and Clark destroyed one of the others, while the third had successfully made a run for it, with Wrigley in pursuit with smoke trailing from its port engine.

We returned to rearm and refuel. We were scrambled again an hour later when Army Intel stated 109s were harassing our MTs near Gabr Saleh, but they were gone by the time we arrived. In mid-afternoon we were ordered to overfly our ground troops now just south of Sidi Rezegh in large numbers and we engaged enemy MTs and armour several times. It was easy to run out of ammunition shooting at MTs. This was our standard ops routine for several days, and it was exhausting. We were doing well and hadn't lost anyone since the operation began, but we found out on the evening of 20th November that the Hun had broken through our lines in a counterattack. Information was confusing, so the CO ordered us to pack away again. I now had a small canvas bag in which I kept my personal effects that I carried with me in the cockpit. First thing in the morning we flew back to LG115 south of Mersa Matruh.

Some of our ground crew never made it to the new destination that night and had to spend a few hours sleeping in the open desert, eventually arriving just after sunrise. Half the squadron were told to land at LG109, five miles east of LG115, and so we did. There were some tents already set up there and we played cards and reread magazines and newspapers as we saw a lot of our aeroplanes flying over, giving the Hun a pounding on the ground. When our erks and their equipment arrived, we joined in.

Early on 21st November, the CO bounded into the mess to give us the quickest briefing I'd ever known: "Follow me; Rommel's being a bastard again!" We dutifully took off, following him like ducklings after their mother. I knew our troops had pushed Rommel back from Sidi Rezegh, but now he was sending his tanks forward again threatening not only there but beyond Sollum and Sidi Omar. It looked like everything we had gained in the last few days might be taken away from us. All twelve of us dropped to ground level following the CO as we sped across the desert heading north-west.

Before we reached Sidi Rezegh we found hundreds of Hun MT and armour and began strafing everything we could until we ran out of ammunition. We were joined by Tomahawks from 112 and we didn't encounter any enemy air activity, but the anti-aircraft fire was as thick as a forest and getting more accurate. I heard the tell-tale pings as the metal parts of the fuselage were hit several times. Small arms fire was not a major problem but there were 88 mm guns joining in, and we all knew that one hit from these and there was no chance of survival. Flying through this was a living nightmare and created plenty of twitch. I'd never seen it quite as thick as around Sidi Rezegh that day.

We landed back at LG109 to rearm and refuel. My aeroplane had indeed taken a few minor hits from small arms as Ernie pointed out, but nothing serious. We flew more ground strafing ops for the next few days relentlessly until late on 27th we heard some wonderful news. That evening, just after dark, we were in the mess drinking whiskey with our tea when we heard on the wireless that the Tobruk garrison had finally been relieved; a cheer went up that was probably heard in Tobruk itself, two hundred miles away. We drank to the success of Operation Crusader and the eventual defeat of Rommel.

Just before everyone turned in, I was grabbed by the arm and shoved to one side of the mess next to Clark, who was also being restrained in a similar manner as everyone began gathering around us. What on earth was going on? Clark and I were each handed a tin mug that I could see was half-full of whiskey. The CO appeared wearing his hat, which was very unusual and so I was sure the two of us were in for some sort of public reprimand. As the CO began to speak there was gradual hush with some shouts and cheers.

"When it gets hairy, it also gets twitchy," he said, looking around the tent to serious nods of agreement. "So it follows when there's a good deal of hairy twitching there's also twitchy hairiness," he said, smiling, now to some raucous laughter. "But it brings us all closer, fighting the Hun and the twitch together, united as one, *Celer et Fortis*, members of the same club." Everyone was now suddenly very serious and there was a hushed silence. "Gentlemen, raise your glasses to our two newest members." He lifted a mug and there was clinking of tin all around the tent. I was helped to drink all the contents of mine in one with several firm hands underneath forcing a steep tilt in the mug. The CO then handed Clark and me a small card, before shaking our hands with, "Welcome aboard," just before leaving the mess. There were cheers, followed by a round of applause. It was a deep honour, and Clark and I exchanged surprised glances as we read the writing on our new cards:

'This Western Desert Fighter Pilot is a member in good standing of THE RING TWITCHERS CLUB'. Underneath was written 'Proposed by J. Gidman and Seconded by J. Bandinell'. In the centre was a circular shape beaming out from the card like the bright star of Bethlehem, only this wasn't meant to be a star.

The next morning we were on the move again, back to LG124 near Fort Maddalena. The erks left very early in their lorries after fully rearming and refuelling all our aeroplanes. The unserviceable ones were left intact to look like the airfield was still being used. Luckily we found the LG just as we'd left it and sappers were already there confirming there were no mines or booby traps. It seemed the Hun hadn't been there at all while we were away. The rest of the squadron arrived the same day and we resumed regular bomber escorts and ground strafing ops.

The front line was shifting around like *khamsin* sand, but all we needed to know was where our targets were, while being very careful not to hit our own forces. We kept up the pressure until eventually in the second week of December, Rommel gave up and began a headlong retreat westward with our forces in pursuit. On the 9th we landed at an LG close to Sidi Rezegh, the very place we'd been fighting over for weeks. It wasn't triumphalism or arrogance, it was just the next LG on our list, and any thoughts of victorious jubilation were gone in an instant as soon as we touched down. None of us were prepared for what we found; it was the closest thing to hell I'd ever seen.

We were twenty miles south-east of Tobruk. This whole area had been bitterly fought over and the harsh reality of this was clear to see all around us. In the distance I could see smoke still rising from the recently recaptured city and the entire LG was an utter shambles. It had only recently been captured and sappers were still busy clearing mines and booby traps, so they confined us to a tight area at the eastern side of the runway to where we taxied and switched off. I'd landed with my canopy open and so the smell was the first indication. When I climbed out of my aeroplane, I couldn't believe what I saw.

The Hun had fled without burying their dead and so hundreds were lying all around us where they'd fallen. There were also a lot of Kiwi dead, as they'd played the biggest part in driving the Hun away. Attempts had been made to gather many of them together and there were piles of them dotted all around, heaps of rotting flesh wrapped in bits of uniform and old blankets. It wasn't particularly hot, but it was obvious some must have been there for several days. The sappers had become wary of them because the Hun had even left booby traps amongst some of their dead. There was a lot of burned out MT from both sides, including tanks and British Bren gun carriers, most of which still contained their dead occupants, some of whom were plastered to the insides of the vehicles.

41

THERE MUST HAVE BEEN A DOZEN OR MORE apparently serviceable enemy aircraft in various states of repair. The sappers told us not to touch any, just in case, and they were busy checking them over as we arrived. They obviously knew how curious we would be. The larger buildings were the first to be secured with a very enthusiastic thumbs up from an army major. Quite a few tents had been abandoned and we found a huge number of personal effects, ranging from letters and photographs to clothes, blankets and newspapers, both Italian and German. They'd obviously left in a hurry.

We were shouted at by a sergeant major in charge of the sappers who told us to stay well clear of everything, and so we grudgingly obliged. I was standing with Polly browsing through a copy of *Der Adler*, the Hun's air force magazine, when a dull thump and a cloud of dust blew out from a small hut a hundred yards away. Two men ran towards it carrying a stretcher and I was surprised to see Doc Craib amongst them, looking distinctly worried. I ran over to offer assistance, even though I had no idea what was going on. Any sense of urgency quickly evaporated when I saw what had happened. A door had been wired up to at least one grenade, possibly two, blowing a sapper's head right off his shoulders and out the door. There was obviously nothing the Doc could do other than order a burial party. The next moment there was a similar bang from around the corner at the other side of the same building. An airman lay on his back next to an Italian motorbike, screaming in agony. The kick starter had been booby-trapped and had blown his foot off. His desert boot, with his right foot still inside, had hit the wall and ended up ten yards away. We all became a little more wary after that and left the sappers to do their job.

Morley, Carlisle and Alexander took off again, with Sticky leading after a report of 109s nearby. Then before the rest of us could get up we had to take cover behind a wall of sandbags when we thought bombs were falling on the airfield, but which we soon found out was shelling. I think we'd probably landed a little too soon; the enemy was still close by. Army liaison discovered where the guns were and an hour later most of them were silenced, but this was a shock. I'd never been shelled before and it was a terrifying experience. In an aeroplane with flak bursting all around you can at least *feel* as though you have some control, but with this you are a sitting duck. Luckily no-one was badly hurt and none of our aeroplanes were damaged other than a few minor skin punctures from shrapnel. As soon as the shelling stopped, we took off again and headed for the remaining Hun MT around the western side of Sidi Rezegh and Bir el Gubi to continue what we had started. The Hun was now pushed behind a rough line which ran from the western fringes of Tobruk, just west of El Adem and down through

Bir el Gubi, twenty-five miles south of the city, but it was very fluid and subject to change at short notice. We had to be very careful when strafing ground troops in this situation, making doubly sure who the target was at all times.

Imshi Mason's 112 Squadron were already in action and as I lined up to follow one of their Tomahawks on a strafing run, to my horror, I saw it explode in front of me, immediately striking the ground in a high-speed ball of flaming wreckage. I didn't see anything of the pilot; there wouldn't be at that height, the poor chap had no chance. I felt immediate revulsion but then a sudden wave of gratification swept over me; for a few shameful seconds this was a great sight. I know it's an awful thing to say, but it meant that because he had been clobbered my own chances were immediately better. Three seconds later, I was in the same piece of sky he'd just occupied and I passed through it without incident. He'd been just in front of me and by pure chance he was clobbered instead of me. Even if you were a brilliant pilot, you couldn't do anything about this random bad luck. I felt sick, but I just kept on flying at three hundred miles an hour, skimming the ground at fifty feet, pressing the gun button until I ran out of ammunition.

I pulled up and once I was a safe distance away, I wondered if it had been quick for the Tomahawk pilot or whether he had known what was happening, spending his last few moments in sheer terror. I couldn't stop thinking about this and dwelt on it far too long. With silent guns I headed for home, landing with a bumpier-than-usual touchdown. I sat for a while in the cockpit, thinking of the Tomahawk pilot and how close I had been to taking his place. The moment his aeroplane spun into the ground and exploded was on constant repeat in my mind and it was there every time I closed my eyes.

It wasn't until late afternoon that the sappers declared most areas of our new LG to be safe. We were so close to the front line we'd been on permanent standby, but now it was extended to an hour, which was long enough for a much-needed visit to the new thunder box. To avoid any nasty surprises, we stayed clear of the old Hun latrines and created our own. This one was merely three large buckets surrounded by oil drums filled with sand, initially with no roof of any sort. The user's head and shoulders would therefore stick up over the top and when I first shared it with Doc Craib, a Kiwi sapper came from behind and saluted him, marching off with a German MP40 hanging over his front and a mine detector over his left shoulder. The Doc was taken completely by surprise and instinctively saluted back, despite his position. Frank Tregear arrived and took the third space, passing around a bottle of Chianti in its own straw basket which he'd earlier liberated from one of the tents. I took a quick slurp, keeping an eye out for the CO. "It's getting pretty hairy, isn't it?" he said, staring into the desert. "Lots of twitch." I nodded.

A hundred yards away, my parachute was hanging on the left wingtip of my Hurricane, topped with my leather flying helmet. We were often flying in cold weather attire now: fur-lined flying boots, long trousers, battle dress top and Mae West, but I could still dress and undress in double-quick time. I carried my Italian Beretta in a holster all the time too, but even with this I could be ready in my aeroplane from thunder box to cockpit in less than two minutes.

Later that afternoon, when we were finally taken off standby, we all went on the prowl for something interesting as a much-needed distraction. Under a camouflage net surrounded by shoulder-high sandbags, we found a Hurricane in German markings, the huge black crosses on the fuselage and hated swastika on the tail looking really odd. The sappers cleared it for us and so Gidman sat inside. It looked perfectly serviceable, but it wouldn't start due to a completely flat battery, but what idiots they'd been to leave it for us! We also found a fabulous 109F that seemed undamaged; when it was safe Harry managed to get it started, beaming like a child, but he shut it down straightaway. It was another trophy for 260 Squadron. He was rebuked by the CO for even going near it and had to be ordered not to take it up until the erks had painted roundels on it and the squadron letters HS, which they did for him the next day, along with a yellow question mark on the fuselage. There were two Italian CR42 biplanes and a Macchi C200 that looked airworthy too, only lacking a few important engine parts, so the erks told us, as though their owners either couldn't be bothered to repair them or didn't have the tools. They really had left in a hurry.

The rest of the squadron and all our possessions finally arrived safely later that night and so we spent the next day setting up our tents in the usual way, just how we wanted them. Burial parties finally finished their gruesome task and the smell promptly disappeared. There were slit trenches everywhere as we found out this particular LG had changed hands four times already. As well as aeroplanes, there were some useful fully serviceable vehicles, both Italian and German, which we now claimed as our own, along with lots of other kit such as beds and blankets.

The Kiwis who captured the place took the best stuff, but some of it that appeared immovable became useful after a little coaxing. The best of the tents we found still erected was an enormous rather sweet-smelling Italian tent that became our new mess. There was some beautiful white bedroom furniture inside, a huge wrought iron double bed and at the far end sat a large tin bath. Curiously there was also a very shiny, dark brown upright piano in much better condition than our own. It had obviously been the temporary home to a high-ranking officer who would have been very sorry to have lost it.

A chandelier hung from the centre of the roof and the whole thing looked very opulent. Harry Curno quickly discovered the piano and from that moment the desert echoed to the sound of jazz, Glen Miller, Mozart, Beethoven and snippets of George Formby in a very strange mix. It seemed really odd to hear all this played live amongst so much destruction and it was very welcome.

42

CHIANTI WAS THE DRINK OF THE DAY AND EVERY night in our new mess, after several full barrels were discovered half-buried in the sand. We were a lucky squadron and hadn't lost a single pilot since Op Crusader began, and I wondered how long this could last.

I'd never drunk so much wine before and I woke up with a really bad head and raging thirst. Warm, chlorinated water was all we had in the tent, and as disgusting as it was, it helped. Tea with plenty of sugar followed, with bully beef and biscuits, supplemented by boxes of dates someone had left behind. Morley and Wareham called me over to the wreck of a Messerschmitt 110 among a mixed pile of airframe wreckage. The engines were missing and I wondered why they wanted me to see it. The tail plane was riddled with .303 bullet holes from either when it was shot down or used as target practice. They explained that it wasn't to see anything; they just needed my help carrying a large part of it towards the mess. A sapper had obligingly used a metal saw on the fuselage and we lifted the entire tail plane a hundred yards to our new mess, placing it just outside on two large upright Chianti barrels. With storage boxes behind looking like shelving, we now had a pretty decent outside bar on which to lean while drinking our beer, and it quickly became known as 260's 'Messerschmitt Bar'.

There were other more permanent operational arrangements made at Sidi Rezegh. When the CO's three-ton mobile office arrived, he showed us his new system for putting the squadron on readiness, involving a flagpole he'd rigged up on the outside of his office. He had three flags: white, green and red. The white would mean a low state of readiness of an hour, green half an hour and a red flag meant five minutes. I suppose it saved shouting all the time, and it certainly looked more professional.

That same afternoon just after tea I was approached by Polly and Cundy. "Come with us," Cundy said, after nudging me on the shoulder. He had one of his cheeky smiles, so I knew they were up to something. I followed them past a pile of Hun aeroplane wrecks, past the Me110 from which we'd taken the tail plane, and beyond a huge pile of debris and abandoned vehicles. Parked quite separately and appearing to be perfectly serviceable was a Heinkel 111 twin-engined bomber. There was an enormous flare fixed to the starboard wing root obviously intended to destroy it, but it hadn't gone off properly and so the damage was negligible.

"It's a mark four, or five, probably," Cundy said, "but it's not been used as a bomber, come and have a look." I climbed inside and to my surprise I discovered it was incredibly spacious. There were seats and even a small table and the gun was missing from the dorsal turret. There was an ashtray with cigarettes and cigar butts still in it. This had clearly been used as a taxi.

How did Rommel get away if he hadn't used this? It was interesting, but I wondered what I was doing there until Cundy said, "You can fly twins, can't you, Copping?" I looked at him, astounded.

"No. Who told you that?"

"You've flown a Blenheim to Alex," he said, "so you can be our pilot."

"Who told you that?" I repeated, surprised but already knowing the answer.

"Murray told us," Cundy replied. "You can't deny it, he told us you are a fully qualified Blenheim pilot," he said. I laughed. I suspected they knew the truth and were pulling my leg, so I didn't feel inclined to argue. I looked at the controls and the instrument panel. Everything was in German, of course. The Nazis were terribly selfish; they didn't build any of their aeroplanes with English translations in case we wanted to fly them. "What do you think this means?" Cundy said, pointing to a word next to a red-handled lever: *flugzeugklappen*.

"No idea," I replied.

"What about this?" he said with his right hand on a lever, above which was written the word *druckerhohungspumpe*. Same answer. Cundy sat in the pilot's seat and I sat next to him, but it was no good; if we were to do anything with this aeroplane, we would need someone who could translate at least a few of these words around the cockpit. We could no doubt start it up through trial and error, but it would have been foolish to carry on. We'd probably all have been willing to give the 109 a go, because fighter cockpits are forced to be very similar, but this seemed much more complex. As we were sitting there to my surprise we were joined by the CO with Harry and Gidman. "How hard can it be?" Gidman said.

"That's the throttle, I think," Harry said, leaning forward. "It looks similar to the Stuka."

"Are you sure?" Gidman said. "It's nothing like that in the 109."

"What about this?" Cundy said, pointing to another lever.

"Sorry, no, the Stuka didn't have that, not as far as I can remember."

"So we think we know where the throttle is, but we aren't sure?" Polly said. "It's a start, I suppose." The basic instruments common to all aeroplanes were there, but it was a twin-engined machine, and so required a little more work. Where were the fuel pump switches, booster switches, magnetos, and where were the landing gear and trim levers? I hadn't noticed before, but the altimeter was hard to spot because it was in thousand metre units subdivided into hundreds, looking nothing like ours. The CO wasn't saying anything but was now standing between the pilot's seats staring at the instrument panel, which, just to complicate matters, was fixed to the ceiling above our heads. He looked up, tapping a few of the dials while muttering, "Mmm," and, "Aahh," occasionally.

Some erks had opened the engine cowlings and had their heads buried inside.

"I've asked them to give it a check over, just to be sure," the CO said, glancing outside. "I suppose it could be useful," he added finally.

An erk joined us in the cockpit; his hands and fingernails deeply ingrained with oil and scarred all over from years of working on engines. He was a wiry, cheery chap who introduced himself as Corporal Williams and asked how he could help. We were wondering the same until he said, "I can speak some German, do you need a hand?"

He was thrust between the seats immediately and instructed to point around the cockpit, methodically translating everything we could see. To our astonishment the first long word that had baffled us was translated as 'flaps', and the second was 'booster pump'. We were getting somewhere. Cundy pulled out a scrap of paper and made some hasty notes as the translations continued. Williams pulled out a booklet, smaller than a magazine but quite thick. He was reading from it and nodding to himself, pointing around the cockpit as he did so.

"What's that?" Cundy asked.

"Oh, they left us an instruction manual, in German, of course, but very decent of them, eh?"

I've no doubt we'd be better able to follow the instruments once we took off and saw them in action because most were similar, but it was such an odd cockpit that Williams' help was priceless. After fifteen minutes he left us, shortly followed by the CO.

"I'll leave you to it but come and see me before you do anything with it," he said as he clambered out. Williams had clearly enjoyed lecturing half a dozen pilots, and to be fair to him, he was very good at it. His German mother would have been proud.

I knocked once on the door into the CO's office and ushered Cundy inside first.

"It's ready, Sir," Cundy said.

"Right, either of you flown a twin before?" he said, staring at us both.

"Just briefly," I said. "A Blenheim, but never landed one or anything," I said.

"How hard can it be?" the CO said in reply. "It has two engines so it's just two of everything, surely," he said, laughing while lighting a cigarette. "The bottom line is, do either of you feel confident enough to use it? There are no twin-rated pilots here at the moment as far as I know, and you two are the only volunteers," he looked at us with his serious briefing face, exhaling smoke from his Chesterfield through his nostrils. I wasn't aware that I'd volunteered.

"I'm happy to give it a go, Sir," Cundy said, looking at us both.

"What about you, Copping?"

"Why not?" I said, with an almost involuntarily nod of the head. "I'll give him a hand," I added.

"That settles it, then, she's ours, or rather, yours. The erks have told me she has new engines and is in tiptop condition, so god only knows why they left it. We'll use her for leave trips, supplies and so on. But first you've got to make her look like she belongs to us and not the bloody Hun, alright? Get the erks to give her a paint job, anything will do, like they did with the Stuka, and before you go anywhere in it, I want to know, right?"

Ten minutes later I sat with Cundy at the Messerschmitt bar, discussing it. We were in urgent need of more beer and whiskey, some decent bread would be nice too, and cigarettes. We began compiling lists and we were bombarded with requests. Christmas was coming, so it would be nice to get hold of some decent meat. I thought of Tim Murray and his Greek friend Agnides. It seemed 'Olympus Minerals' would soon be having a new set of customers, if we could find the proprietor.

43

EVERY DAY TOWARDS THE END OF NOVEMBER, 260 Squadron were engaged in ground strafing of Hun MT wherever we could find it, often with 112 Squadron on several ops a day until 3rd December, when it appeared the Hun had really had enough and began a full-scale withdrawal westward. The ops were shared between us, but I was still involved most days, and it was exhausting. Every night when I shut my eyes, I saw my bullets tearing into the enemy, with the terrified occupants jumping from their shattered vehicles running for cover with their uniforms burning and then being churned up into the dirt with nowhere to hide. They did it to us, so we did it to them. They strafed our troops and our airfields, so we did the same. What else were we supposed to do?

It was around this time that I stopped having dreams, at least not pleasant ones. I began having the same recurring nightmare where I was running along a vast empty road on which I couldn't move forward despite looking down to see my feet moving quickly below me. The road was hot and I was melting into it with no shade from the sun and no escape. The only other dream I had was a little more pleasant but still very odd; I'm always alone in the back of an open lorry on a beautiful day when the lorry passes the Eastern Harbour in Alex but doesn't stop when I desperately want it to and we end up driving right past and I'm screaming with frustration in the back. I would wake up from these nightmares very suddenly and always just for a moment I'd think I was at home and not lying in this foul-smelling tent stinking like a disgusting old goat. Often I would get up and wander around the LG, and I would always bump into other pilots doing the same. Some were obviously sleepwalking, mumbling to themselves, cursing, even shouting out loud, but others were wide awake but quite drunk, like the time I found Saunders draped over the wing of his Hurricane with a bottle of whiskey. It was always worse at times of high twitch when you'd see ghostly shadows wandering around in the darkness making the sentries nervous.

By 7th December, the Hun had completely fled the area from Tobruk right down to Bir el Gubi and was continuing a rapid retreat west. This was great news to us, along with another piece of news that hit us completely by surprise from the wireless that night: the Japanese attack on the US base at Pearl Harbour. I remember we were aghast at this and were all listening open-mouthed in disbelief. We knew this could change the course of the war. Our friends in 112 were already flying the American-built Tomahawks obtained through Lend-Lease; there were other modern American aeroplanes like Boston bombers now in the desert too and so we thought the Japanese must have been mad to attack America. They would surely get what was coming to them for this. A war between those two nations across the Pacific wouldn't affect us directly, but then America declared war on Japan's allies in Europe, and so hopefully this would eventually make a real difference to the desert campaign.

Sunday 14th December began with dawn patrol over the thunder box as usual followed by briefing at the gaggle board after breakfast. With Tobruk back in our hands and the Hun on the run westward, we were happy to help make his retreat as uncomfortable as possible. Sixteen of us were to provide top cover for some Fleet Air Arm Albacore torpedo bombers attacking Hun shipping as it fled along the coast. Troops and supplies were being evacuated, as well as fresh supplies of ammunition arriving from across the Med. They still held the ports of Bardia and Sollum despite being surrounded twenty-five miles east of Gambut, so we were called upon to assist in attacks on these.

The CO put us on five minute readiness in order to test his new flag system; nothing happened and no-one noticed until Harry Curno saw it and came charging into the mess and began bashing out a tune on the piano that I thought was Mozart or Beethoven but then recognised as 'The Red Flag'. The same tune is also ironically known as the 'Tanenbaum', or Christmas tree, a German tune. He sat on a barrel, playing it as loudly as he could with all his flying kit on and his parachute on top of the piano. We suddenly realised and jumped into our aeroplanes.

I was with Saunders and Morley, with Flight Lieutenant George 'Sparky' Black as leader of Red Flight. The CO took off first with Polly, Gidman and Wareham as Blue Flight; with Harry leading another three, Carlisle, Curno and Alexander as Yellow Flight; and Sticky leading Dunbar, Clark and Cartwright as Green Flight. We were well used to this new finger-four formation and the CO admitted it was working much better than the Vic formation. We headed north where we waited over the coast flying orbits until the Albacores arrived. I had a vague idea what these aeroplanes looked like, but I was shocked when I saw them chugging along far below, barely a few hundred feet up. They were large biplanes similar to the famous Swordfish, each one with an enormous torpedo slung under the fuselage. They were following the coast excruciatingly slowly and I knew they would attract interest from the enemy. We flew past Tobruk and towards the port of Gazala which was still in enemy hands and where the target shipping was located. We knew a large number of 109s were based around there too, and sure enough, before the Albacores could line up to attack, we were pressed into service as twelve 109s appeared from directly ahead of us heading straight for the Albacores. We broke formation and engaged them immediately.

I was on Sparky's starboard side and together we fired at a 109, which briefly showed us his underside in a steep turn. I thought I'd taken some hits until I realised the rattling sound was some of Sparky's spent cartridges hitting the leading edge of my port wing. There was an explosion of smoke and flame from the 109's engine and he rolled onto his back and bailed out. His parachute opened and as he drifted down towards the sea a hundred yards from the shore, his 109 plunged into the water vertically with a huge splash but no explosion.

A 109 then fired at me, the flashes from his guns clearly visible as he shot overhead from my port side. I pulled back on the stick and pushed the throttle forward to follow him. I fired and missed and fired again, but he turned westward and I let him go. Blue Flight pursued the other 109s and down below I saw four of the six Albacores lining up on three ships, their anti-aircraft fire blazing away at them. I dropped down with Sparky and Morley, and together we made the ship's gunners keep their heads down for a few moments with a long burst until the torpedoes ran on to their targets. Two of the ships took hits while the third had turned and made off. I could see dozens of men with their clothing on fire jumping into thick, burning oil on the surface of the water and so we left them alone. The last two Albacores had a go at the third ship, but their torpedoes missed, or at least there were no detonations. Having used up all their munitions, the Albacores turned eastward for home, with us circling overhead for a while.

The 109s dispersed and we returned to the LG, where we rearmed and refuelled, and in the afternoon, we were sent in the same formations further west to provide close cover for Blenheims attacking Hun airfields around Martuba. The weather wasn't great, with intermittent low cloud and rain, and I couldn't tell if the target had been hit. I was used to flying in clear blue skies and not such poor visibility, and so it all seemed confusing when just as we were about to leave, we were bounced by a large force of 109s and Macchi 202s. There must have been a dozen of each and suddenly the sky was filled with aeroplanes and bullets flying around everywhere. This was no longer a bomber escort but a dogfight for sheer survival. There were desperate warning shouts over the R/T, and I saw Harry and Yellow Flight in trouble below, but I had a pair of 109s on my tail and so I couldn't do anything to help. I pulled around and fired a few long deflection bursts at them and then my guns were silent.

I was weaving around and pulling steep turns to the limits of both myself and the aeroplane and made a few dummy passes at a Macchi 202 which caused him to head off west, but I was really no good to anyone without ammunition. In amongst all this, I caught a glimpse of a Hurricane trailing smoke and losing height, but I was too far away to see who it was, and I couldn't hang around to find out. I caught up with Sparky and Saunders who were now heading for home, so I followed, throttle wide open and nose down. With so many enemy fighters around, I was sure we would be pursued, but after an agonising few minutes heading south-east at high speed, I realised they had decided against the idea. As suddenly as they had arrived, the 109s and Macchis were gone, so I eased back on the throttle, drew back the canopy and searched for home.

I followed Sparky in alongside Morley and Saunders and taxied over to dispersal. I shut down the engine and when the aeroplane was silent I just sat there, wet through and exhausted. Dave and Ernie came up and helped me out, and when I jumped off the wing, my knees almost gave way. I'd flown in my battle dress top and long trousers, which were now sticking to my skin.

Blue Flight landed followed by Green Flight, and they taxied over and shut down their engines, but the CO didn't emerge from his cockpit, so it was clear something was wrong. An erk jumped onto the wing, peered inside and immediately began shouting for help. I then saw Doc Craib running over with his bag. Several Hurricanes were badly shot up, including the CO's. He was lifted from the cockpit onto a stretcher and taken to Doc Craib's tent. All in all, it had been a pretty tough show.

Yellow Flight had still not returned. Twenty minutes later, Carlisle, Curno and Alexander came in, but Harry wasn't with them. They had hung around in order to try and find him but had to come away. All three looked glum as they trudged over to us. "Harry's missing," Carlisle said as he walked past me, staring ahead. When any serious incident happened, we'd usually meet at the CO's office for debriefing and mutual consolations, but of course he wasn't there. Our mother hen was lying injured in Doc Craib's tent.

Flight Lieutenant Hall immediately assumed temporary

command of 260, and the first thing he had to do was to list Harry Bandinell as formally missing. An hour later a Blenheim arrived and the CO was carried aboard for transport to hospital in Alex. After tea the atmosphere in the mess was subdued to say the least. Harry Curno played the piano for a while and Sticky tried to lighten the mood with his gramophone and some rarely played records, 'South of the Border' and 'Elmer's Tune,' and 'Salome' and then generous amounts of Chianti was issued for medicinal purposes by Doc Craib, who faced a grilling when he arrived in the mess. "He'll be okay," was all he would tell us as he reached for the wine. He sat down and took his pipe from his breast pocket, tapping the ash out on the edge of the table onto the floor before filling it up. He then hid from the rest of us in great clouds of sweet-smelling tobacco smoke, prompting everyone else to light up.

I was in the middle of a copy of *Der Adler*, wondering what hilarious derogatory comments Goering was making about the Spitfire when an hour later Vanderkamp came in with the new CO. They spoke briefly to Doc Craib who was talking to Gidman and Sparky. The CO was still on his feet when he turned to face the rest of us. I think we knew what was coming. Everyone stopped talking and was looking at him as 'Amapola' on Sticky's gramophone crackled to a halt.

"Army Intel just confirmed that Harry's aircraft has been found, and he was still inside. He didn't make it, chaps, I'm sorry."

44

THREE DAYS LATER OUR NEW PERMANENT CO ARRIVED from Cairo: 'Barney' Beresford, or Squadron Leader Tristram Barnard de la Poer Beresford, as I noticed on his luggage. He was obviously from a very well-to-do family, and his accent confirmed this. He was the polar opposite in every way to Derek Walker. When he introduced himself in the mess he hinted there might be some leave coming up, but nothing specific was mentioned. With Tobruk relieved and the Hun retreating fast, we wondered if the next flight we'd make would be a much-needed trip to Alex. The Heinkel 111 was now a beautiful bright yellow, looking like an enormous twin-engined canary with hand-painted roundels and we were all itching to use it for leave trips but there was nothing going at the moment. The new CO was very busy with Doc Craib, Vanderkamp and the other officers.

We weren't allowed official leave but perhaps we could take a trip to the coast, not far away? Squadron Leader Walker's Italian staff car was still with us, standing idle next to his office, and so we could only ask. We were in dire need of a break and our new CO knew it, so we weren't too surprised when permission was granted.

We set off for Tobruk just after breakfast, with Bernier, Colley, Gidman and I sharing the driving, and even though it wasn't far, at about twenty-five miles we were reduced to a crawl on several occasions. Colley entertained us with some of his jokes. "I say, I say, I say, I just took my wife to the West Indies. Really? Jamaica? No, she went of her own accord. When a clock goes forward it goes tic-tac, but when Rommel goes backwards it's tactic." We laughed because we wanted to, not because the jokes were funny. We needed the distraction, and Colley was always there to provide it, whether we wanted him to or not.

The drive began well and was straightforward enough; we followed well-used dirt roads, never straying off them even for a few inches for fear of mines, and the same on the tarmac roads which were still largely intact. We bumped into some Kiwis who warned us the mines were particularly thick around the Tobruk perimeter and so for a couple of miles Bernier and Colley walked ahead, scanning the surface just to make sure.

The closer we came to the city the scenes became truly awful. We had certainly given their MTs a severe bashing, and the sappers were still catching up with disposal of the dead. Wrecked vehicles lined the road; most of them burned out and reduced to twisted metal hulks. The Hun had booby trapped more of his own dead and so the sappers decided to burn many of them in pyres by the road, causing a bitter smell of death that lined the back of the throat and stayed there.

We reached the outskirts of Tobruk by mid-morning. At first sight the city resembled a vast wasteland of rubble with hardly anything left intact, but recent rains had created an abundance of purple bougainvillea clambering up walls and around the shattered remains of buildings. How lovely it must have looked before the war.

Indian soldiers wearing turbans filled the streets, casually leaning on their MTs and tanks; the Punjab Regiment had played the biggest part in the city's liberation relieving the Poles and the Czechs after the Aussies had held it so well for five months. It had been a truly international effort. They pulled us over at a roadblock to check who we were before waving us on. We then parked the car in the long, narrow harbour and were relieved to get out and stretch our legs. The Italian cruiser San Giorgio sat forlornly near the harbour entrance, scuttled in shallow water by its crew in January. The grey weather and destruction were now reflecting our mood, and no-one had any thoughts of going in the sea for a dip, even though for the time of year it looked inviting. It was cool but certainly not cold by British standards. We couldn't guarantee there weren't munitions lying around on the beach, or even human remains, and so we contented ourselves with sitting on the promenade smoking. It was enough to give our eyes something else to focus on other than the endless desert, aeroplanes and each other.

A group of about a dozen middle-aged and elderly women approached us, some with hands outstretched, sobbing and bringing with them a dreadful stench. They seemed to be arguing until they came close to us when all went quiet. One was holding a baby; another was pulling a toddler by the arm that was silent and looked utterly miserable. They spoke to us in what I first thought was Spanish but of course it was Italian. I had no idea so many Italian civilians were still here until Gidman filled me in on the local history. Libya was a favourite spot for Italians before the war and Mussolini even had a holiday home somewhere on the Libyan coast he visited regularly before he decided to take on the British in Egypt.

The women gathered around us and communication was impossible at first. They spoke very little English, but Bernier stepped forward straightaway and began speaking to them in French, which some of them understood. Warrant Officer 'Stan' or Joe' Bernier was a slight, calm, softly spoken, blue-eyed French Canadian, probably a year or two older than me at about twenty-five and was the sort of man you would love to have as your older brother. He had problems occasionally due to his height, he was six foot three at least, and was easily the tallest pilot in the squadron, with a wispy moustache that had probably taken him years to grow. He was renowned for his selflessness; he would readily give up his seat at the thunder box if you were in more urgent need, and would share his last cigarette with anyone, so he was well-liked by all of us. This pleasant disposition was deceptive, however, because like so many combat pilots, he was a determined killer when at the controls of his aeroplane.

Bernier immediately translated, speaking with great empathy, and two of the women then took his hand and one collapsed to the ground in front of him. It seemed they were starving and were begging for food. Bernier tried to explain that we were just visitors and couldn't help them. The youngest of the women, probably in her early forties, pushed her way up to Bernier, smiling, straightening her long, black hair with both hands and then pulling her dress down off her shoulders, revealing some very generous cleavage.

Bernier was unimpressed and to my surprise he took out two tins of bully beef from the pockets of his flying jacket like a magician and handed them over, both of which were seized immediately. He then gave them his half-empty packet of Chesterfield cigarettes, so perhaps they could be used to barter for food.

Apart from the translations, Bernier didn't make any comment to us and there was no expectation we should do anything, but when someone performs a spontaneous act of kindness right in front of you, you find you have only two choices; you ignore it or you take part, if you can. Colley was first. He emptied his pockets – cigarettes and a small amount of Egyptian piastres – and we followed, handing over what we had, which wasn't much. The women gathered their composure and began to move away muttering, *"Grazie, grazie,"* over and over. It wasn't enough, but it was all we had.

We climbed back into the car, with me at the wheel because it was my turn. "The baby's been dead for almost a week," Bernier said. "But she won't part with it. That's what the smell was, and why they were arguing before they came up to us." No-one spoke. I started the car and turned it around in the road to find our way out of there. Our day out at the seaside hadn't quite turned out the way we intended. We were checked again by Indian soldiers as we left Tobruk, and they pointed out a quicker way back through the perimeter heading south-east along the coast road, which we gratefully took.

A mile outside the ruined city, we saw what at first appeared to be a huge shifting herd of grazing animals with a few shepherds standing watch. We were pulled over at a British Army checkpoint by two stern-looking MPs with fixed bayonets on their Lee Enfields. Satisfied as to our identities, they let us through. We then realised what the enormous mass of livestock was on our left. They were hundreds, perhaps thousands of POWs, guarded by just a handful of British soldiers.

When we arrived back at Sidi Rezegh, all four of us headed straight for the Messerschmitt bar and shared a bottle of whiskey between us, neat. We didn't even bother with our tin mugs.

45

FOR THE NEXT FEW DAYS WE WERE CALLED ON FOR bomber escort ever deeper into Libya. On 18th December we escorted a raid on Mechili, a hundred miles inland west of Tobruk. We were a flight commander short because Flying Officer Osgood Villiers 'Pedro' Hanbury was now in Cairo recovering from a bad case of jaundice, and wouldn't return until the end of January. He never made any complaints until Doc Craib insisted he seek treatment when he began turning an odd shade of yellow. His place was taken by a newly arrived officer called Bradley who seemed to be a really nice fellow, always smiling and helpful. Except for us pilots, even in the desert it was generally frowned upon for officers to mix closely with non-commissioned ranks, but this chap was soon spending a lot of time with the erks and even the sappers.

Fifteen of us took off heading west across the desert with our new CO leading, one aeroplane short due to battle damage. Most of the land en route to the target was in our hands and when the Beaufighters delivered their payload without encountering any enemy fighters, we dropped down to low level looking for MT. We soon found a small column of mixed MT and we were surprised when first passing they didn't open fire on us. We swung around and pressed home a long strafing run when they began to wake up, hurling a lot of flak at us. Luckily there were no 88s amongst it all, mainly light stuff and a lot of Bofors, but it was soon pretty thick and I heard a couple of our pilots over the R/T saying they'd been hit so we then headed for home. We'd inflicted plenty of damage with the usual dreadful sights of men running around with no chance of finding cover. They did the same thing to our troops, and so you couldn't think of compassion or empathy. At least this was what we kept telling ourselves.

Thirty minutes after landing back at Sidi Rezegh, Gidman still hadn't returned. Two hours later and with no news, he was officially listed as missing. That night in the mess he remained a missing pilot with no evidence he was anything else, so the mood was optimistic. Pilots had been known to crash-land and find their way back to our lines, and so this was what we had assumed had happened to Gidman.

First thing in the morning a Photo Reconnaissance Blenheim landed and two very stern-faced army types stomped across the dispersal area demanding to see the CO. They disappeared into his office and unusually, the doors were slammed shut behind them. We assumed this was another lengthy intel briefing, but we were wrong; it was much worse. This was the kind of news that when I first heard it, I felt physically sick. I wanted to scream and get blind drunk, both at the same time. The two army officers left in the Blenheim and the CO then called us into the mess for a briefing. He was holding a slip of paper in both hands. "'A' Troop, First Light

Anti-Aircraft Regiment of the Desert Rats was attacked yesterday by fifteen Hurricanes south-east of Mechili. Two men were killed and eleven injured. They were forced to return fire and one Hurricane was hit and was last seen heading off in a southerly direction." He was clearly reading directly from the intelligence report, and when he'd finished he folded it over twice very precisely and slipped it into his breast pocket. "It would be a reasonable assumption that the Hurricane that was hit was Pilot Officer John Gidman. This has been a lesson for us all, gentlemen, a reminder that we must read the intel reports and study the maps in greater detail so that we can at least try to avoid this happening again." He turned around, leaving the mess in absolute silence.

In the morning the CO lightened the mood instantly by issuing leave passes, obviously a deliberate policy on his part. We wondered how anyone would get to Alex and hoped for the appearance of a passing Blenheim until we remembered the Heinkel, which we had now affectionately named 'Delta Lily'. It had been thoroughly checked over and was ready to fly, and even had her name painted on the port side near the cockpit. We were all still reluctant to be the first to pilot it until that afternoon when some visiting RCAF pilots, showing an interest in our acquisition, informed us that one of their contingents was twin-rated.

An American calling himself Captain Margolian admitted in his broad Texan drawl that he had five hours on Bostons, so Cundy promptly grabbed hold of him and with all due respect marched him over to the Delta Lily. Five hours wasn't much, but it was a lot more than anyone else. They both climbed aboard and ten minutes later it was waddling towards the threshold with both engines turning over very smoothly. The engines then roared without any movement from the wheels until the brakes were released a few seconds later for a short field take-off. Empty and pointing into wind, it climbed very well as we watched closely. They kept it in the circuit and came in for final approach with thirty degrees of *flugzeugklappen* successfully applied. Margolian then flared the Heinkel far too high, probably thinking he was still in a smaller aeroplane, and then corrected it with a quick roar from the engines before throttling back again, but still touching down with a bump. The throttles were pushed open again and they took off without stopping. They did this three times before pulling over and making a running change of pilot. I could see Cundy climbing into the pilot's seat before he taxied it to the threshold. Delta Lily took to the air again this time with Cundy at the controls and he brought it back down after a wide circuit without a problem. We were in business.

Curno, Saunders, Morley and Alexander climbed aboard, and Cundy took off heading east, with everyone glaring with envy. They would not be missed operationally because we were five aeroplanes short with two damaged and three in urgent need of de-choking from sand. There was only one op that day, which I wasn't chosen for, and those who took part returned safely, with everyone still twitchy after our recent losses. News was spreading of the rapid advance of our troops and the erks began loading the lorries again with the CO confirming another imminent move. Five hours later Cundy returned in the Delta Lily with boxes of dates and some beer, apparent gratuities from Agnides who had spotted our aeroplane and cleverly realised the commercial potential.

Next morning half the squadron headed west to Mechili and before we had settled in, we moved again to Msus, even further west. With our help, our ground forces were advancing so fast we were landing at LGs that we had been attacking only a few days before. Even though we had no idea how long we'd be at Msus, we decided to make it as comfortable as we could.

All our stuff was unpacked and tents pitched before deciding which abandoned equipment we could use for ourselves. Until very recently Msus had been Zeit Msus, a Hun LG, and so the usual precautions had to be taken with booby traps. They and the Italians had left a lot of kit behind, including eighteen Fiat G50 fighters, but sadly most of them were badly damaged. In their haste to leave they'd obviously driven a heavy vehicle at the tail of each one but the last was missed and appeared airworthy.

There were unexploded munitions everywhere and two sappers each lost a hand when they were clearing some of it; whether these were deliberate booby traps or not I wasn't sure. It was around this time that Doc Craib told us not to use any more of the blankets and bedding we found; cases of body lice had begun to appear and so the advice now was to burn anything that wasn't issued by us from Cairo or Alex.

Early on 23rd December Cundy and I were called into the CO's office before breakfast for what was described as a special briefing. One of the cooks was standing there smiling, nodding at the CO.

"I want you to fetch something from Alex," the CO said to us, glancing at the cook. "Are you sure you can do this?" he said to him, and the man nodded with a self-assured, "Yes, of course, Sir," in reply. The CO turned back to us. "Take the Heinkel to Aboukir and liaise with Pilot Officer Murray, he has something very important for us," he said, without initially saying what it was. "Make sure the cargo is back here no later than 0900 hours on the 25th, okay? Go this morning and make arrangements to collect the items tomorrow afternoon, then fly back either tomorrow night or on the morning of 25th, understood?"

"Yes, Sir," Cundy said. "But what is it?"

"It's fresh meat and veg, for the 25th," the CO replied. "Just get it here by then, and for god's sake, don't be late."

46

WE TOOK OFF HEADING EAST AT A THOUSAND FEET flying very low, as pre-arranged with Army Intel. It was over five hundred miles to Aboukir near Alex and the flight was eventful to say the least. Suddenly we were buzzed by RAF fighters near Tobruk who lined up on our tail in what appeared to be final preparations to attack. I'd never before been inside a bomber in these circumstances and I felt completely helpless. They would destroy us in seconds if they fired on us, so Cundy threw the aeroplane around violently before trying another recognised tactic of submission, lowering the undercarriage. He pulled back the speed, lowered some flaps, and the wheels clunked down into position just as we were suddenly surrounded by the shark-mouthed Tomahawks of 112 Squadron, the pilots with their canopies open giving us the thumbs up, with one of them clearly laughing. Much later we found out they knew all along who we were but just wanted to shake us up a bit, the bastards. We were then shot at briefly from the ground as we passed a few miles south of Sidi Barrani, but that was the final problem we had until landing in one piece after two hours in the air.

Tim was standing with Agnides at his lorry. Like me, Cundy had met them both before and they greeted us like old friends. I was amazed Agnides even remembered me and after handshakes with a bear-hug that almost crushed the breath from me, he disappeared into the back of his lorry, emerging a moment later with a small wooden crate which I assumed was meat but was actually whiskey. Where was the meat?

Instead of being given meat we were led to another lorry that was producing a distinct odour and some very odd noises. The CO would be furious if we didn't bring meat back; he stressed several times how important it was to the squadron, and I could see a growing look of concern on Cundy's face too. The back flaps of the lorry were parted, revealing a dozen crates of very noisy animals and birds. The smell was far worse than our own latrines on the hottest day of the year.

"I've got two-sixty down for three crates of turkeys, six sacks of veg and a goat, is that right?" Tim looked at us both, beaming. I looked at Cundy.

"What?" I said.

"Meat, we've come to collect meat," Cundy said with some urgency. "Not animals."

"Yes, well, this is it. You can't get fresher than this," Tim said, standing with Agnides, also looking very pleased. "Each crate contains ten turkeys, and the order was for thirty, so pick which ones you want and you can take them with you now, or if you want, we can arrange for them to be here at 0700 tomorrow. You could then spend tonight in Alex if you want to; it's entirely up to you."

Listening to everything he just said, however absurd some

of it sounded, buried in amongst it all was an offer of a night in Alex. He knew this would never be refused.

"Yes, for a small additional fee we can keep them fed and watered for you until the morning and have them ready first thing," Tim said.

"This is no problem," Agnides added, nodding. The deal was done and we shook hands. We selected the first three crates and the largest, plumpest goat. We then hitched a lift with some Aussies into Alex.

It was wonderful to push open those lovely weathered green doors to see Florence again. She was wearing a plain white cotton apron, there was flour all over her hands, and there was an appetising smell of baking that added to the usual aromas inside *Pension Crillon*.

"Just two?" she said, glancing at the door in case more emerged. I shook my head.

"Just us, and only one night, I'm afraid," I said. "We must leave early tomorrow, six o'clock." She nodded. We didn't tell her about Harry or Gidman, and she didn't ask. She made us tea and we tossed a coin for who was first in the bath, arguing in her kitchen to the point where she raised her hands: "Boys, boys! Please, there is no hurry, *calmez-vous!*" she said, shaking her head. Cundy was first in while I drank more tea with Madame as she then brought a glass of Lebanese Arak with a small jug of water. This was the aniseed liquor I tried before, like French Pernod, and just like before it burned my throat. Gabriel was away in Cairo, so she said, and his enormous presence was missed.

Almost an hour later Cundy bounded in, sweet-smelling, clean-shaven and looking like he was about to collect a medal on parade. Ten minutes later I plunged into a deep, luxuriant bath and my own goat smell dissolved as my head sank under the water.

We both had a haircut in one of the many barbershops before finding a restaurant overlooking the Eastern Harbour and eating enormous pieces of spicy fish that was the best I'd ever tasted. Afterwards, with boyish enthusiasm and our sharp new hair, we settled for the Carlton, where the same group of musicians were playing, and I noticed the barman who served us was the same. We were both conscious of our early start the next morning when the lorry to Aboukir would be outside at six o'clock, but it didn't change the pace of our drinking.

Our last call before bed was The Monseigneur. There were pilots from 94 and 112 Squadrons that Cundy knew and so for the last beers of the night I stood watching the band. Suddenly there was loud cheering and applause as Imshi Mason took to the stage with his saxophone and began blasting out some Glenn Miller. Dancing ensued with loud shrieks of delight from the women present, swirled around by men in various uniforms. Leaning at the bar, on my left shoulder a hand snaked its way around my right arm from behind, followed by a small, wet kiss on my right cheek.

"Copping," Ayesha said in my ear. "I knew it was you."

She hauled me up the steps and out into the street. The sea breeze was cool but in no way could anyone have described it as cold. I was flattered she remembered me, but more than that, she wanted to be with me. "Where have you been?" she said, and without waiting for a reply she added, "I looked for you every weekend, but you were never here." I felt oddly guilty about this, but at least I wasn't in the lamentable state I was in at our previous encounter.

We walked for less than five minutes before turning into a street called Borsa el Qadima, written in white letters on a blue background on the wall. It looked oddly familiar. She pushed open a small black door, dragged me inside and then up a narrow flight of stairs. She unlocked her door with a tiny key around her neck and I followed.

I sat in a very solid armchair that was threadbare in parts but was clearly well-loved and she put a kettle on a stove in the corner, lighting it with a match. A huge double bed dominated the tiny room and she reached around for a button and zip at the back of her neck, undoing them both before hauling the green cotton dress over her head in one, folding it neatly before laying it on the bed. "I hate it all," she said, removing her bra and pants before slipping a nightdress over her shoulders that was so thin as to be almost invisible. *What did she hate?* I thought, watching. I could smell tea just as she looked at me. "Sugar?" she said with one of her lovely smiles.

"Yes, I will, if you have it, thank you," I replied. I fumbled around for my Chesterfields and without thinking I lit two. She handed me a china mug of sweet black tea and, moving over to the bed, she cradled hers, sitting cross-legged facing me, taking a pull on her cigarette. Holding it briefly between her lips, she unfastened her hair and it tumbled around her shoulders, longer than I remembered.

"I want to fly, just like you," she said, shaking her hair before smiling, "far away from all this." I thought she was just thinking out loud but then I realised she was deadly serious. I wondered if I was missing something or whether I'd made a commitment I wasn't aware of. "I'm so glad to see you," she said, taking a sip of her tea. "I will always remember that night," she added, smiling. To my shame I could hardly remember any of it, but I did recall the bath and everything else the next morning. She had behaved like we were married, walking around naked and confident; that part I remembered well. I wondered why she did this, and why me, so I asked her. "Because I can, with you," she said, glancing into her tea, swilling it around as though reading the leaves.

"I knew it from the first time I saw you." I crushed the end of my cigarette into the tin ashtray with rather too much gusto. She noticed but just smiled. "Don't worry," she said, "I am your friend, Copping, your *girlfriend*," she said with emphasis. "You are safe with me."

47

We sat up and talked for half the night. She didn't ask about my combat duties or anything specific about the war and I didn't tell her; this was understood between us both. We spoke about Egypt, Madame Pericand, whom she apparently knew well, and some distant future when the war would be over and the world was peaceful again. "Do you think it will be finished in five years, or could it be ten years?" I didn't reply. She sensed reluctance on my part to even discuss it, so she quickly changed the subject. "You must come with me to Cairo," she said, rising from the bed and placing her mug in the small ceramic sink with a clunk before lighting a cigarette without offering me one. The dense clouds of blue-grey smoke lingered around her in the airless room as she exhaled, unmistakably French, probably a Gitanes or Galloises. This could be an attic room in a tall Parisian tenement, I could be a struggling English artist studying somewhere in the bleakest parts of the city, and she was my exotic, unpredictable French mistress that I spent occasional erratic weekends with. "It's where I'm from and where my parents are. I want to show it to you. Will you come, tomorrow?" She looked so pleading that I nodded, though god only knew when this might actually happen. She obviously thought I was on leave now. *I ought to tell her*, I thought, but I let her continue planning this trip of ours to Cairo and our grand tour of the pyramids. It was something I'd always meant to do anyway and now with Ayesha's prompting it was much more likely.

"Of course," I replied, "I'd love to."

"Tomorrow?" she said as she saw me looking down. She knew.

"I have to return in the morning." She rubbed her forehead with her right hand, clearly disappointed, as though I'd just cancelled her birthday party.

"I'm going to bed," she said suddenly. "Do you want to stay here, or are you going back to the Pericand's?"

"I have an early start, but I'll stay for a while, if that's okay?" She stubbed out her cigarette and placed the ashtray on the floor. She then pulled back the bedsheet and lay on the bed, legs together, arms outstretched, like Jesus on the cross. I took off my shirt and boots, leaving my shorts on and lay next to her on my back. I knew she was disappointed, perhaps even angry, but she moved up to me anyway and laid an arm over my chest.

It was five-thirty and still dark when I woke up. I hadn't moved and Ayesha's arm hadn't moved. I'd slept really well, with no nightmares. I wanted to stay forever in that room with her and never leave. Was this what married people had? I envied them if it was; this sense of belonging, of safety and security. But I knew I had to get back to the war, so I moved her arm and laid it by her side. My sense of duty was operating my limbs now; I was merely a string puppet moving around under orders from above, and without these strings I'd collapse back onto the bed in a heap with Ayesha and never get up again, but I couldn't miss the transport to Aboukir, so I dressed and left without speaking. As far as I knew she was still asleep. I noted that I had spent most of the night in number seven, Borsa el Qadima. My footsteps echoed around the empty streets as the first call to prayer began rousing the city, and just then I remembered it was Christmas morning.

Madame was in the kitchen. She made toast and marmalade with thick butter that melted over the sides of the bread, and hot tea with real milk. She never questioned where I'd been but just smiled, saying nothing. At ten minutes to six Cundy walked in, fully dressed. He winked at me as he sat at the table before feasting on Madame's toast. We were in a rush and so she kissed us both, hugging us tightly. She then walked us to the door and before I stepped outside, she whispered, "*Bon courage*," deep into my ear. The lorry arrived at exactly six o'clock and we trundled noisily to Aboukir as the sun rose over the white flat-topped buildings and palm trees lining the road.

At six-forty-five there was still no sign of Tim Murray or Agnides. We climbed aboard the Heinkel and began pre-flight checks, dreading the thought of returning empty-handed.

"You do know the CO will shoot us both with his own revolver, don't you, Copping?" Yes, I did.

"Perhaps we could fly over the wire and surrender? We'd probably receive better treatment," I suggested, only half-joking. We were just about to start the port engine when a lorry sped around the corner and thundered to a halt next to the Heinkel. Agnides jumped out and ran around the back. A minute later he emerged with a goat on a lead, like he was taking his dog for a walk.

"Keep the damned thing in a crate," Cundy shouted through the cockpit window. "What the hell is the man doing?" Agnides found the loading hatch underneath and launched the goat inside. I immediately heard it banging around, running the full length of the aeroplane and ramming into the sides, obviously frightened to death. The next minute three crates were loaded aboard and half a dozen sacks before I heard the cargo hatch slam shut. Agnides then gave us an exaggerated salute before jumping into his lorry. Tim was nowhere to be seen as he sped away out of sight.

"Did you pay him?" Cundy asked me.

"No, I thought you did," I replied. There was more banging from behind us.

"If that bloody thing sits on the control cables or chews them or something we're buggered," Cundy shouted. He was right. I unfastened and braced myself for the worst.

The port engine started wonderfully, as did the other, just as I entered the rear of the aeroplane. The three crates of turkeys were noisy, but at least they were contained. The goat, however, was charging around the cabin, obviously terrified.

It had a rope lead and collar, and so I reached out to grab hold of it. If only it was that easy. The damned thing ran past me, heading for the cockpit. We were short of time, so Cundy was busy pressing on with the take-off procedure.

Just as we began hurtling down the runway about to leave the ground, the goat ran amok in the Perspex nose of the Heinkel. To his credit, Cundy stayed calm and instead of chasing around after it I waited for it to emerge, which it duly did after only once jumping over Cundy's legs. I've never played rugby before, so this was the first time I'd ever performed a rugby tackle. With its back legs secure, it did the only natural thing it could do: it evacuated its bowels. I was doused in yellowy green liquid and foul-smelling, barely solid shit that blew out under high pressure as though the animal had a severe case of jippy tummy.

I hauled myself over the top of it and grabbed the rope, all the time the damned thing was kicking and writhing around, bleating and screeching. As I stood up, I felt the Delta Lily becoming airborne and I caught a glimpse of Aboukir disappearing beneath us. I dragged the goat to the back of the aeroplane and tethered it securely to the legs of a chair, well away from any control cables. My hands were covered in shit but then I realised I had piss dripping from my head onto my shirt front. I was now doing things entirely in reverse; I was returning from Alex stinking like an old goat.

One of the sacks had been ripped open by the goat and a dozen large cabbages were rolling around like bowling balls. The goat loved it, taking a quick munch on any that came near. I gathered them all up as best I could, anxious to return to the cockpit, but Cundy was doing fine when I returned to my seat. He laughed when he saw me, wafting his right hand in an effort to drive away the smell. I found an oily rag with which to wipe my hands and collected most of the shit from my uniform. We then remembered we'd forgotten to pre-warn Army Intel we were coming, so we flew down to five hundred feet and tried to avoid any known landing grounds en route. Luckily we later found out the CO had already contacted intel to ensure our safe arrival with great expectations of meat for Christmas dinner.

Passing from Bir Hacheim to Msus over seventy-five miles of open desert was tricky, as we'd followed a track from Mechili on the trip in. We saw nothing below us and it was a huge relief to see the coast and eventually Msus, thirty miles from the sea. We landed without a problem a little late at almost nine-thirty and were immediately surrounded by the cooks who carried away the turkeys. Cundy shut down the aeroplane and we were about to return to dispersal when I remembered the bloody goat. Cundy flatly refused to have anything to do with it, so I climbed back aboard and grabbed hold of the thing again. I had to hug it to my chest to get it out the aeroplane so it didn't injure itself jumping out, and then walking with it on the rope lead I felt particularly absurd, but the poor thing hopped along, happily unaware of what was to come.

48

THE COOKHOUSE TENT WAS LOUD WITH TURKEYS screeching their final moments until the last one was despatched. A gang of erks willingly assisted in plucking the feathers which, after some initial tuition, continued at a great pace until they were soon ready for the pot. I washed my hair and left my shirt in the *dhobi* to soak and was sitting in the mess when one of the cooks appeared holding a very large knife. It was still dripping blood and when he saw me, he took hold of the blade, offering me the handle.

"What's this for?" I asked, slightly bemused, taking it from him.

"It's for the goat," he replied. I looked outside. I'd not seen it for half an hour and assumed it had already been despatched. "We're very busy with the turkeys and so we wondered if you'd do the honours, Flight." I was horrified. I'd never killed an animal before and wouldn't know how. He could see my obvious reticence. "You just grab it by the head and slit its throat under the chin, like this," he said, drawing his left hand across his Adam's apple. "We're going to roast it; we've got the fire ready, only we need it for the gravy. We'll gut it and trim it, but it just needs despatching." I looked around, speechless. Saunders was nearest to me and he grabbed the knife.

"Here, I'll do it," he said as he stomped out the mess with me and a few others in close pursuit. It was tethered to a guy line at the back of the mess tent, munching on something obviously very tasty. It seemed someone had given it some cabbage leaves and potato peelings. Saunders stepped forward, talking to it. "There there…" he said. "This won't hurt," he said, crouching down next to it. To my astonishment he started stroking it as though it was his Labrador. "Right," he said, standing up, ten seconds later. "Not really my cup of tea." We looked at him and one another. "Anyone else want to do it?" he asked, holding the knife at arm's length. No-one spoke. The goat stood there victorious over a half a dozen veteran RAF fighter pilots.

We all dispersed back to the mess. Five minutes later the CO emerged from his office. He had a Webley revolver in his right hand and was dropping cartridges into the chamber before clicking it shut with a sullen stare. He'd obviously found out and was chuntering to himself as he passed us.

"I'll do the bloody thing," he said as he walked up to the goat. "I've done plenty of game shooting in my time, leave this to me." Most of the mess had turned out and were standing behind him. He took aim and pulled back the hammer. Nothing happened. There were a few murmurings. The goat looked at him and carried on eating. "Not used to things standing still," he said, "and it's too dangerous to let one off so close to the mess like this. Can someone untie it for me?" Tom Hindle reached forward and unfastened the rope. The goat began strolling away towards the runway. "That's more like it," the CO said, and as the goat was less than ten yards away, he pulled the trigger and missed.

Now the goat was wise to it, he ran headlong into the desert at high gallop and it seemed certain that we were going to lose our gravy. *Bang!* Another shot rang out, followed by another, and then another. The goat was weaving around as though he had read our tactical manuals, dodging every one of the .455-inch bullets, until the last one, which struck him somewhere in the chest area and he dropped with a thump in a cloud of dust. His legs quivered for a moment and then he was still. There was a huge round of applause. I expected a bow from the CO, but he just turned and walked back to his office with the Webley still in his right hand.

We had turkey, cabbages, cauliflower, carrots, potatoes, peas, some rather odd stuffing, smothered in wonderful meaty gravy, all washed down with plenty of very nice Chianti. As is RAF tradition, the officers served the rest of us before they too sat down and ate. It really was quite wonderful. Thankfully the Hun must have been sitting down to Christmas dinner too, because we didn't hear a sound from him all day. In fact, we were fairly quiet for a few days after that as news kept coming in of our ground forces pushing further west. We celebrated the New Year in high spirits; it seemed Rommel had given up and at this rate we'd all be in Tunis by Easter.

We were back at work on 28th December when we were involved in ground strafing Hun MT wherever the army could find it for us. Sergeant Dave McKay took a hit from ground fire and we saw him put his badly smoking Hurricane down safely in the desert dangerously close to enemy positions. Barney saw what happened and shouted up over the R/T straightaway: "Can you chaps cover me for ten minutes while I make a collection." He dropped down and made a slow pass over the patch of flat ground where McKay's stricken Hurricane was parked. McKay was standing next to it, waving and no doubt contemplating captivity. But we knew immediately what the CO was intending to do as we circled overhead just in case. He couldn't order anyone else to do it, so he would have to do it himself.

He lowered his flaps and undercarriage, and landed as close as he could to McKay's aeroplane. Even at a hundred feet you cannot be sure of the surface and he took a huge risk of pranging his own aeroplane and getting put in the bag along with McKay. Before he climbed into the CO's Hurricane, McKay set fire to his own and the CO took off with both of them aboard. The cockpit of a Hurricane is barely big enough for one, and so the trip back must have been tricky to say the least, but they managed it. The CO received a rapturous welcome with several rounds of 'For He's a Jolly Good Fellow' and was given free drinks in the mess all night.

At the beginning of January, we took part in top cover for Blenheims bombing targets at Agedabia more than fifty miles south of Benghazi.

The Blenheims were led by Squadron Leader 'Buck' Buchanan, whose fearlessness was legendary. He flew his aeroplanes into dense flak at six thousand feet in order to make sure the target was hit, instead of sweeping in low and getting out quick. We did this with them several times and we'd always hang back from the target because the flak was so thick. Each time at least a couple of Blenheims were hit, but Buck refused to change tactics because he knew his men would follow him everywhere.

He was noted for his charm and it was rumoured he was holding a female American reporter hostage in his tent, but no-one I knew had actually seen her. My flight commander on these ops was Pedro's replacement Flying Officer Dave Bradley, and he proved to be an excellent pilot and leader, and we didn't lose a single aeroplane. After the third such op, Bradley bought me several beers at our wonderful Messerschmitt bar that we'd brought with us and I found him to be a lovely man. When he realised I was sharing a tent with half a dozen others, he offered to put me up in his, saying, "It seems such a shame you are crammed in when I have a tent to myself." I declined his offer, not just on grounds of superstition, even though I was tempted.

There were wells of fresh water at Msus and so it was wonderful to have such huge quantities at our disposal. We filled oil drums and submerged ourselves in it and washed all our kit while throwing water around at one another like kids on a hot summer's day in England.

I don't know whether it was this water or not, but Ron Cundy was taken ill and left us in the back of an army lorry, poor sod. Doc Craib said it was a nasty case of pleurisy and he was gone for nearly three weeks. We were all disappointed because he was our main Delta Lily pilot. I didn't feel confident enough to fly it alone, and neither did anyone else at the time, and so in the second week of January 1942 when we moved to Benina just a few miles east of Benghazi we had to leave it at Msus.

The LG at Benina, like most in the area, was mainly an Italian airfield also used by the Hun and the sappers were busy clearing booby traps that were all over the place. We were getting wise to them, but they kept trying sneakier ways to kill or injure us. A sapper lost three fingers when a fountain pen blew up in his hands and so now everything became suspect. We decided to avoid anything they had left behind; it was just too risky. Quite by chance and to our amazement, a NAAFI canteen wagon appeared the same day we arrived stocked full of goodies; that was compensation for losing the Delta Lily. They were incredible people and were a very welcome sight.

By now the front line was somewhere near El Agheila in the Gulf of Sidra, and we were unaware of what Rommel had planned for us and just how fragile this front line would be. The second week of January was marked by several huge *khamsin* that lasted for days at a time but at least they were keeping the Hun on the ground too. In the third week of January we moved to a landing ground at Berka on the coast just south of Benghazi, and we didn't know it at the time, but this would be our last significant move forward because from then on it was only back.

49

WE WERE CLOSE TO THE SEA AND IT WAS MUCH greener, with a near-constant breeze, making a welcome change from the desert. There were dozens of wrecked Italian aeroplanes at Berka, deliberately torched by their owners in retreat. Sadly we would soon find out what this was like.

On 17th January Cundy returned, and to our delight he touched down in our old friend the Delta Lily, with three new pilots aboard. He'd returned to Msus in an Anson and found the Heinkel still airworthy, so the Anson was sent home. Sadly they found us in a terrible state, bordering on panic. Army Intel informed us that Rommel had broken through at El Agheila and was rapidly heading this way. Half the squadron was immediately told to leave and as yet no-one knew where, provided it was east. We packed quickly and loaded the lorries and half our Hurricanes took off. The CO called a meeting of everyone remaining, which was most of the erks and pilots. It was mid-afternoon and we could hear artillery in the south-west that made everyone a little twitchy because it was so bloody close. We stood, as a fairly large untidy crowd in front of the CO as he addressed us in reverential silence.

"I need a few volunteers to stay behind for as long as possible to destroy some aeroplanes and make sure the serviceable ones can get away. You'll then be able to get in a couple of lorries and make a run for it. I know I'm asking a lot, it'll no doubt be pretty hairy and there's a risk you'll get put in the bag, but I wouldn't ask if it wasn't absolutely necessary." Just then a shell exploded only half a mile away, and we all knew it wasn't one of ours. "Will any volunteers please take a step forward now." Without any prompting and as though it was all well-rehearsed, every single one of us stepped forward.

I could see the CO was moved. "For Christ's sake, I only need twenty men!" he shouted, as we all laughed. "Flight sergeants, pick who you need and the rest of you, will you kindly bugger off!"

Warrant Officer Rixon, Flight Sergeant Bill Cartwright, and Aircraftsmen Gough, Davrell, Cable, Patton, Scully and Best were among a handful of erks that I knew who stayed behind. I strapped on my parachute and stood clutching my little sack of possessions with all the other pilots at dispersal, wondering what to do like new boys at school. Where were we going to go? It was decided we'd head to LG141 near Gasr el Arid. I'd never heard of it and I was shocked when I saw on my map just how far away it was and so close to Tobruk. There was an obvious risk involved in falling back to Msus or Mechili, in case Rommel crossed the desert and cut us off, so a fall back of over two hundred miles was ignominious but probably very wise. We wished everyone luck and strapped in. The Delta Lily was crammed with whatever it could safely carry and was escorted east across the desert.

LG141 at Gasr el Arid had long been abandoned by everyone, which meant it was reasonably safe from fresh booby traps, but we still had to begin again with slit trenches and latrines and so on. The sappers had a slightly easier job, but we had to join in with some of the heavy work. There was a cool breeze which helped and occasional showers which were welcome. Most of the erks made it safely to LG141, but some were still missing.

Flight Sergeant Bill Cartwright and a cargo of airmen in a three-ton lorry were the last to get through before the Hun cut the road. Somewhere along the line, Cartwright picked up a lively Collie dog which he named 'Blitz', immediately enriching the lives of everyone at 260 from then on.

At the end of January, our flying capabilities were again greatly reduced by poor weather, but this time it was strong winds and heavy rain. With this in mind, on the 31st, the CO organised a huge party in the mess for everyone, including the erks, and we all had a wonderful time. He knew the conditions that prevented us from flying also stopped the Hun and so he very cleverly used this to cheer everyone up. In the beginning of February, there was an unusually cold wind and we conducted as many ground attack duties against the Hun as we could, but it didn't seem to make any difference to the pace of his advance. The 109s were always ready for us and we were very lucky not to lose anyone. Our LGs were constantly strafed, either by 109s or Ju88s, and so talk of us having parity in numbers was hard to believe. The constant shifting of LGs made it difficult to maintain full strength but all our erks worked supremely hard to keep us airborne. Our latest new pilots, Sergeants Bob Wilmott, Lionel 'Shep' Sheppard and Flight Lieutenant Kenneth 'Hawkeye' Lee were very keen, the latter a very experienced flight commander from 112 Squadron.

We all wanted to keep up the pressure on the Hun and stop his advance, but then at the end of the first week of February, we were sent away in small groups to LG101 and 115 south-east of Mersa Matruh for 'type conversion', which is flying terminology for learning how to fly another aeroplane. Amongst everything that was going on, we were abstracted from the front line for three weeks to learn how to fly the Curtiss P40 Tomahawk. The timing really couldn't have been worse. We were happy with our Hurricanes and were very familiar with them. I'd been flying the same machine for weeks now and I knew it back to front, but we were told of the increased speed, firepower and manoeuvrability of the P40, and so we went along with it. Besides, 112 Squadron seemed successful with theirs. But I couldn't help thinking the Hun was very happy in his 109E and his new 109F, and had been flying the same aeroplane type since before the war and he knew it incredibly well. Those who don't fly don't realise that total familiarity with an aeroplane makes the flying instinctive and a split second spent hesitating while looking down in the cockpit was enough to get you killed.

The Tomahawk is a formidable beast close up. At three tons fully loaded and with an almost all-metal skin, it's bigger and heavier than the Hurricane. At the start of my first day at LG101, we were assembled in the mess for a briefing on the new aeroplane. There were some smiling faces among the instructors, but these were outnumbered by frowns and shaking of heads. We were each handed a copy of the Pilot's Operating Manual and several instructors stood at the front to reveal their experiences of flying it. There was praise for it, but some words of warning: 'No spins' and 'it has a tendency to yaw hard to port when throttle is applied, so use the rudder and trim levers'.

They also said 'watch the narrow undercart when taxiing,'

but on the plus side 'it does have a steerable tailwheel'. At least there was some consolation. I wondered what sort of aeroplane it was that didn't like spins. I found this very odd.

We were sent away with orders to study the manual, and I noticed in the pages about handling, 'NO SPINS' was written in capital letters. The next morning, we faced a written test of fifty questions about the aeroplane, like a formal exam. I knew I wouldn't do well; I can't remember cold facts, but some of the more technical questions I remembered, like those about the radio and electrical systems, which seemed far more extensive than the Hurricane. I don't know how many I got right; they never told me. I kept on reading the manual whenever I could, as we all did, but I needed to fly it to get a better understanding. I first sat in the huge cockpit of a Tomahawk on 9th February 1942. Even though it clearly wasn't brand new, it smelled of fresh grease and leather.

An instructor stood on the wing next to me and went through the controls.

"Watch it on start-up; keep an eye on the temperature and pressure gauges, and the mags as normal. When you taxi, you'll find it alright because of the tailwheel, but you can't see forward, obviously. Once it's off the ground, use plenty of rudder. Engine torque pulls the left wing down, so keep it level with plenty of right stick and keep it trimmed. Glide speed is around 100 mph, approach 105 mph. No flaps over 140. Don't forget the rudder trim one and a half turns to the right for take-off. Take it up for a circuit then bring it back here, alright?" I nodded in reply and began the start-up procedure as the instructor jumped down and walked towards the dispersal. I had the checklist in front of me, and I worked through it systematically:

Flaps neutral, gear handle neutral, rudder trim two and a half degrees right, elevators trimmed for take-off, mixture set at idle cut-off, throttle one inch open. Fuel set to fuselage tanks. Carburettor air set at full cold. Battery switches on. Generator switches on. Fuel pump on. Three right-hand circuit breakers on, and gun switches off. I primed the engine with three strokes. Fuel pump off, so as not to flood the engine on starting. Ignition switch to both, then starter engaged. The propeller turned several times before the V12 Allison burst into life with masses of smoke and flames briefly shooting from the exhausts.

50

With my left hand already on the throttle, I set it back to 800 rpm, and I noticed the fuel pressure was perfect at sixteen pounds per square inch, just as it should be so I moved the mixture control to auto and set the throttle at 1,200 rpm, and then turned the fuel pump back on. The oil pressure was good, and I ran the engine up to 2,300 rpm and checked both magnetos. Everything seemed fine, with all electric switches rather than hydraulic as in the Hurricane. Fuel pressure was stable at fifteen pounds, as I ran through the checks again. Elevator trim rechecked at take-off position, and ailerons at neutral. I lined up at the end of the runway, pulled the canopy closed and locked it before gently applying full throttle.

Acceleration was swift, but the pull down on the left wing was startling, even with all that rudder trim, and I had to hold the stick firmly just to keep it level. This was a huge shock and felt like someone was sitting on the end of the wing.

I climbed up quickly to circuit height and turned to port before levelling out and throttling back. Re-trimming was then essential as it now yawed to the right. The trim wheel is next to the left hand and is a horizontal wheel six inches across, so thankfully it's not hard to reach. I raised the undercarriage and then lowered it again, observing the instruments as I conducted the downwind checks. I deliberately gave myself plenty of room to turn in on final approach, at least a mile away from the airfield. I needed every moment to familiarise myself with the landing procedure. I lowered half the flaps and then full flap at five hundred feet, and they came down so quickly it caught me by surprise. With the throttle only open an inch by this time, I crossed the threshold at 115 mph. At the round out, ten feet above the ground, I closed the throttle completely and the main wheels touched, followed by the tailwheel. I knew I'd come in a little too high and too fast, but rather that than too slow and stall it. I wasn't taking any chances. I'd touched down a third of the way down the runway and braked fairly hard to stop myself overshooting and noticed how powerful the brakes were.

I taxied over to dispersal and an erk gave me the thumbs up. I opened the canopy and as I came to a stop the instructor jumped onto the wing.

"How was it?" he shouted, the engine still running.

"Fine," I shouted.

"Good," he said, "then go up and do some more." So I did three more circuits before pulling over and shutting it down. Compared to the Hurricane, there was probably twice or three times as much to do in the cockpit. Along with the pronounced yaw to the left, this would take some getting used to. Sadly with what was happening at the front line I wondered how we'd be able to do this.

The Tomahawk was obviously the only subject of

conversation in the mess that night. There were a lot of mixed emotions about it, some very positive, but others downright hostile, with some of the chaps saying they would rather fly the Hurricane, even if it was an older machine. They may not be given the choice. With this in mind, like many of the chaps I decided to make the most of it. I didn't dislike the new aeroplane, it had some great features, but we'd only flown it in the circuit so far and had not really seen what it could do. This would come later. First impressions were common to us all, that it was labour-intensive in the cockpit, with too much trim needed when varying the power. I could only imagine all this happening with a well-flown 109 on your tail; taking your left hand off the throttle to use the trim wheel would be the last thing you needed.

I was willing to give it a chance and after another day of circuits and bumps we were allowed an hour's free time with the aeroplane for general handling tests. I didn't hesitate and took it straight up to five thousand feet for some real flying.

I started with some steep turns, sixty-degree bank, and I was pleasantly surprised at how manoeuvrable it was, more so than the Hurricane, in my opinion, so this was a good sign. I worked my way up to some more robust aerobatics and I found rolls were faster and it was more responsive than anything I'd yet flown. My biggest shock was when I came out of my first loop, when the Tomahawk started falling like a rocket-propelled brick. Within seconds the ASI stated I was doing over 400 mph. This was quite exceptional and it stuck in my mind from that very first moment. I would later use it to my advantage frequently in combat. I know the VNE speed was supposedly an impressive 480 mph, and I must have come pretty close to that. Stalls were gentle and predictable, both clean and with gear and flaps down, and I resisted the temptation to try a spin; we had been warned countless times not to, and I remembered the bold lettering in the manual. We all found it really odd that a fighter aeroplane was not safe in a spin. I can't say this didn't worry me, as it did a lot of the chaps. You could put a Tiger Moth, a Harvard and even a Hurricane into a spin all day long and recovery would be no problem. It was obviously connected to the fact it gained speed so very rapidly in a dive.

Before I finished I climbed up to ten thousand feet, just because I could, and took a long look around. From up there the world was simply blue at the top and a brownie-yellow at the bottom. I throttled back and pulled the canopy open to take in the breeze. It was still warm, even up there. I flew a few more steep turns and spotted a tiny wisp of cloud, so I dived through it, cutting it in half. I then throttled back for a cruise descent to the airfield.

We repeated the exercises we had done in the Hurricane: formation flying, ground attack practise with lots of low flying and chasing each other around the sky in practise dog fights. It was a lot of fun to be flying again while not being shot at and I was getting used to moving that damned trim wheel every few seconds when in practise combat situations. If you didn't, then you'd need both your knees to help keep the stick hard over and the wings level. This and the fact that spins were forbidden caused a great deal of consternation.

A lot of pilots submitted formal applications to come off the Tomahawk. I admit I wasn't entirely happy with it; there was just something about it. I'd seen a lot of Fleet Air Arm aeroplanes based around Alex and so that same afternoon, along with several others, I submitted a report for a transfer, without telling anyone from 260.

While we were playing around with the Tomahawks on 10th February, we heard that Rommel had reached Tmimi, only fifty miles west of Tobruk. This didn't cause too much alarm, as he'd been stopped near there before, but again we wondered about the wisdom in sending us away at such a time. A few days before we were due to return to ops, another aeroplane arrived at LG101. I thought it was a Tomahawk until I noticed the guns were missing from the nose and the air intake underneath was huge.

It was a Kittyhawk Mk I and it had a formidable array of six .5-inch guns, three in each wing. We were all offered the chance to take it up, so we drew lots and watched one another in turn.

I took it up to five thousand feet and found it a little better than the Tomahawk, but it was still a P40, and I missed the simplicity of the Hurricane. The next day other Tomahawks arrived and we were told that some of us would not be returning to ops in our Hurricanes but in Tomahawks. The P40 was a more modern aeroplane and so we were generally pleased with this, but to be honest the performance wasn't much better than the Hurricane and we seriously wondered why there were no Spitfires in the desert. Surely with the threat of imminent invasion in England now receding, they could send some over to us? We were told we now had superior numbers to the Hun and a superior aeroplane, but we didn't believe either of these claims.

I climbed into a Tomahawk IIb and started her up. There was an overwhelming smell of new leather and fuel mixed with gun oil and there was not a scratch on any of the controls. Bradley led us back to LG141 on Friday 20th February and yet again on our right we could see the ominous sight of Tobruk burning. The CO looked drawn when he welcomed us back and only an hour after landing we understood why when a pair of 109s appeared, sweeping over at ground level, the unmistakeable dull thump of the nose cannons blasting one of our new aeroplanes to pieces. Most of us didn't even have time to find a slit trench. Half the squadron was away, which was a blessing, and they only made one pass before disappearing. The CO informed us this was now the usual pattern of life at a forward LG. That night we were bombed from some height, probably by Ju88s, but only minor damage was caused to the runway. The 109s strafed us again before breakfast in another single high-speed pass damaging a few vehicles but missing our aeroplanes. The Hun clearly knew exactly where we were and was keen to keep us awake. Probably with this in mind, the next day we moved to LG109 near Gambut, most of the move conducted in one night. For a few days after that he left us alone and it gave us chance to settle in.

51

WE WERE NOW BECOMING ACCUSTOMED TO MOVING house and wherever we went we replicated everything just as it was before. In our tent Carlisle and Saunders were at the back, with me and Wareham further down towards the middle, then Wrigley and Morley near the door. I knew who snored the loudest and whose farts stank the most, usually after a lot of beer. They said I snored too, but how was I to know? We each had either a wooden crate or a metal ammo box for personal possessions and we'd lean on these to write letters. There were candles in the bottom of four petrol tins in our tent which the avid readers such as Saunders and Wareham used to keep near them, but their late-night reading was becoming less frequent. It was interesting to witness the different morning rituals some men had; sitting on the bed for ten minutes staring at the ground before moving, or springing out of bed full of energy, or rolling onto the floor and crawling out the door half-asleep, usually after a heavy night in the mess. It was always possible to tell when we'd all had a bath or a spot of leave because for a few days afterwards the tent didn't stink like a barn full of old goats. We'd rarely discuss any of our ops, other than to perhaps acknowledge the varying levels of twitch we encountered, but even then it wasn't in great detail. Nobody bragged about what they did, or what they thought they did, we just didn't talk about it.

My first op in a Tomahawk was the following Sunday when eight of us conducted fighter sweeps across the front line, which was now fairly static again from Gazala down to Bir Hacheim. We saw a group of 109s ahead of us but instead of engaging they flew west back across their lines, and we didn't pursue them. That night in the mess some semblance of normality returned when Harry Curno entertained us on the piano, in-between Sticky treating us to the use of his gramophone. The CO allowed us to finish off the Chianti, and the whiskey also came out, a little too much. Three days later, just before midnight, the ground shook to the sound of several 125 kg bombs exploding nearby, typical Ju88 stuff, so we all rolled out of our tents into the slit trenches. We could tell the bombs were wildly off target but stayed in cover anyway. Just as silence was returning, I heard Stan Bernier shouting and thought he'd been hit. It was pitch black, so I had no idea where he was and after a few seconds the shouting stopped. We drifted back to our tents and no-one mentioned anything about Bernier, so we all went back to sleep.

Just before breakfast I caught up with him at the thunder box and he said he was okay, he wasn't hit, but he wouldn't discuss the night's events at all. Bernier and Cundy were then seen going into the CO's office and the door was shut behind them. When they came out, they wouldn't say what was going on, but then at about four o'clock that afternoon Flying Officer Bradley climbed aboard a Lysander with all his kit and was never seen again. The CO never mentioned Bradley and so that night in the mess I again asked Bernier if he was okay and what had happened in the night. He refused to say anything and avoided me, so later on when I bumped into Cundy at the thunder box I asked him about it. There was no moonlight and so it was pitch dark as we sat facing the desert.

"I suppose now it's over it doesn't matter, but the CO did tell us to keep mum about it," he said in a half-whisper.

"About what?" I said.

"Bradley's gone," he said, which I knew. It wasn't unusual for pilots to be reassigned at short notice, so I wondered why this had anything to do with Bernier calling out in the dark. He obviously couldn't see the confusion on my face but told me anyway. "He surprised Bernier last night, during the raid. Did you hear him shouting?"

"Yes, I did. I thought he'd been hit or something," I replied.

"No, but he was just as shocked," he said.

"Why?"

"Keep this under your hat, but he put the hard word on Bernier last night in the slit trench," he said, leaning forward. "Do you have any newspaper there?" I passed him some, which he then tore into strips to finish what he was doing.

"Bloody hell," I said, sounding shocked.

"Yes, quite, just what I thought when Bernier told me. I couldn't believe it. We were up half the night wondering what to do about it. But you'll never guess, when we told the CO he said he wasn't surprised. Would you believe that? I had no idea, did you? Such a shame too, he was a really nice chap, wasn't he?"

300

"Yes, he was," I replied, still sounding surprised.

"You just never know, do you?" Cundy said, finished and now pulling up his trousers. "He's been sent to Cairo to some office job somewhere. Such a shame. Now we're a bloody pilot short." With that, he fastened his shorts and disappeared into the dark.

On the afternoon of 25th February, the weather was reasonably pleasant, with no breeze of any kind, but it wasn't baking hot either, rather like a decent English summer's day. The white flag on the side of the CO's office hung limply, indicating not just zero wind but a relatively calm one hour's readiness. Barney loved Derek Walker's flag system, so he continued it with enthusiasm. Cartwright's dog Blitz was asleep at my feet as I was relaxing in the mess when Tregear and Cundy brought in the mail. Like most of us I was still wearing my flying gear and in eye contact with my aeroplane a hundred yards away, with my parachute dangling from the end of the nearest wing. They opened the mail sack and began sorting through the contents, shouting out names. Cundy passed me a letter from Aunt Margaret that when I opened it discovered that it contained a Christmas card. She'd clearly forgotten to allow at least six weeks' travelling time. "You know Imshi Mason, don't you, Copping?" Cundy said, still sorting the mail while looking curiously pleased with himself as though he was about to reveal some great news.

"I wouldn't say that. I've seen him playing in Alex, as you know, why?" I said, placing my Christmas card on the table before resuming my *Picture Post*.

"He's missing," he said. "I found out from Vanderkamp this morning."

"He'll turn up," Tregear said, leaning in. "He's been shot down before, hasn't he?"

"Yes, he's probably in the Monseigneur right now, practising on his bloody saxophone," I said, not giving it another thought.

"That's what I said," Cundy replied. "He's had so many scrapes and always come out on top. Did you know he used to drop handwritten notes in beer bottles on the Italians telling them to come up and fight?"

"No, I didn't," I said, "but it doesn't surprise me one bit."

"If the Jerries have him, they'll need a saxophone or he'll drive them mad," Tregear said.

"He'll drive them mad if they let him have one, that's for sure," I said, to which the three of us laughed. I lit a cigarette and carried on reading. There was no further discussion of Imshi Mason. We all knew we'd see him again, either at five thousand feet leading 112 Squadron or on the stage in a smoky Alex nightclub. He'd been featured in the press several times wearing his trademark white flying suit and goatee beard, and was a hero not just to us but to a lot of people back in Blighty. He was therefore quite indestructible.

In March the weather was hot again. It hadn't changed suddenly, but you realised that shorts were more comfortable and the battle dress top was too much. Some chaps continued wearing long trousers in case of fire in the cockpit, which was very wise, but most of us were willing to take the risk. In the first weeks of March, the Gazala-Bir Hacheim line was holding well and we dared to think we might start pushing Rommel back yet again. We hadn't lost anyone else in 260 and reports from the front line were good. We were getting more used to the Tomahawk, but the yaw to the left was still something that frightened me. What if I forgot about it or was distracted the next time a 109 was on my tail? I was now quite good at using the trim wheel quickly with my left hand at every adjustment of power, but it was a second in combat that was a potentially lethal waste of time.

On 2nd March, four living skeletons appeared at LG109. At first we had no idea who they were; standing there like dead men at dispersal early that morning as Blitz was going mad, barking and growling, frightening the life out of them. It wasn't until one of them spoke that we realised who it was.

52

THE GROUND CREW WE'D LEFT BEHIND AT BENINA who hadn't made it back were assumed to have been put in the bag or lost in the desert, so when three of them turned up having walked over two hundred miles we couldn't believe it. Warrant Officer Rixon was with Aircraftsmen Cable and Scully who all collapsed with relief when they saw us. Doc Craib ran up and was helped to carry them into his tent and for several days all he was seen doing was feeding and watering them like starving stray animals. Eventually Rixon managed to join us in the mess to tell of his amazing story. They'd walked by night, navigating by the stars and hiding from the sun and enemy patrols by day, heading due east all the time. They were going to call in at Mechili until they saw the Hun had retaken it, realising they then had another week of walking still to do, on very little water and a handful of dry biscuits. When they finally reached the wire in a desperate condition and virtually dying of thirst, they bumped into a team of Gurkhas who fed and watered them in exchange for helping them fight their way back to our own lines. Once through, the Gurkhas left them, having told them where we were and precisely which direction to head off in. Of the twenty or so volunteers that we left behind at Benina, apart from Cartwright's lorry these three were the only ones who made it back.

If I could pinpoint the start of when everything began crashing around us in 260, it was Friday 20th March. Harry Curno ran into the mess just after breakfast and began bashing out 'The Red Flag', prompting the rest of us to run for our aeroplanes. Twelve of us were sent to provide top cover for Bostons attacking the Hun at Martuba where the flak was really bad, and a dozen 109s bounced us just after the Bostons left the target area. They came for us in a determined fashion and we confirmed to our sorrow that the Tomahawk was no match for the new 109F as they gave us a serious mauling, creating plenty of twitch on our part. I fired a few hopeful deflection shots at them but for the most part we were on the defensive. The airframe rattled like an old train with the two .5-inch guns in the nose and four .303 guns in the wings and we learned not to follow close behind another Tomahawk when they were firing because the spent cases from the .5-inch guns spewed out underneath in huge numbers and at four inches long they were a real health hazard. I saw Tregear's Tomahawk take a nasty hit to the engine, causing smoke to start puthering out and then the same thing happened to Alexander, probably from the same 109. Both went down and I didn't see either of them bail out, but I couldn't hang around to check, even for a moment. We were dogfighting for our lives for ten minutes until quite suddenly the sky was empty and the 109s had gone. The CO shouted up for us to return home and I was utterly exhausted and soaked through with sweat as I touched down at our LG.

Hindle and Wareham's planes were so badly damaged I was surprised they'd made it back, thankfully unhurt. There were huge holes from cannon shells in their wings and fuselage and if nothing else the Tomahawk could take a lot of punishment.

Our new pilot, Sergeant Wilmott, claimed a 109 on his first op, but that night Sergeants Frank Tregear and Bob Alexander were formally listed as missing. You might think this would be the main topic of conversation, but it wasn't. Nobody spoke about Tregear and Alexander, at all. It wasn't disbelief; it was deliberate disregard, even though we knew them well and they were our friends, we had to assume they were gone, and there was nothing we could do about it.

I'm not sure whether Doc Craib enjoyed his unofficial role as squadron trick cyclist, but it was something that circumstances had forced upon him. The fact that we hid the word 'psychiatrist' in a circus euphemism was an indication of how seriously we took it, but the reality was that however he'd acquired it, the role kept him very busy. He was firstly our MO, medical officer, dealing with anything from prickly heat and jippy tummy to serious wounds, but his role had evolved over time into quite a few other things. I told him a little about Ayesha, one of very few people I'd confided in about her, but none with the truth, mainly because he asked me directly one night while sitting close in the mess, not long after Bradley had made his ignominious departure. He just came straight out with it. "Do you have a woman, Copping?" he said in a furtive whisper and with a sullen stare, searching my face for a reaction. I wondered at first if he was testing me, or even putting the hard word on me, and so I had no choice but to tell him, though of course I didn't dare mention the true nature of our relationship; I just let him make assumptions. Maybe this was prompted by seeing how Bradley and I had been getting on so well, but then he was a lovely chap and everyone else liked him too. He nodded anyway, adding, "Yes, fine, okay," before looking around and offering to fetch me a beer, which Bradley did, very often.

When he came back, he sat close again and after the first sip he said to me, "I have a secret that I'm going to tell you, but you mustn't say a word to anyone else." I was shocked. He was definitely putting the hard word on me now. I was immediately suspicious and on my guard, gripping my beer in both hands so firmly between my legs I could have been landing a Tomahawk in a gusting crosswind. He edged closer and now almost in a whisper, he began speaking. "Imshi Mason is dead. The CO told me an hour ago. It's going in the press tomorrow. His squadron were caught up in a dreadful scrap in their new Kittyhawks and lost four aircraft." He leaned back in his chair, taking another sip of beer. I shook my head a little before he continued, "I thought I'd tell you because you're different, I know you can take it, but the chaps don't need to know yet, eh?" I wasn't sure whether I should be flattered or not. I was relieved he wasn't putting the hard word on me anyway. He stood up and before moving away he just said, "Keep it under your hat for now, Copping," and left the mess just as Harry Curno started pulling the blankets off the piano. He began playing softly at first, slowly and quietly until several of us gathered around and began singing. It didn't matter what, or whether we were in tune, we just wanted to sing.

The next morning Harry Curno was busy at the thunder box when Barney put the red flag up, so no-one noticed. He had to revert to going around shouting in the mess.

We were sent up to keep watch for a gaggle of 109s seen heading our way, but by the time we arrived over the rendezvous point with 112 Squadron in their shark-nosed Kittyhawks, they'd gone, if they'd been there at all. This happened again in the afternoon and I began to wonder if the Hun were now doing to us what we did to them some months ago before and during Op Crusader, keeping us up and awake, and very tired. We never gave them any peace as they retreated, and so now it was our turn to understand what this felt like.

On 22nd March a lorry-load of battle-weary New Zealanders heading east pulled up at LG109, demanding payment for being used as a taxi service. We wondered what on earth they were talking about until Frank Tregear and Bob Alexander jumped out the back of their lorry, fit and well, as though they'd just returned from leave. Frank walked up to me and said in his broad Aussie drawl, "Get the bloody kettle on, mate, my throat's as dry as a dingo's backside." Men are not supposed to show emotion, at least not publicly, but we were all very obviously relieved to see them, particularly the CO. Frank had successfully crash-landed at Gazala on our side of the wire, and Alexander managed the same at Tobruk. They'd both hitched various lifts until the last stage when they were reunited quite by chance in the Kiwi's lorry.

That night in the mess the CO gathered everyone around for a special presentation to our two returning pilots. We'd heard what this might be and when we found out we were delighted. Since June 1941, Desert Air Force pilots had started a great tradition which quickly spread to every squadron. We all stood in reverential silence as Tregear and Alexander were presented with certificates of membership of the Late Arrivals Club, along with their silver pin badges, a winged flying boot.

"I had these brought to me from the silversmith in Cairo for Harry Bandinell, and then Gidman, but now at last I've put them to good use, so congratulations, chaps," the CO said, shaking their hands in turn. There was a tumultuous round of applause and great cheering. I handed Frank a whiskey and took a look at his certificate.

"In as much as he, Frank Tregear, in the Western Desert

on 20th March 1942, when obliged to abandon his aircraft, on the ground or in the air, as a result of unfriendly action by the enemy, succeeded in returning to his squadron, on foot or by other means, long after his estimated time of arrival." At the bottom of the certificate, written in red capital letters, was the line, "IT'S NEVER TOO LATE TO COME BACK."

Though it was well deserved, Rixon and his fellow erks' trip across the desert seemed far more deserving, but sadly there was no certificate for them, though the CO insisted they take part in these celebrations. It would be weeks before Rixon and the others were fit again, but Tregear and Alexander were fit to fly the next day.

53

PEDRO HANBURY WAS PROMOTED TO FLIGHT Lieutenant as Flight Lieutenant Hall was repatriated on health grounds. We were not told exactly why this was, but we could guess. The sleep-walking ghosts were thick around the LG every night due to the amount of twitch we were experiencing, and I was no exception, waking up most mornings at around four o'clock, only getting back to sleep after half a hip flask of whiskey. It was about this time that 'Hawkeye' Lee adopted his chicken, Henrietta, which he insisted on taking up with him in the cockpit of his Tomahawk. Nobody minded at all, that was his business, and because he was a brilliant shot and a great pilot nobody cared, but no-one had the heart to tell him there was no chicken. He was seen having long chats with Doc Craib, who seemed to make light of it at first, but I could tell he was worried. No-one said anything to Hawkeye about it, even when Henrietta was apparently sitting with him in the mess.

The next day we were all up again, escorting twelve Bostons on another raid over Martuba. Yet again we were bounced by a large formation of 109s from behind and above, and four Bostons were shot down. There wasn't much we could do to prevent this because the 109s were all over us and we had to fly to the limits just to stay alive. So much for the Tomahawk being superior; it clearly wasn't. We waited for the CO's shout and then we hauled our aeroplanes around in 360-degree turns in an effort to get behind the 109s while still trying to keep a watch on the Bostons. Despite firing off most of my ammunition, not a single 109 was seen to go down or even sustain any damage. Whoever those pilots were, they were bloody good.

While everything was happening, I caught a glimpse of Saunders' Tomahawk spinning earthward, but I couldn't hang around to see what happened. Tom Hindle went down too and like Saunders, no-one saw what happened to him. Frank Tregear was hit and shouted over the R/T that he had a complete hydraulic failure and was intent on belly-landing back at the LG. I returned five minutes before him and watched as he brought it in fast and low in a flapless approach before stalling it onto the ground, churning up dust and debris all around before heaving to a stop.

A group of erks started running up to him but suddenly they were shot at from inside the cockpit. What on earth was he doing? Had he gone mad? Everyone dived for cover until the shooting stopped and the aeroplane was finally approached with great care. He waved at them and shouted, and it seemed he couldn't get the canopy open and so he'd been shooting at it with his pistol in frustration but still failing to get it open. It was incredibly claustrophobic being stuck in a damaged aeroplane like that, as I can remember. They eventually managed to smash it open and haul him out uninjured. Many of us kept the canopy open just a little from then on.

It had been a bad day, just one of yet another of the same, and it ended with Flight Lieutenant Tom Hindle and Sergeant Sandy Saunders being listed as missing. We'd be lying if we said we didn't look out for strange lorries arriving at dispersal at odd times, with grateful hitchhikers aboard.

The CO broke the latest news from Army Intel about our missing pilots on 25th March: Tom Hindle had safely force-landed at El Adem and was on his way back to us, but Sandy Saunders had been killed. The army found his aeroplane and buried him in the desert next to the wreck. Hindle returned on 27th, fit and well, and was duly made a proud member of the Late Arrivals Club amid much cheering and celebration. We all wished everyone shot down could become a member. Saunders was never mentioned again.

On 28th March a lone Tomahawk landed at LG109 because the young pilot was complaining over the R/T that it was running badly. I didn't see where he was from, but I saw him sitting in the mess drinking tea and chain smoking while he waited. I couldn't help notice he was shaking badly, not just his hands but his entire body, shivering as though he was sitting in an ice-cold wind. I'd never seen the shakes as bad as this before, and I felt really sorry for him. I wanted to sit with him to give him some reassurance, but the erks called him back and he walked over to his aeroplane, staring at the ground. He really was unfit to fly, in my opinion. We were all frightened at times, but to carry on when so utterly terrified showed a huge amount of courage. Those who said they weren't frightened were liars.

I watched as he climbed in and started it up, then bounced down the runway without any engine checks and was veering off when suddenly he either throttled right back to abort the take-off or the engine failed because the tip of the starboard wing hit the ground and it crashed straight onto a tent and exploded. There was one man, an erk, fast asleep in the tent who wouldn't have known anything about it. Neither of them could be saved.

Nobody questioned you if you turned back occasionally. I did it twice, only once when it was genuine. If your fuel pressure drops or the engine sounds as though it's rough running, there could be a serious problem with your aeroplane and so it was necessary to turn back. If it really was faulty, you'd be a liability to yourself and your colleagues if you pressed on. But we all knew that turning around more than a few times would create suspicion. No-one wanted this, and the subsequent shame and humiliation. We lost a sergeant pilot in March, not through enemy activity but what was called LMF: Lack of Moral Fibre. After the sixth occasion when he returned with some sort of problem that mysteriously fixed itself after landing, he was seen going into the CO's office. He'd already been given the ignominious nick name of 'Boomerang Bill' in the short time he'd been with us, and some chaps hated him. He had a family and small children back in Blighty, unlike most of us, and was always talking about them, so was it only right that he wanted to stay alive for them? I had mixed feelings about it, and some sympathy, but if your wingman disappears just before going into combat, he puts everyone at risk. Anyway, it was decided he was bad for morale, and it couldn't be allowed to spread, so we never saw him again.

Barney Beresford was promoted and posted to command 233 Wing on 31st March while Pedro Hanbury was promoted to Acting Squadron Leader, becoming our new CO. Despite Pedro being with 260 longer than me, I'd never really spoken to him; unlike my first CO Derek Walker, this Eton-educated chap seemed more than a little aloof and now he was CO he moved into the office lorry and was seen even less. He kept up the flag system started by Derek Walker, but there was a noticeable change in the way the squadron was run. He was forthright in his opinions and unequivocal in his attitude towards the Hun. One night in the mess I heard him discussing this with Ron Cundy and I could see he was getting really angry. Cundy was suggesting that there was no personal hatred of the enemy, but Pedro stood up and rebuked him loudly, shouting, "You've got to hate them, Ron!" before storming off. I don't know his personal circumstances, nobody did, and whether this was a factor in his attitude was debatable, but it was certainly reflected in the air when he was facing them in combat. He was a brilliant fighter pilot.

Our first op with Pedro in command was 1st April, when eight of our Tomahawks joined up with ten Kittyhawks from 112 Squadron to escort Bostons on a raid over Derna airfield. Bernier never made it up because his Tomahawk caught fire on take-off, which must have been a terrifying experience. It was a good job it didn't happen five minutes later because he just managed to shut it down and get out before it burst into flames and exploded. The temperature warning light was something we got used to seeing on the Tomahawk, but clearly it shouldn't be completely ignored!

Some 109s and Macchi 202s came up to defend Derna and an almighty scrap ensued. Hindle claimed a 109 destroyed and a Macchi 202 damaged, and Pedro worked with Carlisle to damage a 109 together. I fired a two-second burst at a 109, which I thought was surely damaged as bits flew off and a deflection shot caught another, but I wasn't sure. The enemy were different here and we managed to get the better of them from the start. I flew with Hawkeye Lee, 'Shep' Sheppard and Clark, and thankfully we all returned undamaged, except for one of our newest pilots, Flight Sergeant Burrill, a Canadian, who caught some damage to his cockpit and his legs on only his second op. Doc Craib ran out with his bag and Burrill was eventually taken to Cairo. After I'd shut down my Tomahawk, Dave and Ernie asked me how I got on, which they always did. I jumped down and was explaining how I thought I'd hit two 109s when Pedro heard and came up to me.

"Do you have any verification for this, Copping?" he said, sternly and quite loud, in full hearing of a number of other pilots walking back to dispersal. I didn't know quite what to say. Had he not been the new CO I'd probably have laughed and dismissed it, but I could see he was serious.

"No, I don't, skipper, I don't think so…" I looked around. No-one volunteered any help.

"Then keep your bloody mouth shut. I'll not have anyone shooting a bloody line like that, do you hear?" I felt terribly embarrassed and didn't know what to do or say in reply.

"If you think you've damaged a 109, then register it in the correct manner so it can be verified by Army Intel, otherwise keep it to your bloody self." He turned and walked to his lorry, climbed the steps and disappeared. Morley was the closest and he rolled his eyes at me before walking away. This was the new Pedro, and I was very wary of him after that and avoided him whenever I could.

On 2nd April we escorted Bostons again on a second raid over Derna Airfield. This time the Hun seemed better prepared and sent up a dozen 109s who really knew what they were doing. We had all on to keep them off the bombers but still they damaged three, which luckily managed to crash-land on our side of the wire. Sergeant Jim Morley didn't return and was listed as missing that night.

54

I was not called on for ops for a few days and spent most of this time sleeping, or at least trying to. My sleep patterns were all over the place and my concentration levels were dropping as a result, and I was not alone. I slept whenever I could and yet I was still exhausted. On 7th April I was up with eleven others on a fighter sweep across the front line when I saw Sergeant Bob Alexander's Tomahawk take a hit, either by an 88 mm shell or a lucky shot from a 109, which were all over us at the time. Again I had a perverse twinge of selfishness that fate had got the other chap and not me. This was a shameful thing to think and I never discussed it with anyone. I watched in snatched glances as his aeroplane immediately caught fire and fell into a dive that just kept on accelerating. No-one saw him get out because there just wasn't enough time. I wondered if he was aware of what was happening as his aeroplane headed inexorably into the ground and exploded. I couldn't get this out of my mind.

Two-sixty were up on fighter sweeps like this almost every day at the request of the army, and the line was holding, partly thanks to our efforts of continually harassing the Hun as we switched to ground strafing whenever we could. The destructive power of the Tomahawk's two .5-inch guns and four .303s on MT and armour was better than the Hurricane. As a result, the Hun became very adept at throwing up everything they could, from small arms to Breda 20 mm and 88 mm. Ground strafing became full of twitch on every single occasion and none of us wanted to do it, but it was just what the army wanted, so we had to. They called for even closer support, so with this in mind on 13th April and with what was probably a huge dollop of false optimism, we moved west to El Adem, just south of Tobruk. The day we moved in we were strafed by four 109s that also dropped small anti-personnel mines all over the airfield, causing a lot of panic because many of them didn't explode immediately. These rotten things we nicknamed 'butterfly bombs' were not much bigger than a tennis ball and I assumed the pilots had simply chucked them out the window by hand as they flew past.

We set up the large EPIP mess tent first, put the piano at the back as usual and made fresh latrines. El Adem was a base for 109s and 110s before November and so there were dozens of wrecks lying around and we could have easily made ten new Messerschmitt bars, but we still set up our existing one next to the mess. By now we were wise to the Hun's booby-trap tactics, but because it had been in our hands for months, we were careful but not too worried. The Hun was now making very determined efforts to retake Tobruk, and it was our job to help stop him.

On our first full day at El Adem, Harry Curno could only rattle off the first few bars of 'The Red Flag' at breakfast before we were scrambled to intercept enemy bombers heading for Tobruk.

We climbed to five thousand feet and headed due north, only to be bounced by a dozen or more 109s from above. We didn't see any bombers and had to fight our way back to El Adem after Polly Parrott was mauled by three 109s and took a hit to his engine that began smoking badly. The 109s cleared off and Polly managed to crash-land back at El Adem without undercarriage. He was badly shaken but otherwise okay.

On 17th April a Tomahawk from another squadron appeared overhead on its own and we could hear the engine was rough running very badly. It was clear the pilot had genuine problems and so it was no surprise when he turned in to land at El Adem. I watched it come in on a reasonable final approach, if a little too high, but then when it touched down it bounced back up fifty feet, stalled, hit the ground hard and exploded. The pilot, whoever he was, must have been killed instantly. By the time anyone got to him there was nothing left to save.

The Hun was constantly reminding us that El Adem was once his airfield and I think he was keen to take it back, because he never left us alone. We were losing enough aeroplanes to the sand and engine burnout without him flying over every two minutes and strafing us. Ernie told me one of the Tomahawks was already burned out with ninety-five hours on the engine, which was apparently very good for the desert. With no spare engines, there was only so much even highly skilled erks could do.

Both 250 and 112 squadrons were now flying the new Kittyhawk Is and very soon we would be joining them. They began replacing our Tomahawks with these throughout March and April, also telling us the drop tank release handle on the left would soon be used to release a 500 lb bomb under the fuselage. We were stunned by this, but we were assured the more powerful Allison engine was very capable of lifting this and more. We were ordered to spend a few days familiarising ourselves with the Kittyhawk, but to be honest, nobody was keen because we'd already flown one and it was still a P40, if a better version of it. But after Imshi Mason's disastrous first op in Kittyhawks in February, at least a few hours of conversion training was mandatory.

I flew to LG115 in a Tomahawk IIb on 20th April 1942 and returned three days later in a brand new Kittyhawk I, serial number ET411. It had six .5 inch-machine guns in the wings and was a big, heavy, fearsome machine.

My first combat op in a Kittyhawk was 24th April. I was in Red Flight with Tregear and Wareham with Wylie as Flight Commander; Hindle led Blue Flight with Clark, Wrigley and Carlisle; Pedro led Yellow Flight with Dunbar, McKay and Shep; and Sparky led Green Flight with Bernier, Colley and Wilmott. The op was ground strafing of MT near Mechili, which was over a hundred miles behind the lines. If we were hit and went down in a forced landing we'd be put in the bag, but that would be a lucky escape. The further over the wire we flew, the flak was usually much worse. With this in mind, the thunder box was oversubscribed and the spades were therefore called into use followed by the customary pee on the tailwheels. There would be bags of twitch and we knew it.

I grabbed a last-minute seat at the thunder box and couldn't get my backside off the wood until there was absolutely nothing left. It seemed as though everything I'd ever eaten in my entire life splashed down onto the shit heap that morning. A hip flask was being passed around and I took a long, grateful swig to take the edge off.

We took off a few minutes later and assembled in climbing

turn orbits up to five thousand feet before heading west. We dropped down to five hundred feet in a shallow dive near Mechili looking for targets and spotted a long column of MT heading north. The sight of sixteen Kittyhawks hurtling in at fifty feet and close to 400 mph, with all our .5-inch guns blazing, must have been a terrifying sight. The occupants of the vehicles were abandoning them and running headlong into the desert as one after the other, they exploded and flipped over. The rattling of my guns was incredible as the whole airframe shook and actually slowed the aeroplane down the recoil was so immense. They didn't have time to fire back at us and so we went in again but this time we weren't so lucky. As Frank Tregear passed over a line of MT, one of the lorries exploded just by sheer bad luck at the exact moment he was overhead, hurling his aeroplane into a spin straight into the ground. He had no chance. I saw it happen in a terrible blinking moment on my port side and knew it was Frank, and I was gripped by a deep sense of panic and terror.

The CO also knew what had happened but never mentioned it over the R/T; he simply called us up and led us back across the desert. He later stated that it had been a very successful op without mentioning Frank. He was officially listed as Missing Presumed Killed, but those of us who saw it knew of the certainty. No-one was willing to argue with Pedro, so it stayed like that. Perhaps the CO himself didn't want to admit the truth. Cundy was the only other Aussie in 260 and I know this must have hit him hard because they were always seen together, but he didn't show it, at least not publicly, no-one did.

Frank's personal effects were gathered up in a box from the tent he shared with Shep, Colley, Patterson, Stebs and new lad Trickey, and added to his valuables in the CO's office for repatriation to his next of kin. His name was wiped off the gaggle board, never to reappear, and he wasn't spoken of again. He was gone.

There's nowhere to go in a desert landing ground. You can't take a stroll through the woods or go stomping off up a high hill on your own to gather your thoughts. You have to content yourself with a few careful yards around the perimeter, using a spade as a prop to steal some solitary moments. Other than that, the night provides sufficient cover for all the sleepless murmuring ghosts coming to terms with another loss, and the constant nagging thought: *Who will be next?*

55

THE HUN NEVER GAVE UP AND WE WERE SCRAMBLED early the next day after a report of Stukas heading for Tobruk. We were joined by Kittyhawks from 2 and 4 Squadrons of the SAAF and just as we found the Stukas, a huge number of 109s and Macchi 202s came at us from the west. There must have been fifteen or twenty at least and they really knew what they were doing. We didn't get a chance to have a go at the Stukas because the fighters were all over us. Within seconds I saw a 109 go down trailing smoke, pursued by the CO, and two of our new chaps, Miller and Black, took on a Macchi 202 which caught fire, in what became an almighty scrap south of Tobruk.

The R/T was busy with warning shouts and I fired a few hopeful shots at a 109, but he was quick to get out of my sights, wary of our new firepower. Miller's Kittyhawk was then hit and he went down trailing thick, black smoke, and then, much to our surprise, the rear gunner of a Stuka caught a lucky shot on the CO's aeroplane which sent him down in what could be a forced landing. We organised ourselves on the remaining 109s and they dispersed heading west at high speed, so we let them go. During this frantic melee, I hadn't noticed Rhodesian Bill Wareham was missing.

When we landed, there was a lot of frenetic activity to find out what had happened to our pilots. We were taken off ops for the rest of the day, and indeed for the next few days, until we knew what had happened to the CO. By mid-afternoon we heard he was fit and well after successfully crash-landing east of Gazala and was delayed while waiting for transport, but Miller trudged back in time for tea, having caught a lift with some Indian troops. The next day the CO arrived and those who dared gave him some gentle ribbing about being shot down by a Stuka, which for a fighter pilot is a dreadful sin as well as an embarrassment. That night they became the latest proud members of the Late Arrivals Club amid great celebrations that were a much-needed tonic after recent events.

On 27th April we held our only formal parade at any LG when to our astonishment we were visited by a royal VIP. It was the worst time for such a visit and the sky was suddenly thick with our fighters providing a protective barrier, including some from 260 who missed the parade. I couldn't believe it when a twin-engined Hudson bounced onto the dusty hard ground of our LG and the Duke of Gloucester stepped out. We were lined up at dispersal for him to shake our hands and he must have wondered who the hell we were. No-one was dressed the same, even though we did try, our hair was as wild as usual, and the last time we'd washed any of our kit thoroughly was months previously at Msus. God only knows what he thought of us. One of our chaps suspected he had lice again and so the thought of some of these nasty little creatures jumping onto the royal body made some of us smile. He didn't stay long because after a quick tour and a cup of desert tea, without even sitting down to enjoy it, he was soon heading off back east out of harm's way. Ron Cundy took a few pictures to add to his collection and was snapping a lot with his faithful little camera, getting the shots developed later in Alex at huge expense. He took photos of us all in and around our aeroplanes, and all over the LG.

Just after the Duke left us, Vanderkamp delivered the solemn news that the army had found the shattered remains of a 260 Kittyhawk and its pilot near Tobruk. They buried Sergeant Bill Wareham beside the wreckage where he'd crashed. Some of us were still chewing the biltong he'd given us in his last parcel from home. Just to finish off another bad day, one of our new pilots, Sergeant Andy Trickey, botched his final approach in his Kittyhawk and crashed at the end of the runway and was killed. I didn't see it, but I heard it, and we'll never know what happened. He was a keen young lad and had only been with us a week.

The CO knew we were all desperate for leave. Morale was on the floor and we were all exhausted. Doc Craib picked up on this and the end result was a rolling two weeks of forty-eighters for everyone, to be taken in groups of six. I was in the first batch and needed no encouragement to climb aboard the Delta Lily the next morning with Wylie, Hindle, McKay, Viesey and Clark, with Cundy at the controls. We had a pleasant, uneventful flight to Aboukir and a quick transfer courtesy of an RAF lorry straight into Alex.

Madame Pericand fussed around us as usual as we settled in the green wicker chairs outside the French doors at *Pension Crillon*. We drank *arak* and water as we took turns in the bathroom and put on our crisp, clean uniforms from the wardrobe. There were name tags on uniforms that would now never be claimed, and I wondered just for a very bleak moment if someone might soon be looking at my name in the same way.

I shared a room with Dave Clark, who I had arrived with at 260 all those months ago. We were no longer the naïve, young, fresh-faced pilots we once were. Clark's movements were slower, his demeanour was heavy and laboured, and he walked with a noticeable stoop in his gait. He looked ten years older. I wondered if he thought the same about me.

After a wonderful meal of roast chicken and vegetables that very definitely did not include bully beef, we dispersed into the late-afternoon glow that was now descending across the streets of Alex. I really did love this place now, and I wondered if the war ever came to an end and if I survived, I might live somewhere like this where the summers are long and the winters are short. Clark knew his way around and so I left him with Viesey as I headed for number seven Borsa el Qadima. I found it easier than I anticipated and discovered the main door to the street was open. I remembered the steps up to Ayesha's apartment, so I took them three at a time.

Expecting the door to be opened immediately, I was surprised when there was no reply to my knocking. I tried the handle, but it was locked. I didn't know what to do. There was no-one around to ask about Ayesha, so I made my way back down the stairs and into the street. I lit a cigarette and began walking to the Carlton, occasionally glancing over my shoulder just in case.

I found Viesey and Clark at the bar with the others. Despite the prices, the pace of our drinking accelerated as the evening wore on. We stumbled our way into the Monseigneur, where whiskey and *arak* were the drinks of choice. I was a willing participant and after only a couple of hours, the oblivion we all sought swallowed us up.

It must have been quite late in the morning when I woke up because the sun was well-established in warming the room. Clark was snoring in the next bed and I could hear vehicles in the street below and the shouting of traders, all the usual Alex noises.

Just after ten o'clock, I staggered to the bathroom and then downstairs. Madame made toast and butter with a real fried egg on each slice, and I sat on the wicker chairs alone with my tea and cigarettes. I began to feel human again and politely refused an early glass of *arak* with Gabriel, who simply shrugged and threw his down in one. He then dragged a pedal cycle through the kitchen and kissed Madame tenderly on the check before wheeling it through the hallway and out the front door. The others appeared and Madame was busy cooking again. There was a subdued atmosphere and by now midday was fast approaching. We had arranged transport back to Aboukir at three o'clock because Cundy was bringing in the Delta Lily at four. This was the only certain opportunity to be back on time, so we had to take it.

I didn't feel like doing anything, so I lay on my bed and nodded off. At two o'clock Clark had a bath and stuck his head around the door offering me his water, which I declined. Before he returned, I had a sudden dreadful thought that I'd never be there again, which I immediately tried to dismiss. In a state of panic, I found a scrap of paper and scribbled a few lines on it, then ran down the stairs and out the front door. I ran non-stop into seven Borsa el Qadima and banged on Ayesha's door, but there was still no reply. I shoved the note under the door and made my way back to the *Pension Crillon*.

McKay, Dunbar, Stebbings, Carlisle, Wrigley and Meredith alighted from the Delta Lily, all smiles as we climbed aboard looking sullen. Sacks of veg were pulled up through the loading hatch underneath and propped up with crates of beer, tins, cheese, eggs and bread. There were also lots of chickens, dead this time and already plucked, thanks to Agnides' latest special offer. Since the Christmas episode, he didn't supply us anything live again.

The first week of May was a complete dead loss due to the *khamsin*. No sooner had one come to an end than another blew up from the south, covering everything we'd just dug out. The thunder box filled up with sand, which wasn't a bad thing because we simply moved it to the left a little and so it saved us a job, but the aeroplanes remained covered the whole time. Obviously the Hun was going through the same and so it was a chance to relax and catch up on sleep.

We had some other visitors in May too: a team of Gurkhas arrived in their lorries and set up camp with us all around the LG. There was a hell of a flap when Vanderkamp told us of intel reports stating the Hun was about to drop paratroopers on several of our forward LGs, hence the added security.

56

FOR THE FIRST FEW DAYS THE GURKHAS DIDN'T SEEM to do much due to the *khamsin*, apart from wander around the LG looking impossibly smart and eerily handsome, yet at the same time darkly fierce with their kukri knives and wide smiles, but then we saw them disappear at night on several occasions when we were turning in, returning in the morning with tales of derring-do behind the lines that frankly we thought might be a little exaggerated.

We were proved wrong in the middle of May when a badly shot up Kittyhawk from 250 Squadron crash-landed at our LG with a loud metallic thump and a cloud of dust. The pilot had shouted up over the R/T that he'd been hit by ground fire not far away from us and when he didn't get out, we ran over with Doc Craib to take a look. He was a young lad who looked as though he was still in his teens, and when we lifted him out and laid him on the ground, he was conscious and was trying to speak. He wasn't screaming or groaning in pain even though he was clearly injured, but he had a distant look in his eyes and was actually smiling. Doc Craib leaned him on his knee and after opening the lad's shirt, he just shook his head. He knew straightaway. A few seconds later, the poor lad died in his arms. We searched his blood-soaked pockets and then wrapped him in a blanket and buried him the same afternoon. There were a surprising number of people in attendance, even though we'd never met him.

We knew there was a very active Hun AA battery not far behind the wire from us and Vanderkamp confirmed this. The CO was incensed and the death of the young pilot sent him into a quiet rage, even though we were unsure it was they who got him. The lieutenant in charge of the Gurkhas was seen going into his office with Vanderkamp and they didn't come out for over an hour. That night they were despatched into the desert to find this rotten AA battery.

They returned before dawn and were in the mess eating when I walked in, still a little bleary-eyed, to the extent that I missed what was hanging from the entrance of the EPIP tent. How could I have expected it? Viesey arrived and stood at the entrance where I heard him say, "Jesus Christ," before sitting down with me, a mug of tea in one hand and cigarette in the other.

"Have you seen that?" he asked me. No, I hadn't.

"What?" I replied. He didn't say anything but nodded towards the entrance. I looked across at a length of rope hanging limply with a few items attached. I looked again and realised what it was. We found out from Vanderkamp that the particular AA battery that had been giving us problems would no longer do so, not for a few days at least. The Gurkhas had found them asleep in their tents and slit their throats as they slept, except for one, who they despatched towards his comrades with a message.

It was our fault that the next part happened because we had been so sceptical. They'd cut the right ear from five of the Huns and it was these that were now gently swaying in the morning breeze on our mess tent, catching the wind like tiny pink sails.

The leave relays continued throughout May, along with the arrival of new pilots until most had taken a spell in Alex, thanks to Cundy and the Delta Lily. The exhausted and dishevelled were replaced by fresh-faced young men in clean uniforms so new to the desert that they were still brushing the sand off their uniforms and combing their hair. We also had transferees from 94 Squadron, namely Canadian pilot Sergeant Jim Edwards, Flight Lieutenant John Williams, Flight Sergeant Bill Stewart and Irishman Sergeant Pete Meredith. Their arrival was not best-timed because near the end of May we had to move east and leave El Adem because it was getting far too hairy. In the next few days we nicknamed the area around it 'The Cauldron' because it was so damned hot. The Hun really did want it back, so we let him have it.

We were now at Gambut, thirty miles east, but the Hun followed us and didn't give us a moment's peace. We'd been bombed in the night and strafed twice in the morning, and I found Tom Hindle fast asleep with his head on a table in the mess just as we were scrambled to intercept prowling 109s. I knew Hindle was exhausted because he took off without any flaps and nearly didn't make it into the air. The Hun was desperately trying to push east and we were at the sharp end, trying to stop him. He was hurling everything our way and we'd only been in the air a few minutes before we were bounced by a dozen 109s, three of which caught Hindle hanging around on his own at the back and was subjected to a fierce assault as they began picking him off like vultures. We tried to help, but it was all over in a few seconds. He wasn't flying to his usual standard and was hit very quickly as his aeroplane was seen going down trailing smoke, but no-one saw where he went. Once everyone knew what had happened, we stopped talking about him and he was listed as missing that afternoon.

On the 28th we were involved in ground strafing the front line again at the request of the army to keep the Hun busy, and the next day it was more of the same. There was plenty of twitch created by all sorts of stuff, and I heard over the R/T that Viesey had been hit and then Wylie shouted up that he was going in. I could only think, *Shit*, and kept repeating this in my head as I carried on flying to the best of my ability, straining my neck from constantly looking around, when suddenly I heard an almighty bang from my engine and smoke began puthering into the cockpit, obscuring my vision. This was it. This was how it was going to happen. I knew I'd been very lucky, but now my luck had run out. I was about eighty feet above the desert, hurtling along at 300 mph, so I couldn't even consider bailing out. At any moment my aeroplane would explode and I'd see the desert close up for a second before it was all over.

I waited for the inevitable explosion, but it didn't happen. The smoke didn't get any worse and the engine sounded fine. A minute later I was still okay, so I turned east and headed for our side of the wire for somewhere to put down. If flames began licking my feet, I'd get down immediately, but I hung on and waited, as the smoke was now starting to die down so I stayed with it. I opened the canopy and could hear the engine had now started rough running and vibrating terribly, but I still had power, so I pressed on. When Gambut appeared on my nose I pulled the undercarriage lever, but nothing happened. I had no flaps either. I tightened my shoulder straps and braced myself.

To avoid a stall, I came in fast and low and hit the ground with such a terrific noise and shower of dirt I thought the engine had exploded. The prop blades were bent and stopped immediately, and I skidded along the flat desert LG with such horrendous force the friction began ripping the front air intake apart, taking the radiators with it. When I eventually came to a grinding halt after a few awful seconds of metallic screeching, I turned all the switches off and got out as fast as I could.

Curiously it didn't seem as bad as the time I came in on a collapsed undercarriage leg, perhaps because this time I was ready for it. It still shook me up, though, and we'd lost another aeroplane. I staggered back to dispersal and then to the mess for a drink. Ten minutes after my crash-landing, 'Shep' Sheppard came in badly shot up and did the same thing, and luckily he was unhurt too. Later we stood in the mess drinking tea and whiskey together, both a little shaken and relieved but also angry, as though we'd just been bowled out for a duck on the village green.

We still had no news of Wylie and Viesey, and so they were formally listed as missing. I was off ops until another Kittyhawk arrived, or until I could fetch one. The new Kittyhawks we were now acquiring had strengthened wings and so we were to begin carrying a 250 lb bomb under each wing and another bomb under the fuselage. The idea was that 260 still had to provide escort for bombers, which we did, before dropping our own bombs on any MT and armour we could find.

On 1st June I flew to LG115 and collected a brand-new Kittyhawk IA serial number ET569, complete with bomb racks and a cockpit that smelled like the rich leather seats of a brand-new Rover. The controls were a little stiff, but it was now my aeroplane and so I tried very hard to get used to it as quickly as possible. There were a lot of eager young men over the other side of the wire that had been flying their 109s for years and were very familiar with them, and so we had some urgent catching up to do.

That same afternoon, Dave and Ernie very carefully loaded a 500 lb bomb under the fuselage of my aeroplane and after giving me the usual thumbs up, I trundled from dispersal to the end of the runway, extremely conscious of what was hanging beneath me. Ernie very kindly sat on my starboard wing to guide me before jumping off at the end of the runway. This could also have been reassurance that he'd fitted the bomb correctly, of course.

The pull on the aeroplane by the extra weight was incredible and we were aware it would significantly raise the stall speed, so I kept the nose down and the power on as much as possible until I got used to it. A dozen Bostons were en route and when they came close, we climbed up to three thousand feet to meet them, with Sparky leading with me as his wingman, and Wrigley and Carlisle on his right.

The Bostons dropped their bombs along a line of MT and as soon as they did so we lined up in a shallow dive, releasing our bombs at fifteen hundred feet onto the head of the column. The Hun threw up a lot of anti-aircraft fire and we got out unscathed as quickly as we could.

57

Dropping a bomb was entirely different to simply using the aeroplane as a gun platform. I couldn't see it fall because release was timed, so it dropped somewhere beneath the port wing, and the rise in the aeroplane was tremendous, so the instinct then was to get the hell out rather than hang around to see what the bomb had done.

The next day was similar, with two ops every day for the next few days, dropping our bombs and getting used to flying the new 'Kittybomber', as it became known. Ernie and Dave were now taking it in turns to ride on my starboard wing as far as the threshold area, and then after landing they did the same to help guide me around, and I was incredibly grateful.

At the end of the first week in June we had news of our missing pilots. Flight Lieutenant Bob Wylie had successfully crash-landed but on the wrong side of the wire and so had been put in the bag. At least he was alive. The same day we heard Flight Lieutenant Tom Hindle had been killed, along with Flight Sergeant Dick Viesey. Two-sixty was being badly mauled but we knew it was the same at other squadrons. Their names were wiped from the gaggle board.

On 9th June, Flight Sergeant Dave Clark, my friend from Ma'aten Bagush, went missing on ops. No-one saw what happened. He didn't shout up on the R/T; he just didn't come back. We took off again later the same day and his place was filled as we carried on with our offensive patrols protecting our ground forces that were now in full retreat. We were forced to move further east to an LG at Bir el Beheira near the Egyptian border, losing a lot of our equipment that couldn't be moved or repaired, including the CO's Italian staff car that wouldn't start. Regrettably we had to leave it, so we set it alight along with a couple of Kittyhawks with engines choked up with sand. We just didn't have the time to sort them out; it was our turn to abandon stuff to the enemy. I didn't see anyone leaving booby traps the way the Hun always did, which doesn't mean it wasn't done, but we seemed more concerned with getting out safely than hanging around.

Whatever we threw at the Hun, including our new bombs, it didn't seem to slow him down, and in the air we faced ever-increasing opposition. On 12th June I saw Jimmy Wrigley tangling with a Macchi 202, which Waddy eventually shot down, but after that Wrigley disappeared. When it's all going on, you haven't time to keep tabs on everyone and so I didn't see what happened to him.

Around this time, we discovered a shocking problem that no-one foresaw; I couldn't believe it when it first happened to me. I was pulling a couple of steep turns to get behind a Macchi 202 when to my horror nothing happened as I pressed the gun button. I had him dead centre in my sights, but there wasn't a bloody sound from any of my guns. I couldn't have run out because I'd only fired a few short bursts earlier and so I kept trying but still nothing happened. I had no choice but to return to the LG.

I immediately spoke to Dave and Ernie about it and to my astonishment they both shrugged and shook their heads.

"It's a common fault with this kite," Ernie said.

"Were you pulling G, aerobatics?" Dave asked me. *What? How could this be?* "It doesn't happen every time, only occasionally," he said. I found this really worrying, as did everyone else.

Jimmy Wrigley never returned and was formally listed as missing. It now seemed inevitable that I would be next on the list.

In the early days I counted up my combat hours religiously, but now my logbook was looking very scrappy. I knew I had accrued more than a hundred front line hours, but the ops were much shorter now due to the Hun being so close, often just a few minutes away, and so reaching the golden 200 hours was looking much less likely. Because of this I forgot all about the OTE; it wasn't a realistic way out of there. Who was to say they'd honour it anyway? I'd never heard of anyone going home after it was reached, and who's to say they wouldn't simply increase the number of hours required? I continued filling in my logbook as always, but now every other entry had a note in the margin, 'Lost another today', with the name of a friend next to it. I filled it in without any sense of purpose or enthusiasm because the end result was impossible.

There were only twelve of us left now and our current LG was wide enough for us all to take off together in slightly staggered line abreast. The mess tent was still our main refuge as the June sun beat down on us and we also spent a lot of time between ops resting in the shade under the wings of our aeroplanes at five-minute readiness. There was no rendition of 'The Red Flag' on the piano because it was still in the lorry; no-one had unloaded it yet. I think we knew by the thumping of Hun artillery that we probably wouldn't be staying long. Without the piano we had no music at all; Norman 'Sticky' Glew had left us at the end of May for Cairo before a posting to Malta, and he'd taken his gramophone with him, which we missed terribly.

The CO looked as drawn as the rest of us and sleep became something very precious, with most of us snatching three or four hours at best, but despite our continual efforts there was no slowing the Hun and his armour as they came ever closer.

Amidst all the exhaustion we were given a huge boost when the mail arrived, with four letters and a parcel for me, delivered by a Beaufighter on its way to an op. We eagerly awaited these mail drops and cherished every single item, rereading the letters dozens of times and so these couldn't have arrived at a better time. The parcel was from my mother and consisted of a lovely big slab of homemade fruit cake that looked and tasted as fresh as the day it was baked two months before. As was customary I shared it with Carlisle and Doc Craib after I mentioned it at the thunder box. The Doc came round with a cup of tea ready in one hand and eager anticipation all over his face. In exchange, the Canadians amongst us handed round packets of Sweet Caporal cigarettes, a welcome change from Woodbines, and Coca-Cola extract for the chlorinated water. Two of my letters were from Aunt Margaret telling me that at the time of writing, which was April 1942, Southend had not yet experienced any air raids this year. I was delighted for them and oddly enough I wondered if my efforts in the desert were making a contribution to it. I was also thrilled to receive a letter from Bill Short, the chap I knew at Cranborne in South Africa. He said he was in Singapore enjoying a wonderful life with a Hurricane squadron, with servants, great food and even a swimming pool at their disposal. I was envious until I remembered Singapore had fallen to the Japanese in February.

I checked the date on the letter: 23rd January. I wondered if he'd managed to get out in time. I knew thousands had been captured when it fell and I just hoped he wasn't one of them. The other letter was postmarked Alexandria and simply addressed to 'Copping – 260 Squadron RAF'. Inside was just an address in Cairo written in blue ink. I had no idea what this was until I saw the signature at the bottom: '*Ayesha*'.

When I woke up in the early hours as usual, I couldn't stop thinking about home. One of the oddest thoughts I had was that I'd never walk along Southend Promenade ever again. Perhaps I'd dreamed it without remembering, like the nightmare of never seeing Alex again, stuck in the back of a lorry forever driving past, but it seemed so frighteningly real. The most startling thing about this was not alarm at the prospect of it, but my surprise when I realised I had accepted it and that my never seeing home again was no longer a worry.

In the morning we climbed up to three thousand feet to join Beaufighters, Blenheims, Bostons and Hurricanes hurling whatever we had at the enemy. The heat haze was as thick as fog rising well above ten thousand feet which made navigating and bomb aiming difficult, forcing us lower. We had our full bomb load as usual and were dropping it all on their MT and then strafing everything that moved until we ran out of ammunition; but still they kept coming.

When we came down, we were forced to move yet again because Gambut had become too hairy to hang on to. This time we flew to an LG near Sidi Azeiz just west of Bardia but we didn't even unpack before we were moved further east after reports the Hun were only twelve miles away. Our erks in their lorries were diverted before most of them had even arrived. The Free French army couldn't hold the Hun and eventually fell back despite valiant efforts and this time on 18th June, we flew a long way east to LG76 south of Sidi Barrani. Stan Bernier, probably as exhausted as the rest of us, mishandled his approach and his Kittyhawk overturned when he touched down. We ran out to him with fire extinguishers fearing the worst, but luckily all we found was a disgruntled expression in a cloud of dust as Bernier was pulled out uninjured.

In the relative safety of our new LG, we managed to pitch all our tents as usual and even unload the piano. Carlisle set up his bed at the back of our tent and I put mine where it always was, about halfway along on the right, where the canvas in the middle hangs low above my face. I could move my bed nearer the entrance, or to the other side, or even next to Carlisle, because the other four beds usually in our tent remained stacked up on the lorry, but I stayed put. There was something inexplicably comforting in familiarity, and I didn't want to change anything, just in case; neither of us did. Unpacking our tent box, I found Saunders' copy of *Wuthering Heights*. It wasn't really his book; it belonged to the tent, so that's why it had remained, but there was a letter from England at the back that he'd obviously used as a bookmark. I had an urge to read it, but now it would be disrespectful to read a dead man's mail. I made a mental note to take it to the adj for sending on to his next of kin, but then I forgot. Nights were quiet in our tent now. It seemed Carlisle didn't snore or fart very much. The other four had obviously been the main culprits after all.

58

MORE PILOTS WERE ARRIVING USUALLY IN ONES OR twos, and all were very welcome: Flying Officer Vic Thagard, a Canadian from Winnipeg; Flying Officer Grant Aitchison; Sergeant 'Red' McClive, an American from Flint, Michigan; and Flight Sergeant Mel Arklie, also Canadian and also from Winnipeg. The Canadians were great pilots, as Sergeant Jim 'Stocky' Edwards was already proving. A few days later even more arrived: Flight Sergeant Ody, Flying Officer Gilboe and Sergeant Mockeridge. Now all we needed was more aeroplanes. Sergeants Rob Mockeridge and Pete Meredith helped fill our empty tent by moving in with Carlisle and me; they had no choice because space was getting tight.

By a small miracle we still had the Delta Lily, and I was despatched the next morning with three others to LG100 near Wadi Natrun to collect new Kittyhawks. As the desert fell away beneath us, I wished we were heading off on leave,

and despite the noise, I fell asleep in the back of the Delta
Lily and only woke up when the undercarriage clunked into
place for landing. It was incredibly hot at Wadi Natrun and
we said goodbye to Cundy as he flew back immediately via
a stop at Aboukir to pick up supplies. We trudged over to
dispersal to sign for the new aeroplanes, which we assumed
were the ones lined up sparkling in the midday sun. "They're
not yours, gentlemen," the adjutant told us, sifting through
his papers. "You're two-sixty, aren't you?" Bernier nodded.
"Yours will be ready tomorrow, later on; ET574, 575, 576 and
EV113, tomorrow afternoon, gentlemen, at the earliest." We
looked at him, probably very blankly, wondering what to do
until he decided for us. "If I were you, I'd take advantage of
this and do a bit of sightseeing in Cairo, it's only a short hop
down the road. I know you lot have had it up to your ears. I'll
clear it with your CO, it's Pedro, isn't it?" He was a squadron
leader, so who were we to argue? "Be back here by 1700 hours
tomorrow, no later, right?"

We couldn't believe our luck. I fumbled in my pocket for
my wallet and for a terrible fleeting moment I thought I'd
lost Ayesha's address, but it was still there, crushed up at the
bottom behind a ten-bob note. Transport to Cairo was fast
and frequent and we were approaching the western suburbs
in the back of an army lorry in just over an hour. We found
the city in something of a panic, with talk of evacuation. Some
people had apparently already left and were heading east into
Palestine. I can't say I blamed them; we were not stopping
Rommel at all, and if he made it to Cairo, god knows what
would happen. I met a lot of nervous people and I tried to
find a map of the city to locate Ayesha's address. I parted with
the others and made my way to the train station as a good
place to begin. I found a map, but it just showed to remind
me how big the city was. I was beginning to despair until two

MPs joined me and one of them knew where the suburb was, so I took a taxi for a twenty-minute ride east. The taxi drove into an area where domed churches filled the skyline and it pulled up outside a huge house with high walls around the front garden and palm trees gently swaying in the afternoon sunshine. I banged on a pair of green steel gates but there was no answer and they were locked. I banged again and eventually a middle-aged man opened them with a rattling of keys. To my astonishment he simply said, "Copping?" and ushered me inside with a handshake and warm smile.

I was abandoned in an enormous living room feeling rather lost until Ayesha appeared and kissed me warmly on my cheek.

"You've met Papa," she said, taking my hand, leading me over to some easy chairs. We sat opposite one another as the afternoon shadows lengthened and she lit two cigarettes, handing one over. It was unmistakeably French, as was her perfume that I hadn't noticed before. She looked different, younger and happier. She sat in a chair beside me, staring intently at me before smiling. "Did you visit my flat in Alex?" she said, pulling long and hard on her Galloises before blowing the smoke across the dead air in the room where it gathered in the middle like a huge blue-grey cloud big enough to fly through.

"Yes," I said, "very recently," to which she laughed. I thought of my note lying on the floor of her empty flat, never to be seen.

"I'm sorry, but I had to leave quickly. They've closed the building. Do you know why?" I looked blank. How would I know? I shrugged.

"No. Tell me," I said, tapping the ashtray.

"Because the Germans are coming," she said in a serious, almost chastising tone, as though I should know, which of course I did.

"They're not," I said, lying, and I suddenly wondered about the Pericands in the *Pension Crillon*. It seemed much worse than I thought. "I left you a note," I said, "but you must have beaten me to it, and I'm glad you did." She smiled.

"I had to leave anyway, I couldn't stay, I missed my parents," she said, just as a woman entered the room wearing a long black dress: Ayesha, but twenty years older, stylish and beautiful or even more beautiful than her daughter. She sat near me and took one of my cigarettes. "Mama, this is Copping," Ayesha said proudly. She gave me her perfectly manicured and very slender left hand, which I took awkwardly with my right hand and shook it gently without speaking. She lit her cigarette in the same way as Ayesha, blowing the smoke high across the room the way Ayesha did.

Papa walked in with a tray of glasses, a bottle of *arak* and a jug of water, gently placing it on a coffee table between us. He poured four glasses, adding just enough water to turn the liquid cloudy before handing them around.

"*Salut!*" he said, raising his glass and tipping it all down in one. We all followed. "My wife and daughter are leaving Egypt," he said in excellent English, pouring another for himself. "There's no time to waste," he added, indicating for me to help myself. I reached over and poured a large one, filling the remainder of my glass with water.

It was certainly strong liquor, but not ideal for sipping. "We are losing the war," he said, staring into his glass. Then, turning to me while looking deep into my eyes and at my uniform, he said, "*You* are losing the war." I didn't argue because I knew he was right. It could all be over in Egypt in less than a month.

I had a long soak in their bath and Ayesha took my uniform to wash. She called me to the table and we ate tender pieces of lamb with boiled potatoes and fresh salad with fruit to follow. All through the meal Ayesha's father spoke in Arabic and French to his wife and daughter, and often in another dialect I didn't recognise, to which they both frequently nodded. Whatever it was, they knew he was right. I heard my name mentioned a few times and before I was allowed to feel uncomfortable, he threw me reassuring glances and kept topping up my glass, this time with red wine. I caught my reflection in a mirror behind Ayesha and I wondered if I looked like her father or was it just because I was wearing some of his clothes?

The room began to take on a different atmosphere; the way a room does when consuming a lot of alcohol. It became smaller and the rest of the world was now gone, with only the four of us remaining. Everything her father said seemed important as he began explaining in English what they intended to do. "I will stay," he said. "I will be okay with the Bosch; they will have no quarrel with me. I am Egyptian, yes, and I am Coptic, they will leave me alone, but Ayesha and her mother are not, so they must leave." I saw Ayesha nodding, and suddenly her mother began to cry.

"There may be no need to leave," I said hopefully, trying to project some optimism and clearly failing.

"I don't wish to know in detail what is happening to you and your colleagues, Copping, but I know it's not good." He shook his head and smiled. "With respect, there is nothing you can tell me that would persuade me otherwise. Even if I was blind, I could see what is happening." With that he stood up and tipped the remainder of his glass in one before moving away from the table. Ayesha's mother followed, no longer crying but clearly still upset. I was deeply conscious that I'd landed in their lives at the worst possible time.

"We will go into Cairo tomorrow," Ayesha said, walking around the table and taking my hand. "I will show you the real Egypt," she said, leading me away from the table.

59

I woke up in an east-facing bedroom as the sunlight began filling the room. There was quiet outside, with only a very distant call to prayer and no traffic noise. It was warm already and I couldn't sleep any longer. If I was to be back at Wadi Natrun by 1700 hours, I had barely twelve hours left. I dressed and then walked down the stairs to the kitchen and sat down. There were boxes everywhere dotted around the house filled with belongings: bric-a-brac, decorations, pictures, with an enormous golden candelabra protruding from one of them with writing on it that wasn't Arabic or Greek. I wondered what it was, and where Ayesha was, just as she walked in. She took hold of my head from behind with both hands and kissed the back of it before sitting down. She made coffee and lit a cigarette, then she boiled some eggs and made toast. I was starving.

After breakfast I took a shave and Ayesha brought my

clean uniform, freshly pressed. She was moving quickly and I sensed an urgency that I was also feeling.

At nine o'clock we were on a bus across the city. I was shocked to find British troops and civilians clogging up the main roads, with everyone moving at double speed. The bus took us over the Nile and very soon I could see the points of the Giza pyramids, high and incongruous above everything else.

We stood like tourists with our backs to the Great Pyramid as Ayesha took a camera from her bag. A British Army officer with a woman on his arm came strolling by, so Ayesha asked them to take our picture. I saluted and thanked him. Ayesha dropped the camera back into her bag. "I'll send it to you," she said to me, taking my arm.

We walked back over the bridge towards the city, jumping on and off buses when we needed a break. We found a shady pavement café and drank coffee, and were happy to watch the busy world continue without us for a while. Midday passed and yet I had no appetite. There was so much I wanted to tell her that I couldn't, but which I suspected she already knew. I had to be at the railway station to catch the transport, so we walked in the general direction.

"Where will you go," I said, "if you leave Egypt?"

"My mother has family in Palestine, they are waiting for us, so we are going there," she said. She stopped and squeezed my hand, looking into my eyes. "Come with us." I froze when she said this, the directness of it and the sheer relevance almost causing my legs to give way. I regret that I shouted at her, angry that she'd even suggested it because the truth hurt so much. I dearly wanted to escape.

"You know I can't," I repeated, shaking my head.

"You can, just don't go back."

"I must."

"You don't."

"I'm part of it, part of the squadron, they all need me. I can't just leave."

"You can, your friends will understand, I know they will."

"My friends are all gone," I said, standing trance-like by the busy road, oblivious to everything else except Ayesha's stare. I thought of Jimmy Wrigley, Saunders, Wareham and the others from our tent who were now gone, and then Harry Bandinell, of Gidman and the argument in the armoury about whether to shoot the Italian Stuka pilots. Then there was Frank Tregear and his comment about Ayesha, and Wylie, Viesey and Tom Hindle, all gone. It was the first time I truly realised what it all meant.

"Then you will be killed too if you go back, horribly, just like them, you can't go back." I didn't know what to say. I knew she was right.

It was a certainty that I would be next, but I didn't want to go like the others, facing my end in abject horror, sitting there helpless in a flaming wreck, a prospect that was far worse than death itself.

"I can't do this," I said, breaking away from her and walking on. In the next moment I saw the railway station with lorries outside, and the others from 260 were gathered around one of them, smoking. Ayesha grabbed my hand.

"Promise me you'll come," she said, adding, "Promise me you'll escape." I couldn't answer. I couldn't even speak; the words wouldn't form and I had no energy left. All my friends and all my war was now gone. I knew at that moment that I'd lost it all and she was right, and her father was right.

"I promise," I said as I turned around into my own nightmare, walking towards the lorry on that hot Cairo street, unable to stop or turn around, with my feet moving beneath me, but I wasn't moving at all. I climbed aboard the lorry and dared to look back across the street for one last time, only to see that Ayesha had gone.

We arrived back at Wadi Natrun with thirty minutes to spare and it was still baking hot. I picked up my kit from dispersal and strapped on my parachute. We were shown to our aeroplanes and I was about to climb into EV113 when I noticed it was already taken, so I ended up in ET576.

It started beautifully, and it was obviously a new aeroplane. The flight back was easy and relatively short, and we arrived in time for food, which by now I was ready for, even if it was the usual bully beef and biscuits.

The piano was back in action in the mess and Harry Curno was virtually tied to the ammo boxes and plied with beer to make sure he couldn't stop playing. Afterwards Carlisle had half a bottle of whiskey and we both sat in our tent drinking until it was all gone while our other two residents came and went, before I passed out.

Just after dawn 'The Red Flag' was bashed out on the piano and we took off still half-asleep, heading west lugging full bomb loads. I dropped my 1000 lbs of high explosives on advancing Hun MT and then turned around to strafe them until we ran out of ammunition.

We tore up and down their lines, killing all in our path, raking everything with our .5-inch machine guns. I wasn't bothered anymore; I just wanted to kill them all. I heard the pinging of small arms on the metal skin of my aeroplane and flew through the pom-pom bursts of 88 mm shells, watching them all run for their silly bloody lives.

In an effort to kill more of the bastards, our erks fitted twelve-inch steel rods into the front of our bombs so they would detonate on the surface, spreading the red-hot shrapnel even further, ripping the bloody Hun to pieces. Taking off with two 250 lb bombs and a 500 lb bomb was always hairy and we had to ensure the fuel load was minimal or we'd never get off the ground. The front line wasn't far away and so dropping these bombs became a pleasure, in more ways than one.

But he just kept on coming and we grew used to a new way of waking up: the dawn take-off and retreat. On 26th June, amid a terrible panic, we took off and were astonished to see Hun armour to the *east* of us and even rolling onto the western edge of our LG. Most of the lorries had left in the night and we'd folded up our tents and belongings, throwing them into the back of any lorry we could still find. I grabbed my little canvas bag and threw it into the roomy cockpit of my Kittyhawk and took off.

We landed at LG115 near Mersa Matruh with just enough time for a toilet break before we were sent up to escort some Blenheims over the front line, wherever that was. On our way back three 109s bounced us from behind and Carlisle was hit and went down. I screamed and turned around, desperately firing wide deflection shots at the 109s, not knowing whether I'd hit any of them or not. I kept on firing and screaming at the bastards until my guns fell silent. Carlisle never shouted me and I didn't see where he went.

I hoped he'd manage to put down somewhere, but the likelihood of him getting caught in the bag was high. I landed back at LG115, utterly exhausted. I sat in the open cockpit with the sun on my face and almost fell asleep until Dave and Ernie jumped on the wing, shouting, thinking I was injured. I climbed out, leaving my parachute on the wing and rolled underneath the aeroplane, lay down and passed out.

The erks arrived in their lorries, having only just evaded the advancing Hun and then all the remaining aircraft, including the Delta Lily, arrived, loaded with our kit and anyone else not finding a place on a lorry. Amongst it all, Cartwright's dog Blitz found it very exciting, running around barking at everyone, and I heard the CO shouting on more than one occasion, "For God's sake, will someone keep that damned hound under control."

For a few wonderful minutes as I dozed, I thought I was laying on a beach somewhere, with distant conversations and the sound of a barking dog drifting on a warm breeze, familiar beach noises common to a hot summer's day in England. Ernie shouted me awake when he told me my Kittyhawk was ready again. I saw Edwards, Shep and Cundy, so I hauled myself up to go and speak to them and find out what was happening.

60

JUST THEN A YOUNG ARMY LIEUTENANT IN A BREN gun carrier heading east in a desperate state pulled up in a cloud of dust, very surprised to see us standing around our aeroplanes.

"What the hell are you lot doing here?" he said, standing up, looking totally bemused.

"Waiting for orders," Cundy said.

"You'd better bloody well get a move on then, the Hun is only two miles behind us," to which we immediately ran for our aeroplanes and took off.

We landed at LG09, a few miles west of El Daba less than a hundred miles from Alex. It was chaotic to say the least and we wondered how long we'd be able to stay, probably just a few hours before we were forced further east. At this rate Rommel would be driving his tanks into Alex in another day or so, and then on to Cairo. Ayesha's father was right; it would all soon be over.

That night we slept under the wings of our aeroplanes and we shit in the open using our spades. We drank warm, sloppy bully beef straight from the tin and couldn't light fires to brew up at night due to the risk of being seen, so we all drank warm chlorinated water laced with whiskey or gin, and plenty of it. We could hear artillery in the near distance and it seemed the Hun hadn't tucked himself up in bed as usual with his cocoa. Ju88s came over several times throughout the night, slinging bombs at us again, including more of those bloody awful butterfly bombs. The arrogant bastards were even strafing us in the dark as we all dived into whatever slit trenches we could find. It seemed we weren't even safe here and so we knew we would have to move further east very soon.

In the morning, after probably three hours' empty sleep, we watched as some of our lorries began leaving for our next destination, LG85 near Amriyah on the Alex–Cairo road. When the Hun reached us there, we'd be forced to retreat into the Sinai Desert and then into Palestine, gifting him the Suez Canal. Meanwhile our Kittyhawks were refuelled and rearmed, and we took off to find the front line.

We were shocked to discover it was only two minutes' flying time away and we dropped our bombs on whatever we could find before turning around and strafing the bastards. They threw up a hell of a lot of flak and I heard several loud bangs on my airframe and a few others shouted up that they'd also been hit, but when we'd finished it seemed we'd all come through relatively unscathed. At least I was still alive.

I was one of the last to return to LG09 and misjudged my approach, hitting the ground hard and bouncing a little in what I admit was a terrible landing. Had circumstances been different I would have gone around again and made a better job of it as I should have done, but I was just too damned tired. I pulled up and after shutting down the engine, I almost fell asleep again before Dave and Ernie began rearming and refuelling.

Before Ernie began work, he took my arm to stop me. "Corkie's been clobbered, he's dead," he said. "I thought you should know, Dennis, the confirmation came through an hour ago." It didn't sink in at all. I just looked blank; I know I did. He must have thought me totally heartless, but I had nothing to say to this at all. What could I say: "Oh dear, what a shame?" Now Carlisle was gone, I was definitely next. But this wasn't all of it. "You knew Mr Murray too, didn't you?" he said, waiting for a response, and so I nodded. "The Blenheim pilot," he said, as if he needed confirmation. "He was killed three days ago." It was the first time either of my erks had ever used my first name.

I trudged over towards dispersal, looking for somewhere to sit. A large EPIP tent had been erected for us to hide from the sun and I found a chair and collapsed into it.

I don't know how long I'd been asleep, but when the CO came bounding in, shouting, swearing and cursing my name, I thought he was a player in one of my nightmares. When I opened my eyes, he demanded I stand up, which I did, suddenly realising it was real, and he began a tirade of abuse two feet from my face that shocked me to the core.

"What the bloody hell was that, you damned imbecile?!" he shouted, his bright red face glowing with rage, the veins on the sides of his head protruding and his eyes almost popping out their sockets. "We are short of kites as it is without you performing a bloody shit landing like that. What the hell is wrong with you, Copping?" I had nothing to say to Pedro. What could I say? I knew I was at fault and so I just had to take it. But then he got personal. "You're a bloody useless pilot and a damned useless individual; don't ever do anything like that again, do you hear me?" I had nowhere to go and stood there looking at him, wondering what to say, if anything, in my defence. I had no idea and he knew it, so he continued. "Don't stand there staring with that bloody gormless face of yours, what do you have to say for yourself?" He didn't give me chance to reply before he turned, shouting, "You're a blithering idiot, Copping, and if you want to leave this squadron then you can bloody well bugger off," and stomped away. Cundy was sitting opposite me and witnessed the whole thing.

I sat back down, stunned. I thought I'd been doing okay and was a valued member of 260, but it seemed I'd been kidding myself. I was obviously no longer part of this squadron, if indeed I ever was. I didn't want to fly anymore. Why was he being so horrid and shouting like that? My thoughts fell into a deepening spiral, growing darker. What the hell was I doing there? I'd heard rumours about our tent and the fact that everyone was now gone except for me, and that I was a jinx on them and everyone else. I'd always ignored this until now.

I didn't sleep that night at all. Not even for a moment. I lay down in the dirt staring up at the stars, listening to the Hun artillery getting closer. Near the LG, there were constant vehicle movements, mostly heading west, but some were heading east towards Alex and I wondered if I could hitch a ride. I could climb onto the back of a lorry as it moved through the darkness and I'd be gone.

By mid-morning I was incredibly sleepy and found it very difficult to stay awake. I couldn't eat and all I wanted to do was drink whiskey. The gaggle board was blank, mainly because it seemed we would be moving again, so, like everyone else, I tried to sleep under the aeroplanes.

In and out of sleep, I woke up at midday and ate a can of warm bully beef, the first thing I could face, and lay back down in the dirt like a stray dog. At two o'clock 'Shep' Sheppard found me and kicked my right foot. "Oy, get up, you and me are going flying," he said. I thought he meant we were going on an op, so I gathered all my strength and strapped my parachute on. I was about to get in my Kittyhawk when he shouted over, pointing at another. "We're taking these two to Wadi Natrun for repair," he said, nodding at another Kittyhawk at the other side of dispersal.

"They're both damaged and the guns are jammed, but yours is worse, so tough luck, Copping. The undercart won't come up, apparently, and the radio's a bit dodgy, probably thanks to the flak damage in the fuselage." I wondered why we were doing this now, but Shep just looked at me. "CO's orders," he said, as he jumped up onto his wing.

There was no sign of Dave or Ernie as I climbed aboard ET574. I had no idea how much fuel it had, but it started fine, and I watched as Shep began taxiing towards the runway, and then I followed. The fuel gauge indicated there was plenty of fuel for what we needed, and the two of us took off and began climbing, with me supposedly as flight leader. I tried the undercarriage lever but just as Shep had told me, nothing happened. I had to keep the aeroplane down to around 100 mph as a result, and it all seemed very calm up there as we touched two thousand feet.

I throttled back and trimmed the aeroplane as it settled very nicely in the stable air. I drew the canopy back and leaned into my seat. For a moment I shut my eyes and almost immediately began dreaming wonderful things. There was no war, I'd never joined the air force and I knew nothing about aeroplanes. I was laying on Southend beach, looking up at the clear blue sky on a warm summer afternoon.

I opened my eyes to the cockpit and thought about lighting a cigarette but knew I wouldn't be able to unless I shut the canopy, so I did. I held the cigarette in my teeth and lit it. To my surprise I realised on the first drag that it was a Gitanes, and I was back at the *Pension Crillon* with Madame Florence fussing over me and the others, now all dead, their ghosts laughing and joking around the wicker table and a full bottle of *arak*. I wish I'd brought a drink with me, but I hadn't and I regretted this straightaway; not water but whiskey. I wanted oblivion. I hadn't planned this very well; I hadn't planned it at all.

I opened the canopy again. I didn't know where to go, but it certainly wasn't Wadi Natrun, which was about thirty minutes to the south-east. I couldn't fly anywhere east at all; the RAF would see me and find me, and I wanted to get away from them. I couldn't fly west because of the Hun, so I turned south-west, heading for the deepest part of the desert.

61

I HADN'T EVEN BOTHERED TURNING ON THE RADIO and after twenty minutes, I remembered I wasn't alone, as Shep's Kittyhawk flew across my front, waggling its wings, with Shep grinning and waving at me like an idiot. I didn't tell him before we took off because I didn't know, but now I couldn't, so his Kittyhawk hovered around me like a wasp over a glass of lemonade. I ignored him and eventually he flew off, leaving me alone, but suddenly he reappeared a minute later, clowning around again. After half an hour of this he turned off to port and was gone. Shep was a promising pilot and was probably a nice enough chap, but like most of them, he really didn't have a clue about me.

I climbed up to ten thousand feet, throttled back, trimmed the aeroplane again and settled into my seat. There was no wind of any sort, and the Kittyhawk behaved perfectly.

My mind was full of what Pedro had said and I wondered if he'd found out about my transfer request to the Fleet Air

Arm. Perhaps it had come through. *So what?* I thought, and glanced down at the desert two miles below me, vast and empty. It didn't matter anymore, it was all past, and now I must see how far I could get, so I leaned the mixture right off to conserve fuel. I had half tanks and could probably reach a couple of hundred miles to Siwa, perhaps, or even Jarabub, flying slowly, idling like this, using much less fuel. I passed over the full length of the Qattara Depression and so I knew I was now well clear of any Hun bastards.

I almost fell asleep as the warm slipstream blew into the cockpit and across my face. I took off my headset and threw it over the side, and now my hair was in the breeze too, like riding a motorbike along a country lane. I thought of Southend and my idiot father, spending his entire idiot life prodding around at other idiot's teeth. I was glad I'd never see it again. I thought of Ayesha and those wonderful times in Alex. I shut my eyes to see the images clearer and without realising it I fell asleep.

I ran out of petrol once in my father's Austin 8 and the engine stopped quite suddenly, but the Allison in the Kittyhawk spluttered and coughed so much it woke me up. I'd been asleep for almost an hour and was still heading south-west and had dropped to nine thousand feet, but now the fuel was running out so I knew I had to land somewhere.

I trimmed the aeroplane for a cruise descent without power and a dead stick approach, but the prop was still turning as the engine continued to cough and groan. I passed through five thousand feet and from up there the ground looked perfectly uniform and flat, great for a landing. There was a raised area of darker ground and I headed into the prevailing wind and tried lowering some flaps. To my amazement, twenty degrees came down and I lined up for a perfect approach. At a thousand feet it still looked good but then at a hundred feet I could see I was in for a rough landing.

I quickly tightened my straps and held off as long as I could, keeping it up at about 85 mph until the round out when it dropped down to fifty and landed. Just for a second when the main wheels touched, it seemed I'd done it, but then the aeroplane banged forward with a horrendous crunch onto what I could now see were rocks and the nose dug in violently, ripping off the prop as I shut my eyes and held on.

It was as though I'd crashed a bus into a tree at fifty miles an hour, the aeroplane stopped so violently. I immediately sensed a serious neck ache and discovered a gash to my right knee that started bleeding, and so for a moment this was all I thought about. There was no fire, just a lot of hissing and gurgling from what remained of the engine. The prop had gone and so had the wheels. I was flat on the rocks and sand. I unbuckled my seat harness and climbed out.

I took off my parachute and allowed it to fall as I looked around. My knee was bleeding quite badly so I opened my parachute and tore off a strip, wrapping it around my leg and tying it together before sitting down. It was clear the aeroplane would not now catch fire, so I leaned against it on the starboard side in the shade.

I sat for a few minutes, dazed, with nothing at all going on in my head until I took out the map from inside my left sock and opened it up. I was probably somewhere south-west of Siwa, too far out of the way to be put in the bag by the Hun. I stood up again and looked around, but there really was nothing, anywhere, so I sat down and closed my eyes.

When I woke up it was almost dark and it was chilly, so I climbed onto the wing and back inside the cockpit, drawing the canopy closed above my head. Using the parachute as padding, I made myself comfortable.

I slept well all night and woke up just as the sun began warming the cockpit, so I climbed out. My knee was okay and had stopped bleeding and my neck ache was reasonable. I needed some decent shade, so I pulled out my parachute and made a tent, weighting it down at the edges with rocks. It worked very well, but now I was thirsty. I checked inside the cockpit, but there was nothing, so I looked in the fuselage via the radio hatch on the port side, but there was nothing there either, not that I expected anything. So I sat in my shelter and lit a cigarette.

I nodded off again and when I woke up it was blistering hot, even in my shelter. I was so thirsty I had no spit and found it difficult to swallow, and all I could do was sleep. When I woke, the sun was low in the west, so I reached inside the fuselage to see if I could get the radio working. I unclipped it and lifted it out, sitting with it in my shelter.

I couldn't understand why someone had said it wasn't working properly; it looked okay to me, with no visible damage. Sadly I couldn't get a connection to the battery so I was unable to find out. As it became dark, I realised I'd smoked the last of my cigarettes after stubbing it out in the sand next to me. I climbed into the cockpit and closed the canopy.

In the morning I struggled to get out again, with every movement now a supreme effort. My joints ached, my teeth hurt and I had a pounding headache. I slept again for most of the day until late afternoon, when I woke up as the sun was disappearing again. I was very hungry. I managed to climb back inside the cockpit and passed out.

The sun woke me again and I only just managed to get out, drawing the canopy closed more out of habit than planning. It was a supreme effort and once done I collapsed onto the sand in my shelter.

I leaned against the aeroplane facing the desert and despite the circumstances, I was relieved to be there. I was pleased to be on my own. I dozed all day until the sun and the heat faded, and in my new routine I stood up to get back into the cockpit, but now the canopy beat me; I was too weak to haul it back, so I left it and slumped down onto the sand.

Just then I heard an engine approaching; it wasn't an aeroplane, but a vehicle of some sort. A lorry full of noisy New Zealanders appeared.

One of them jumped down and lifted me up, hauling me into the lorry and sitting me next to the driver. The cab was warm and cosy, and the seats were soft padded leather, just like my father's Rover.

"Where do you want to go, Dennis?" the driver said to me, smiling. "Where do you *really* want to go?" he asked as I smiled back, very relieved to have been picked up.

"No idea," I said, "surprise me."

"Shall we take you home?"

"Yes, of course," I said. "I'd love to go home now, I didn't realise I could."

"Of course you can, we'll do that now, shall we, and we'll all go home, right lads?" he shouted behind him and everyone in the back of the lorry roared in agreement.

"Yes," I said, "let's do that." He handed me a huge mug of sweet tea which tasted wonderful, and I lit a Canadian Sweet Caporal cigarette.

"That's settled, then," the driver said, "but what about Ayesha, don't you want to see her again?"

"No, why should I?" I said, shaking my head. "I don't need her anymore."

"Yes, you've done with her now, haven't you, I forgot," he said.

"Yes, it's all done for me now, there's no-one left."

"Yes, sorry, I forgot that too, that's the damned war for you," the driver said, as we passed close to Kittyhawk ET574, now standing on its wheels with its engine roaring but with no-one in the cockpit. He slowed down and nodded his head towards it.

"Leave it," I said. "I don't want it anymore." The driver smiled and dropped it down a gear to climb over a low crest of rocks and then over the top and into Kents Hill Road, South Benfleet, where it was snowing heavily. "We'll drop you here then, Dennis, but get inside quick because it's bloody cold."

"I will, thanks for the lift!" I shouted as they drove away singing, leaving me with my kitbag at my feet. I opened the front door and Madame Pericand was in the kitchen but now with my mother and father, all of them speaking French and laughing. Harry Bandinell was playing cards at the kitchen table with Gidman and Frank Tregear. They looked like scarecrows as usual with their hair sticking up wildly. Frank looked up at me, surprised.

"Where the hell have you been, Copping?" he said. My mother turned and smiled, and then kissed my father sweetly on the lips. He winked at me and then Ernie gave me one of his thumbs up. Ayesha walked through the kitchen with wet hair and a towel wrapped around her body, waving and smiling at me just as Harry Curno began playing 'La Marseillaise' on the piano.

I was at the far end of the room and couldn't see them very well, so I stood up and started walking towards them, but now it was dark and I was cold, and I just kept on walking.

Epilogue

WHAT HAPPENED IN THE DESERT WAR AFTER JUNE 28th 1942 is well-documented. In October the same year at the Battle of El-Alamein, Rommel was defeated and was eventually pushed out of North Africa altogether. The Desert Air Force then pursued the Germans into Italy.

In the six months from June to December 1942, 260 Squadron lost another nineteen pilots, only three of whom were captured; the rest were killed. Those killed included McKay, MacLean, Bernier, Dunbar, Ody, Mockeridge, Thagard and Arklie.

Stebbings, Gilboe and Meredith were captured. Ron Cundy survived the war and returned to Australia, OTE, and wrote a book about his exploits, as did Lionel 'Shep' Sheppard and Kenneth 'Hawkeye' Lee.

Squadron Leader Osgood 'Pedro' Hanbury was shot down and killed on 3rd June 1943. He was twenty-six.

Norman 'Sticky' Glew was killed in Italy on 17th May 1943 aged twenty-seven.

Pension Crillon still exists, so if you ever stay there don't forget to put a review on TripAdvisor.

Kittyhawk ET574 now stands on a plinth outside the El-Alamein Museum in Egypt. It has been preserved and rebuilt, though not in the correct markings. At least it's been saved.

Acknowledgments

I'd like to thank John Pryor-Bennett, Dennis Copping's nephew, and John James Pryor-Bennett, his great nephew, for their help and information, Jeremy Thompson and his wonderful team at The Book Guild, and to David Lloyd for his advice. Thank you to Frank White, Desert Air Force veteran, and Jakub Perka, the man who first found Kittyhawk ET574 after seventy years in the desert, for the use of his amazing photographs.

Bibliography

Douglas Bader, *Fight for the Sky*, Sidgwick & Jackson, 1973

Chaz Bowyer & Christopher Shores, *Desert Air Force at War*, Ian Allan, 1981

Chaz Bowyer, *Men of the Desert Air Force*, William Kimber, 1984

David Braddock, *Britain's Desert War in Libya & Egypt 1940–1942*, Pen & Sword, 2019

Ron Cundy, *A Gremlin on my Shoulder*, Australian Military History Publications, 2001

Roald Dahl, *Going Solo*, Penguin, 2018

Sebastian Faulks, *Charlotte Gray*, Vintage, 2001

Norman Franks, *Fighter Leader*, William Kimber, 1978

Ian Gleed, *Arise to Conquer*, Grub Street, 2010

Ronald Heiferman, *World War Two*, Octopus, 1973

Joseph Heller, *Catch-22*, Vintage, 2011

George Houghton, *They Flew Through Sand*, Sean Arnold, 1991

Bert Horden, *Shark Squadron Pilot*, Independent Books, 2002

Christopher Landon, *Ice Cold in Alex*, Cassell, 2004

Barry M. Marsden, *Portraits of Heroes*, Amberley, 2011

Alys Myers, *Imshi*, WH Allen, 1942

Carl Molesworth, *Curtiss P40 Tomahawks*, Osprey, 2013

Carl Molesworth, *Curtiss P40 Kittyhawks*, Osprey, 2013

Roderic Owen, *The Desert Air Force*, Hutchinson, 1948

Robin Rhoderick-Jones, *Pedro*, Grub Street, 2010

Lionel J Sheppard, *Some of Our Victories*, Compaid Graphics, 1994

Nick Thomas, *Kenneth 'Hawkeye' Lee*, Pen & Sword, 2011

Geoffrey Wellum, *First Light*, Penguin, 2009